BARTH

OUTSTANDING CHRISTIAN THINKERS

Series Editor: Brian Davies OP

The series offers a range of authoritative studies of people who have made an outstanding contribution to Christian thought and understanding. The series will range across the full spectrum of Christian thought to include Catholic and Protestant thinkers, to cover East and West, and historical and contemporary thinkers. By and large, each volume will focus on a single 'thinker', but occasionally the subject may be a movement or a school of thought.

Brian Davies OP, the Series Editor, is Professor of Philosophy at Fordham University, New York. He was formerly Regent of Blackfriars, Oxford University and tutor of theology at St Benet's Hall, Oxford. He has taught at the University of Bristol, Emory University and the Beda College in Rome. He is Reviews Editor of *International Philosophy Quarterly*. His previous publications include: *Thinking About God* (Geoffrey Chapman, 1985); *The Thought of Thomas Aquinas* (Oxford University Press, 1992); *An Introduction to the Philosophy of Religion* (Oxford University Press, 1982);   .

Already published:

Paul
C. K. Barrett

The Cappadocians
Anthony Meredith SJ

Augustine
Mary T. Clark RSCJ

The Venerable Bede
Benedicta Ward SLG

Aquinas
Brian Davies OP

Catherine of Siena
Giuliana Cavallini OP

Teresa of Avila
Archbishop Rowan Williams

Kierkegaard
Julia Watkin

Karl Rahner
William Dych SJ

Bultmann
David Fergusson

Reinhold Niebuhr
Kenneth Durkin

Paul Tillich
John Heywood Thomas

Hans Urs von Balthasar
John O'Donnell SJ

Lonergan
Frederick E. Cowe SJ

BARTH

John Webster

Continuum

London and New York

Continuum
Wellington House, 125 Strand, London WC2R 0BB
370 Lexington Avenue, New York, NY 10017-6503

First published 2000

British Library Cataloguing-in-Publication Data
A catalogue record for this book is available from the British Library

ISBN 0 8264 5078 4 (hardback)
0 8264 5079 2 (paperback)

Typeset by York House Typographic
Printed and bound in Great Britain by Biddles Ltd,
Guildford and King's Lynn

Contents

Editorial Foreword

St Anselm of Canterbury (1033–1109) once described himself as someone with faith seeking understanding. In words addressed to God he says 'I long to understand in some degree thy truth, which my heart believes and loves. For I do not seek to understand that I may believe, but believe in order to understand.'

This is what Christians have always inevitably said, either explicitly or implicitly. Christianity rests on faith, but it also has content. It teaches and proclaims a distinctive and challenging view of reality. It naturally encourages reflection. It is something to think about; something about which one might even have second thoughts.

But what have the greatest Christian thinkers said? And is it worth saying? Does it engage with modern problems? Does it provide us with a vision to live by? Does it make sense? Can it be preached? Is it believable?

The Outstanding Christian Thinkers series is offered to readers with questions like these in mind. It aims to provide clear, authoritative and critical accounts of outstanding Christian writers from New Testament times to the present. It ranges across the full spectrum of Christian thought to include Catholic and Protestant thinkers, thinkers from East and West, thinkers ancient, mediaeval and modern.

The series draws on the best scholarship currently available, so it will interest all with a professional concern for the history of Christian ideas. But contributors also write for general readers who have little or no previous knowledge of the subjects to be dealt with. Its volumes should therefore prove helpful at a popular as well as an academic level. For the most part they are devoted to a single thinker, but occasionally the subject is a movement or school of thought.

Brian Davies OP

Preface

Another introduction to Barth? Barth must be the most introduced of modern theologians (though not necessarily thereby the
best understood). Two factors, however, prompt yet another
attempt to offer a conspectus of his theology. First, over the last
twenty-five years the Swiss collected edition of Barth's writings
has made available a great deal of hitherto unpublished material
from his pen: letters, sermons and, above all, lecture cycles, especially from his early years as a theological professor. As a result,
there has emerged a rather different picture of Barth from that
which has frequently been conveyed in expositions and critiques of
his work. Most of all this is because these early texts show that
much of Barth's mature thinking was already present in germinal
(and sometimes in quite well-developed) form long before he
started writing the *Church Dogmatics*. This makes implausible the
common idea that Barth's work changed gear around 1930 as he
entered what is generally thought to be the 'analogical' phase of
his thinking. There has also been a steady renewal of interest in
Barth, especially in Britain and North America, as he has once
again come to be appreciated as a thinker of incomparable grandeur
and provocativeness. The renewed sense of the dogmatic potential
of Barth's project has both stimulated and been stimulated by
careful and attentive interpretation of his work, which has again
revised some of the earlier geography of Barth's writings. A fresh
introduction offers an opportunity to draw together some of these
fresh readings and indicate how they shape interpretation of his
theology.

I owe a debt of gratitude to Brian Davies OP for inviting me
to write the book, and to the publishers for their patience with
an alarmingly late author. My reading of Barth has profited

enormously from discussions with colleagues and friends, particularly at meetings of the Karl Barth Society of North America and at the biennial conferences on Barth's theology organized by Wayne Stumme through the Institute for Mission in the USA. My greatest debt, however, is to my graduate students in Toronto and now in Oxford, who, term after term, have inched their way through Barth's writings and pressed me to read with greater attention and surprise than I would otherwise have done. I am grateful to them all.

John Webster
Christ Church
Oxford

Bibliography

Primary literature

Barth's collected works are currently being published under the auspices of the Karl-Barth-Stiftung: *Gesamtausgabe* (Zürich: EVZ, 1971–). Whilst the German texts are indispensable for serious study of his theology, a good deal of his work is available in competent English translations. The basic text is the *Church Dogmatics*, 13 vols (Edinburgh: T. & T. Clark, 1956–75), to which there is the important supplementary volume *The Christian Life* (Edinburgh: T. & T. Clark, 1981). Other important academic lecture cycles (mostly published posthumously) include *The Theology of Calvin* [1922] (Edinburgh: T. & T. Clark, 1992); *The Theology of Schleiermacher* [1923/4] (Edinburgh: T. & T. Clark, 1982); *The Göttingen Dogmatics. Instruction in the Christian Religion I* [1924/5] (Edinburgh: T & T Clark); *Ethics* [1928/9] (Edinburgh: T. & T. Clark, 1981); and *Protestant Theology in the Nineteenth Century. Its Background and History* (London: SCM, 1972). There are also many collections of essays: *The Word of God and the Word of Man* (London: Hodder and Stoughton, 1928); *Against the Stream. Shorter Post-War Writings 1946–52* (London: SCM, 1954); *Theology and Church* (London: SCM, 1962); *The Humanity of God* (London: Collins, 1961); *Community, State and Church* (Gloucester, MA: Smith, 1968); *Fragments Grave and Gay* (London: Collins, 1971); *Final Testimonies* (Grand Rapids: Eerdmans, 1977).

Barth's biblical writings include *The Epistle to the Romans* (London: Oxford University Press, 1933); lectures from 1925/6 on John 1, *Witness to the Word. A Commentary on John 1* (Grand Rapids:

Eerdmans, 1986); a study of 1 Corinthians, *The Resurrection of the Dead* (London: Hodder and Stoughton, 1933); a commentary on *The Epistle to the Philippians* (London: SCM, 1952), and the little study, *Christ and Adam. Man and Humanity in Romans 5* (Edinburgh: Oliver and Boyd, 1963). Unfortunately, only a small selection of Barth's sermons are translated in, for example, *Come, Holy Spirit* (Edinburgh: T. & T. Clark, 1934) and the two volumes of prison sermons, *Deliverance to the Captives* (London: SCM, 1961) and *Call for God* (London: SCM, 1967). In this context, his short study, *Prayer and Preaching* (London: SCM, 1964) repays study.

Commentaries on credal and confessional texts include: *Credo* (London: Hodder and Stoughton, 1936); *The Knowledge of God and the Service of God* (London: Hodder and Stoughton, 1938); *The Faith of the Church* (London: Collins, 1960); *Dogmatics in Outline* (London: SCM, 1960); and *The Heidelberg Catechism for Today* (London: Epworth, 1964). There is also an important commentary on Anselm, translated as *Anselm. Fides Quaerens Intellectum* (London: SCM, 1960).

Much can be learned from reading Barth's published letters: early letters to Thurneysen, some of which are available in English, edited by J. D. Smart, in *Revolutionary Theology in the Making. Barth–Thurneysen Correspondence, 1914–1925* (London: Epworth, 1964); the Barth–Bultmann correspondence, *Karl Barth–Rudolf Bultmann, Letters 1922–1966* (Edinburgh: T. & T. Clark, 1982), *Letters 1961–1968* (Edinburgh: T. & T. Clark, 1981), and *A Late Friendship. The Letters of Karl Barth and Carl Zuckmayer* (Grand Rapids: Eerdmans, 1982). *Karl Barth's Table Talk* (Edinburgh: Oliver and Boyd, 1963) supplements this material.

Secondary literature

The literature on Barth is vast and multilingual. A good account of his life is offered in E. Busch, *Karl Barth. His Life from Letters and Autobiographical Texts* (London: SCM, 1976). One-volume studies of Barth include: G. C. Berkouwer, *The Triumph of Grace in the Theology of Karl Barth* (London: Paternoster, 1956); H. U. von Balthasar, *The Theology of Karl Barth. Exposition and Interpretation* (San Francisco: Ignatius, 1992); G. Hunsinger, *How* to Read Karl Barth (Oxford: Oxford University Press, 1991); and J. Thompson, *Christ in Perspective* (Edinburgh: St Andrew Press, 1978). See also J. Webster (ed.), *The Cambridge Companion to Karl Barth* (Cambridge: Cambridge University Press, 2000).

More specialist studies include: I. Andrews, *Deconstructing Barth. A Study of the Complementary Methods of Karl Barth and Jacques Derrida* (Frankfurt am Main: Lang, 1996); N. Biggar, *The Hastening that Waits. Karl Barth's Ethics* (Oxford: Clarendon Press, 1993); N. Biggar (ed.), *Reckoning with Barth* (Oxford: Mowbray, 1988); S. G. Daveney, *Divine Power. A Study of Karl Barth and Charles Hartshorne* (Philadelphia: Fortress Press, 1986); S. Fisher, *Revelatory Positivism? Barth's Earliest Theology and the Marburg School* (Oxford: Oxford University Press, 1988); D. Ford, *Barth and God's Story* (Frankfurt am Main: Lang, 1981) (on narrative in Barth); T. Gorringe, *Karl Barth. Against Hegemony* (Oxford: Oxford University Press, 1999) (a contextual reading of Barth); C. Gunton, *Becoming and Being* (Oxford: Oxford University Press, 1978) (on Barth's doctrine of God and process theology); T. Hart, *Regarding Karl Barth* (Carlisle: Paternoster, 1999); G. Hunsinger (ed.), *Karl Barth and Radical Politics* (Philadelphia: Westminster, 1976); R. Jenson, *Alpha and Omega* (Edinburgh: Nelson, 1963) (on election in Barth); R. Jenson, *God after God* (Indianapolis: Bobbs Merrill, 1969); W. Stacy Johnson, *The Mystery of God. Karl Barth and the Postmodern Foundations of Theology* (Louisville: Westminster John Knox Press, 1997); E. Jüngel, *The Doctrine of the Trinity* (Edinburgh: Scottish Academic Press, 1976); E. Jüngel, *Karl Barth: A Theological Legacy* (Philadelphia: Westminster, 1986); W. Lowe, *Theology and Difference. The Wound of Reason* (Bloomington: Indiana University Press, 1993) (on Barth and postmodernism); B. McCormack, *Karl Barth's Critically Realistic Dialectical Theology. Its Genesis and Development 1909–1936* (Oxford: Clarendon Press, 1995); J. Macken, *The Autonomy Theme in the* Church Dogmatics: *Karl Barth and His Critics* (Cambridge: Cambridge University Press, 1990); B. Marshall, *Christology in Conflict* (Oxford: Blackwell, 1987); P. D. Matheny, *Dogmatics and Ethics. The Theological Realism and Ethics of Karl Barth's 'Church Dogmatics'* (Frankfurt am Main: Lang, 1991); C. O'Grady, *The Church in the Theology of Karl Barth* (London: Geoffrey Chapman, 1968); R. H. Roberts, *A Theology on its Way? Essays on Karl Barth* (Edinburgh: T. & T. Clark, 1991); P. J. Rosato, *The Spirit as Lord. The Pneumatology of Karl Barth* (Edinburgh: T. & T. Clark,

1981); S. W. Sykes (ed.), *Karl Barth. Studies of His Theological Method* (Oxford: Clarendon Press, 1979); S. W. Sykes (ed.), *Karl Barth. Centenary Essays* (Cambridge: Cambridge University Press, 1989); J. Thompson, *The Holy Spirit in the Theology of Karl Barth* (Allison Park: Pickwick, 1991); T. F. Torrance, *Karl Barth: An Introduction to His Early Theology* (London: SCM, 1963); T. F. Torrance, *Karl Barth. Biblical and Evangelical Theologian* (Edinburgh: T. & T. Clark, 1990); G. Ward, *Barth, Derrida and the Language of Theology* (Cambridge University Press, 1995); S. Webb, *Refiguring Theology. The Rhetoric of Karl Barth* (Albany: SUNY Press, 1991); J. Webster, *Barth's Ethics of Reconciliation* (Cambridge: Cambridge University Press, 1995); J. Webster, *Barth's Moral Theology* (Edinburgh: T. & T. Clark, 1998).

Abbreviations

CD	*Church Dogmatics* (Edinburgh: T. & T. Clark, 1956–75)
ChrL	*The Christian Life* (Edinburgh: T. & T. Clark, 1981)
FQI	*Anselm. Fides Quaerens Intellectum* (London: SCM, 1960)
GD	*The Göttingen Dogmatics I* (Grand Rapids: Eerdmans, 1991)
Romans	*The Epistle to the Romans* (London: Oxford University Press, 1933)
ThCh	*Theology and Church* (London: SCM, 1962)
WGWM	*The Word of God and the Word of Man* (London: Hodder and Stoughton, 1928)

Acknowledgements

Some sections of this book draw on material which has been previously published in a different form, and I am grateful to the following for permission to make use of these texts:

T. & T. Clark: J. Webster, *Barth's Moral Theology*

The Downside Review: J. Webster, ' "On the frontiers of what is observable": Barth's *Römerbrief* and Negative Theology', *Downside Review* 105 (1987), pp. 169–80

Cambridge University Press: Introduction to J. Webster (ed.), *The Cambridge Companion to Karl Barth*

1

Barth's life and work

'As a theologian one can never be great, but at best one remains small in one's own way': so Barth at his eightieth birthday celebrations, characteristically attempting to distance himself from his own reputation.[1] None the less, Barth is the most important Protestant theologian since Schleiermacher, and the extraordinary descriptive depth of his depiction of the Christian faith puts him in the company of a handful of thinkers in the classical Christian tradition. Yet Barth's work has, with some exceptions, not become part of the general theological culture, even in German-speaking Protestantism. His *magnum opus*, the unfinished thirteen volumes of the *Church Dogmatics*, is rarely studied with the necessary breadth and depth; his theological commitments are routinely misconstrued and often sloganized. 'Am I deceived', Barth asked in the early 1950s,

> when I have the impression that I exist in the phantasy of far too many ... mainly, only in the form of certain, for the most part hoary, summations, of certain pictures hastily dashed off by some person at some time, and for the sake of convenience, just as hastily accepted, and then copied endlessly, and which, of course, can easily be dismissed?[2]

For all its lack of recognition, the significance of Barth's work in his chosen sphere is comparable to that of, say, Wittgenstein, Heidegger, Freud, Weber or Saussure in theirs, in that he decisively reorganized an entire discipline. But modern Europe and North America have not proved receptive hosts for Christian dogmatics, especially of Barth's variety, and he remains a massive Christian

1

thinker whose contribution to Christian theology is in many respects still waiting to be received.

Barth's life and work are inseparable, and his writings need to be read in the light of his biography and vice versa.[3] Partly this is because he was at or close to the centre of most of the major developments in German-speaking Protestant theology and church life from the early 1920s to the early 1960s. During his lifetime, indeed, Barth's influence was felt as much – possibly more – through his participation in church and public life as through his strictly academic work. Partly, again, it is because – as we shall see – Barth's identity was very tightly bound up with his external vocation, so that public and personal come together in an intimate way. Moreover, even Barth's academic writings are 'occasional', emerging from and directed towards engagement in church life and theological teaching. At least part of the cogency of his writing derives, therefore, from his sheer urgent presence in what is said.

No critical biography of Barth exists, though his last assistant, Eberhard Busch, assembles a great array of raw material in what is so far the standard account.[4] A projected autobiography started by Barth towards the end of his life was very quickly abandoned; but a good deal of incidental autobiographical material is available in letters, published writings and other forms.[5] Barth was highly self-conscious about the course of his life, and especially about his intellectual development. In his mature writings, he often traced the history of nineteenth- and twentieth-century theology by describing his relationship to it and his own role in bringing to a close the era of Liberal Protestant high culture.[6] Moreover, his theological concern not to drift away from hard-won insight into the true nature of the Christian confession disposed him to keep revisiting the question of the continuity of his own work and, on fairly frequent occasions, to look back over the course of his development. All this means that, despite much that remains unknown about Barth's inner life, much can be and needs to be said at the biographical level.

Barth's life

Barth was born on 10 May 1886 in Basel in Switzerland. His family background placed him at the centre of Basel religious and intellectual life. His father, Fritz Barth, taught at the College of Preachers; his mother Anna (née Sartorius) was the daughter of a conservative

Reformed pastor and related to the famous Burckhardt family. When Barth was quite small, his family moved to Bern, where his father had been appointed to teach at the university. 'It thus came about that I spent my youth among the people of Bern, not without some opposition to a temperament and drift of mind from whose paralysing resistance I already saw my father suffer not a few times.'[7] Although Barth often clashed with his parents, in later life he came to regard his father as '[t]he man to whom I undoubtedly owe the presuppositions of my later relation to theology', and as one 'who by the quiet seriousness with which he applied himself to Christian things as a scholar and as a teacher was for me, and still is, an ineffaceable and often enough admonitory example'.[8] Little inclined to the scientific and mathematical content of his Bern education, Barth was absorbed by poetry, drama and history, as well as by skirmishes with his peers. He attended confirmation classes 'with much pleasure';[9] indeed, the instructor 'brought the whole problem of religion so closely home to me that at the end of the classes I realized clearly the need to know more about the matter. On this rudimentary basis, I resolved to study theology.'[10]

Barth began theological studies in Bern in 1904, finding much of the teaching a dull but (as he later saw it) effective inoculation against the excessive claims of historical criticism.[11] Bern did introduce him to Kant, whose *Critique of Practical Reason* he called '[t]he first book that really moved me as a student',[12] and also to the lively excesses of student society life. A plan to study at Marburg was blocked by his father and Barth went instead to Berlin, then one of the great centres of Protestant liberalism, where he 'heard Harnack with such enthusiasm (and with a little less zeal Kaftan and Gunkel) that apart from the work I did for his seminar in church history I almost completely neglected to make use of the many facilities for general education that were available in that foreign city'.[13] After a brief and rather wild semester back in Bern and an internship in a parish, Barth studied with some reluctance in Tübingen and then, finally, in Marburg in 1908.

One thing drew him to Marburg: Wilhelm Herrmann, then at the height of his powers as dogmatician and ethicist. 'I absorbed Herrmann through every pore.'[14] His influence on Barth, both immediate and long-term, was profoundly formative. Partly he offered a commanding example of lived theological vocation; partly he articulated a coherent account of Christianity which took Kant and Schleiermacher with full seriousness. No less importantly, he also enabled Barth to set a limit to his liberalism: Herrmann's stress on the autonomy of the life of faith (*autopistia*) signified to Barth that, for example, Ernst Troeltsch's subsuming of Christianity under the history of moral culture was a point at which 'I must refuse to follow the dominant theology of the age'.[15] After finishing his studies, Barth deepened his immersion in the Marburg theological scene by working there for a year as an assistant editor for the journal *Christliche Welt*, edited by a leading liberal, Martin Rade. From here Barth went on to pastoral work in Switzerland. After a brief period as suffragan pastor in Geneva (where he was led 'to plunge into Calvin's *Institutio* – with profound impact'[16]), he began his work in 1911 as pastor in the small town of Safenwil in the Aargau.

The ten years Barth spent as a pastor were a period of intensely concentrated development, and most accounts of his work (including those from Barth himself) make much of how the realities of pastoral work which were brought home to him during this decade led to his abandonment of theological liberalism and his adoption of a quite different set of commitments. Barth's liberal assurances were initially undermined by his exposure to the Swiss social democratic movement, then at its height. His immersion in local social and political disputes, fed by the writings of Christian social thinkers such as Kutter and Ragaz, not only made his early years in the pastorate highly conflictual but also began to eat away at his confidence in the bourgeois religious ethos of his teachers. The outbreak of the Great War further disillusioned him. On the one hand, most of his former teachers signed a declaration of support for the Kaiser and thereby showed themselves 'to be hopelessly compromised by their submission to the ideology of war'.[17] On the other hand, the socialist movement itself which, 'credulously enough', Barth had expected 'to avoid the ideology of war', fell into the same trap.[18] At the end of his life, Barth described the crumbling of liberal Protestantism which this represented to him:

> An entire world of theological exegesis, ethics, dogmatics, and preaching, which up to that point I had accepted as basically credible, was thereby shaken to the foundations, and with it everything which flowed at that time from the pens of the German theologians.[19]

In the crisis brought about by the loss of his operative theology and the apparent impossibility of pastoral work which this entailed, Barth began to search for illumination. His lifelong friend Eduard Thurneysen, then pastor in a neighbouring village, encouraged him to take seriously the work of the eschatological revivalist thinkers Johann and Christoph Blumhardt; he read widely in the works of those marginal to mainstream Protestant theology; above all he immersed himself in an amazed rediscovery of the biblical writings, especially the Pauline corpus:

> beyond the problems of theological liberalism and religious socialism, the concept of the Kingdom of God in the real, transcendent sense of the Bible became increasingly more insistent, and the textual basis of my sermons, the Bible, which hitherto I had taken for granted, became more and more of a problem.[20]

In the summer of 1916 he began intensive study of the epistle to the Romans: 'I read and read and wrote and wrote.'[21] From his working notes there emerged the first edition of the Romans commentary, published early in 1919, in which he offered an extraordinarily vivid and insistent characterization of Christianity as eschatological and transcendent.[22]

Towards the end of his pastorate, Barth was consumed by the task of reconstructing his account of the Christian faith, as lectures from the time (collected in English as *The Word of God and the Word of Man*) indicate.[23] A particularly crucial address was that on 'The Christian's Place in Society', given at a conference of Religious Socialists in Tambach in Germany in 1919.[24] As a result of this lecture, Barth discovered himself at the centre of a new theological movement. 'I suddenly found a circle, and the prospect of further circles, of people to whose unrest my efforts promised answers which at once became new questions in the fresh contacts with these German contemporaries.'[25] Partly as a consequence of this new-found prominence in Germany, in 1921 Barth found himself appointed as Honorary Professor of Reformed Theology in Göttingen. Deeply aware of his own lack of preparedness for the role – 'at that time I did not even possess the Reformed confessional writings, and had certainly never read them'[26] – he began the work of theological teaching which was to occupy him for the rest of his life.

'These were, of course, difficult years, for I had not only to learn and teach continuously but also, as the champion of a new trend in theology, I had to vindicate and protect myself in the form of lectures and public discussions of every kind.'[27] In his teaching in these first years as professor, Barth was buried beneath the task of acquainting himself with the classical and Reformed Christian traditions, largely under the pressure of the classroom. He took his students through texts like the Heidelberg Catechism and Calvin's *Institutes*, as well as offering theological exegesis of a variety of New Testament books and eventually teaching a full-scale cycle on dogmatics (published posthumously as the so-called *Göttingen Dogmatics*).[28] Barth also positioned himself more clearly *vis-à-vis* his liberal heritage, notably in a lecture cycle on Schleiermacher (which gave a remarkably mature and sympathetic critique of its subject),[29] but also in external lectures, some of which can be found in the early collection, *Theology and Church*.[30] Barth's central role in the new trend which came to be called 'dialectical theology' demanded much of his energy and took him all over Germany, bringing him into alliance with figures such as Bultmann, Brunner and Gogarten. The journal *Zwischen den Zeiten*, founded in 1922, became the chief organ of the group.

Barth moved to teach at Münster in 1925, where he remained until 1930. During these years he consolidated the theological positions forged in the early part of the decade, and became more deeply acquainted with the Catholic tradition, notably through contact with the Jesuit theologian Erich Przywara. Above all, Barth devoted himself to lecturing and writing on dogmatics, publishing the first volume of his *Christian Dogmatics* in 1927 (the project was later abandoned in favour of the *Church Dogmatics*). Around this time Barth also gave a lengthy series of lectures on ethics (which he already understood as intrinsic to dogmatics), published only posthumously: some of the material found its way in a revised form into the *Church Dogmatics*.[31] Barth's immersion in dogmatics was one of the chief causes of friction with other leading figures in the circle around him; Bultmann, for example, suspected Barth of relapsing into arid scholasticism. Barth's increasingly profound internalization of the thought structure of classical dogmatics pushed him to judge his associates as clinging to the wreckage of theological liberalism, whether in apologetic, anthropological or existential form. By the end of the 1920s, the group had all but dissolved (*Zwischen den Zeiten* lingered on until 1933), not without some personal bitterness on all sides. Looking back on the episode shortly before the Second World War, Barth reflected on 'the loss of a host of theological neighbours, co-workers, and friends ... they and I, little by little or all at once, found ourselves unable to work together any more in the harmony of one mind and one spirit. We quite definitely got on different roads.'[32]

This distancing of himself from his 'theological neighbours' was part of a larger process whereby Barth rid himself of vestiges of his theological inheritance and articulated a theological identity formed out of biblical and dogmatic habits of thought with rigorous consistency and a certain exclusiveness. This process had begun, of course, during the writing of the Romans commentary and was continued during his first two professorships: there is substantial continuity between Barth's early dogmatics lectures and the mature *Church Dogmatics*, for example. However, with his move to Bonn in 1930, and especially with the publication of the first part-volume of the *Church Dogmatics* in 1932, Barth achieved a confidence about his theological commitments which made his writing increasingly calm, unapologetic and descriptively rich. He himself identified his study of Anselm at the beginning of the 1930s as a key intellectual episode. In the book which resulted from this study, Barth noted 'the characteristic absence of crisis in Anselm's theologizing',[33] and the phrase says much about the theological style which became increasingly characteristic of his own work. His confidence had many roots: the fact that Barth felt that he had divested himself of 'the last remnants of a philosophical, i.e., anthropological foundation and exposition of Christian doctrine';[34] the fact that by now he was thoroughly familiar with vast tracts of classical Christian theology, patristic, medieval and Reformation, which made available to him compelling examples of theology done in other than a modern mode; Barth's personal self-assurance as the leading Protestant thinker in Germany. Above all, in the course of the preparation of the early volumes of the *Church Dogmatics* Barth discovered the freedom to think and write confessionally without anxiety about securing extra-theological foundations for the possibility of theology. 'I can say everything far more clearly, unambiguously, simply, and more in the way of a confession, and at the same time also much more freely, openly, and comprehensively, than I could ever say it before.'[35]

Barth remained a sharply critical thinker, of course, even when he settled into a more confessional and descriptive manner. His repudiation of the hospitality to natural theology shown by his former associate Emil Brunner, in a rather savage occasional piece entitled 'No!',[36] not only sealed the grave of the former dialectical theology group, but also provided evidence to generations of North American readers that Barth was at heart a polemicist (and a rude one at that) rather than a constructive church theologian. For Barth, a much more important critical task lay to hand in articulating a theological basis for the church's action in response to the Nazi takeover of Germany. In the early 1930s Barth found himself occupying a key role in church politics, in face of 'a gigantic revelation of human lying and brutality on the one hand, and of human stupidity and fear on the other'.[37] His leadership, both in a stream of writings – most of all *Theological Existence Today*[38] – and in active participation in the nascent Confessing Church, symbolized in his major role in drafting the Barmen Theological Declaration in 1934, was of critical significance. More, perhaps, than any other Protestant leader in Germany at the time, Barth was free of the desire to retain the social and cultural prestige of the church at any price, and could bring to bear on the events of the Nazi takeover a startlingly clear theological position in which the church was wholly defined by its confession of Jesus Christ as 'the one Word of God which we have to hear and which we have to trust and obey in life and in death'.[39]

Barth's leadership in German church life was cut short by his dismissal from his teaching position and his return to Switzerland in 1935. 'As it was, I was dismissed in Germany on a Saturday and on the following Monday the Basel Council offered me a professorship, so that I was out of work for that one Sunday only.'[40] Barth stayed at Basel for the rest of his teaching career. His main task there was the production of the *Church Dogmatics*, first as lectures to ever-increasing crowds of students and then in volume after volume of the final text. 'Dogmatics has ever been with me,' he wrote in the middle of the Second World War, 'giving me a constant awareness of what should be my central and basic theme as a thinker.'[41] The task was utterly absorbing for Barth, and massive enough to be a compelling object both for his intellect and his will. As he wrote, the bulk of the project increased. He found himself reworking the biblical and historical grounds for dogmatics; he felt driven to reconstruct some crucial tracts of Reformed teaching (the doctrine of election is a telling example) or to handle topics in a fresh way (the doctrine of reconciliation, for example, weaves together Christology, soteriology, anthropology and ecclesiology in a wholly unprecedented fashion). Above all, he discovered that the portrayal of the Christian confession upon which he had embarked could not be done 'except in penetrating expositions that will necessarily demand both time and space ... Yes, for a right understanding and exposition there is need of a thorough elucidation.'[42] As early as the end of the Second World War, Barth was expressing frustration with his slow progress and wishing that he 'could run his trains on two or more parallel tracks',[43] and the work remained unfinished at his death, largely laid aside after retirement as he and his long-time assistant Charlotte von Kirschbaum became ill and the stimulus of teaching no longer goaded him to produce.

For all its demands upon Barth's energies, the *Dogmatics* did not eclipse other activities. He was constantly in demand as lecturer and preacher; he played a leading role in the ecumenical movement in the late 1940s, particularly the Amsterdam Assembly of the World Council of Churches; he had wide contact with others through correspondence and personal meetings; he devoted a great deal of time to the many students who came to Basel to write theses under his direction; he kept up a constant stream of less major writings. Moreover, Barth never entirely avoided controversy on some front or other. He often found himself at odds with the Swiss political establishment; he spoke out vigorously in the 1950s against American and European anti-Communism and against German rearmament, to a storm of protest. As retirement approached, he became embroiled in a tangle about his successor, and at the end of his last semester of teaching was publicly criticized by the pro-Rector of the university for his political views. Even after his retirement he evoked considerable church controversy by his opposition to infant baptism in the final fragment of the *Church Dogmatics*, observing wryly that the book left him 'in the theological and ecclesiastical isolation which has been my lot for almost fifty years'.[44]

After retiring at the end of the winter semester of 1961–2 (his swan song was the series of lectures published as *Evangelical Theology*),[45] Barth undertook a lecture tour in the United States and kept up a full schedule of writing, speaking and informal teaching until his health broke down early in 1964. For much of the next two years he was in hospital or convalescent at home, and the long illness left him unable to work at major tasks for the rest of his life. He did travel to Rome in 1966 to talk with those involved in the Second Vatican Council and prepared a last fragment of the *Church Dogmatics* for publication, along with a number of minor pieces. But Barth's closing years were often clouded by feelings of 'vexation, anxiety, weariness, humiliation, and melancholy',[46] especially in view of the constrictions imposed on him by old age:

in every respect my feet can now move only in a small compass. Gone are the trips and runs and walks and rides of the past, gone the addresses to large groups, gone the participation in conferences and the like. Everything has its time, and for me all that kind of thing, it seems, has had its time.[47]

Barth felt the loss of his professional life with great acuteness. But there were compensations: at least partial healing of some broken relationships; a brief but intense friendship with the dramatist Carl Zuckmayer; the retention of curiosity about people, books and ideas. At times, too, Barth was able to express a kind of mellow calm and simplicity, along with an untroubled freedom in limitation, as in the little collection of his writings from the months before his death, *Final Testimonies*.[48] Here he describes what it means to him to be liberal:

> Being truly liberal means thinking and speaking in responsibility and openness on all sides, backwards and forwards, toward both past and future, and with what I might call total personal modesty. To be modest is not to be skeptical; it is to see what one thinks and says also has limits. This does not hinder me from saying very definitely what I think I see and know. But I can do this only in the awareness that there have been and are other people before and alongside me, and that still others will come after me. This awareness gives me an inner peace, so that I do not think I always have to be right even though I say definitely what I say and think. Knowing that a limit is set for me, too, I can move cheerfully within it as a free man.[49]

Barth died on 10 December 1968.

Barth was a powerful, complex personality. His life as well as his literary work demonstrate a highly-developed attentiveness and curiosity: he found people, places, events and ideas utterly interesting and absorbing. He was fascinated by all the different manifestations of the secular world. Especially in later years, he took great delight in the international student body in Basel, and students often experienced his teaching in seminars and lectures as something in which they could 'witness the dynamics of newly-created thoughts'.[50] Carl Zuckmayer, who knew Barth only at the very end of his life, reflected that Barth's

> thirst for knowledge, fed from a spring of deep basic knowledge, was inexhaustible. He constantly took up new themes of a historical, literary, or philosophical character, in order, as he put it, to fill long-standing gaps. Everything concerning everyday life and world events and daily politics occupied him and aroused his criticism and lively interest.[51]

This same trait is also found in his *magnum opus*: one of the things which sustains the argument of the *Dogmatics* in its extraordinary length is that Barth's thinking and writing are always mobile, and the passages where Barth does not convey a sense of astonished discovery are few and far between. 'Something within me remained restless,' he wrote at the end of the 1940s,

> driving me ever and again to seek new knowledge, to press forward on certain lines, to take my stand resolutely and see it through, but at the same time bidding me to view all these activities as parts of a process and so not to forfeit my freedom. I have let myself be led and now and then be taken by surprise.[52]

Barth was able to sustain at one and the same time a vigorously active public life and the continuous interior concentration and focus required to produce his writings, above all the *Dogmatics*. Between 1930 and 1940, for example, he published the first three-part volumes of the *Church Dogmatics* (in English, around 2000 pages of text);[53] a monograph on Anselm (*Fides Quaerens Intellectum*);[54] two expositions of the creed (*Credo*[55] and *The Faith of the Church*);[56] two series of Gifford lectures (*The Knowledge of God and the Service of God*);[57] a book of sermons (*God's Search for Man*);[58] and a very large number of polemical and occasional pieces. All this was accomplished alongside a very prominent role in the German church conflict, first in Germany, and after 1935, from Switzerland. Barth clearly experienced intense fulfilment in what he once called 'the necessity and beauty of serious and regular intellectual work'.[59] 'How fine a thing it is to be occupied with this great matter,' he wrote in the preface to *Church Dogmatics* IV/2.[60] And yet he did not resist public activity; however much he felt harassed by the demands made on him, he appeared to need an external counterpoint to the intellectual.

These two strong aspects of Barth, the internal and the external, coalesce in the fact that his personal identity was strongly defined in vocational categories. He thought of himself in terms of the tasks – intellectual, political, and so forth – which he felt called to undertake and which furnished and sustained a coherent sense of who he was. A characteristic autobiographical passage runs:

> One has his hands full with things to do without so much as seeking opportunity. One has continually to stand forth as example and pattern ... One knows that everything is now at stake ...

And one knows that this can only mean for him who still has his time and task that all the contours of things and men outline themselves more sharply, that the problems and needs of one's own career and position, as well as those of the world around us, are felt more keenly, that one is summoned to a prudent haste, to a certain mild but dogged intensity in both one's work and talk.[61]

It is a revealing passage in many ways: the intensity and persistence of Barth's approach to life and work, the sense of the weightiness and urgent uniqueness of the present occasion. But above all, the passage shows how far Barth was from any idea that knowledge of self is awareness of some inner world behind public speech and action. He thinks of himself, by contrast, as agent, and as agent 'summoned', by the circumstances of how the world is, to action and speech of a certain definite direction. As Hans Frei once remarked,

one has the impression that Barth was a man for whom overt force of character and the exercise of vocation, rather than internal self-consciousness, self-probing or the tensions of 'self-transcendence' were the hallmarks of being human and of his own humanity.[62]

Barth had a very firm sense of his own identity, rooted no doubt in the particular cast of his personality, but reinforced by his inhabiting a broad imaginative space peopled with the figures and texts of classical Christian (and European) culture, and maintained by a commanding sense of being called to an engrossing set of tasks. This combination of interior breadth and highly focused vocation afforded him both a rootedness in his particular context and a freedom from its potential inhibitions. It meant, for example, that he could remain committed to his particular heritage in the institutions of Swiss church, academic and political life whilst at the same time viewing them with a certain detachment. Barth was never completely at home in the culture of bourgeois Switzerland, and often voiced his criticisms of it. 'We Swiss lack the Mozartean element, the calm joyfulness so badly needed in a torn and divided world. We lack the ability to see ourselves in our own relativity.'[63] In many ways Barth was more at home in the larger world of Germany, which provided him with a highly responsive climate for the first decade and a half of his teaching and which ensured his place on the wider map even after 1935. Yet: 'I belong to Basel.'[64] This curious blend of commitment and ironic distance was present in many aspects of Barth's life and work and, as we shall see, also characterizes his theological commitments.

There was also a certain alienating effect to Barth's personality. He could be devastatingly critical of people, views and institutions, and in both public and private life he experienced relationships which were strained or which ended in estrangement. Reflecting on one such breakdown – the disintegration of the 'dialectical theology' circle of the 1920s – Barth was painfully aware that 'my lifework seems to be wanting in a certain accumulative power – even more, that a certain explosive, or in any case centrifugal, effect seems to inhere in it'.[65] Experiences here often led Barth to cast himself in the role of outsider and explain his isolation to himself and others in terms of his sense that the primary ideas which drove his work had not been grasped or heeded or were contravened by the teachings and actions of others. At other times, his defence lay in irony and humour, through which he not only evaded his critics but also softened the negative impact which the weight of his own personality could have.

It is this restless, many-sided personality which lies behind Barth's writings. This does not, of course, mean that his theology should be read as a sort of encoded autobiography, for he was a sternly objective thinker. But there is an intensely personal aspect to all that he wrote (he wrote almost nothing in the way of pure, 'detached' scholarship), precisely because his thinking and writing were who he was.

Interpreting Barth

Reading Barth is no easy task. Because the corpus of his writing is so massive and complex, what he has to say cannot be neatly summarized. Moreover, his preferred method of exposition, especially in the *Church Dogmatics*, is frustrating for readers looking to follow a linear thread of argument. Commentators often note the musical structure of Barth's major writings: the announcement of a theme, and its further extension in a long series of developments and recapitulations, through which the reader is invited to consider the theme from a number of different angles and in a number of different relations. No one stage of the argument is definitive; rather, it is the whole which conveys the substance of what he has to say. As a result, Barth's views on any given topic cannot be comprehended in a single statement (even if the statement is one of his own), but only in the interplay of a range of articulations of a theme.

Moreover, many readers of Barth find in him an unpalatable assertiveness, what Tillich called 'a demonic absolutism which throws the truth like stones at the heads of people, not caring whether they can accept it or not'.[66] There are certainly traces of this in Barth (they are not simply restricted to his occasional writings), and there are plenty of places where he is polemical. But this aspect of his work is best read as a way of making a case for strong (and, judged by the canons of the theological establishment, deviant) views by severely critical attention to other voices. Like some feminist writers, for example, Barth often feels the need to undermine dominant intellectual traditions which stand in the way of a proper appreciation of his own convictions. But it should also be noted that critique is usually subordinate to description, especially in Barth's later work. Nor should it be forgotten that Barth is capable of very-finely drawn and generous readings of those from whom he is theologically distant, and that the thinker whom he studied most critically and with the greatest disagreement – Schleiermacher – is also the thinker whom he read with the greatest deference and sensitivity.

Even after the reader has adjusted to Barth's peculiar rhetoric, another substantial issue needs attention. He persistently goes against the grain of some of the most settled intellectual habits of modernity. In his early writings this comes across in, for example, his refusal to allow that 'history' is a more comprehensive and well-founded reality than 'revelation'. In the *Church Dogmatics*, it expresses itself in his rejection of modern understandings of human moral selfhood which focus on ethical consciousness, deliberation and choice as axiomatic. Thus at key points Barth distances himself, sometimes dramatically, from the idealist and subject-centred traditions of modern intellectual culture. Those traditions still enjoy considerable authority in Western Christian theology, both in its liberal Protestant and its revisionist Catholic expressions, and still make Barth's work difficult to assimilate. And, it might be added, where they have waned – as in some recent 'postliberal' theology – a recovery of Barth's thought has often been either a precipitating cause or a significant consequence.

Because of this, one of the most fruitful ways of reading Barth is to look at his thought in the more general context of the breakdown of 'modernity' – the decline, that is, of idealist metaphysics and the philosophical, moral and religious culture of subjectivity. Barth's relationship to modernity is very complicated, and it is too easy to reduce the complexities by making him appear either merely dismissive and reactionary or a kind of mirror-image of modernity who never shook himself free of its grip. Barth is certainly a central figure in the break-up of the modern tradition in its theological expression: for 40 years he mounted a vigorous critique of that tradition, exposing what he took to be its fatal weaknesses and articulating a quite different way of doing Christian theology. What is less often discerned is that Barth was also in important respects heir to that tradition, and that even when he argued vociferously against it, it sometimes continued to set the terms of the debate. Barth was referring to much more than his age when he wrote at the end of his life: 'I am a child of the nineteenth century'.[67]

As we will see from the analysis of Barth's theology in subsequent chapters, one of the major ways in which Barth was in conversation with his nineteenth-century heritage was in his preoccupation with giving an account of the relation of God to humanity. In early work, the preoccupation expressed itself in urgent attempts to find a satisfactory answer to the question: How is God *God* for us? In the mature dogmatic writings, it came across in the centrality of the notion of covenant, through which Barth phrased his answer to a slightly different question: How is God God *for us*? Barth's answers always involved him in denying some of the basic premises of nineteenth-century theology: the priority of religious subjectivity and experience, the identification of God with ethical value, the presentation of Jesus as archetypal religious and moral consciousness. And, as his thought developed, Barth became increasingly confident that no answer to the question of God's relation to humanity can be considered satisfactory which abstracts from the axiomatic reality of God's self-presence in Jesus Christ. The brilliance of Barth's account of that reality was enough to bring large parts of the edifice of nineteenth-century liberalism crashing to the ground. Yet even so, it must not be forgotten that there is substantial continuity, in that, as Barth put it, 'the nineteenth century's tasks remain for us, too'.[68] In Barth, then, we shall encounter a thinker who was both deeply indebted to the intellectual traditions of modernity and also their rigorous critic. If Barth dismantled modern Protestant theology as it developed in Germany in the eighteenth and nineteenth centuries, he did so from the inside.

In what follows, we shall trace major themes in Barth's theological writings, starting from his early writings from the pastorate in Safenwil and his first years as a professor, and then analysing the structure and content of the *Church Dogmatics*. We will conclude with a more extended consideration of Barth's relationship to modernity and the reception and resourcefulness of his work. The sheer magnitude, quantitative and qualitative, of his achievement inevitably means that a book of short compass can only scratch the surface. But by close study of some key texts, it may stimulate the reader to explore Barth's own writings and engage at first hand with this compelling thinker. If it does so, it will have fulfilled its end.

Notes

1. 'Karl Barth's Speech on the Occasion of his Eightieth Birthday Celebrations' in K. Barth, *Fragments Grave and Gay* (London: Collins, 1971), p. 112.

2. 'Foreword to the English Edition' in O. Weber, *Karl Barth's Church Dogmatics* (London: Lutterworth, 1953), p. 7.

3. This is what makes contextual interpretations of Barth (exemplified most recently by T. Gorringe, *Karl Barth: Against Hegemony* (Oxford: Oxford University Press, 1999) important, provided that they are sophisticated enough not to absorb Barth into the factors which supposedly 'influenced' him, and provided that they do not treat his theology as if it were simply the record of the history of his times.

4. E. Busch, *Karl Barth. His Life from Letters and Autobiographical Texts* (London: SCM, 1976).

5. Much material is available in Barth's published correspondence; for example with Eduard Thurneysen (a selection is available in J. D. Smart (ed.), *Revolutionary Theology in the Making* (London: Epworth, 1964); with Rudolf Bultmann in K. Barth and R. Bultmann, *Letters 1922–1966* (Edinburgh: T. & T. Clark, 1982), with Carl Zuckmayer in *A Late Friendship. The Letters of Karl Barth and Carl Zuckmayer* (Grand Rapids: Eerdmans, 1982); and with different correspondents in *Letters 1961–1968* (Edinburgh: T. & T. Clark, 1981). The prefaces to the various volumes of the *Church Dogmatics* often contain autobiographical material. Various autobiographical sketches from the faculty albums of the universities where Barth taught can be found in the Barth–Bultmann correspondence (pp. 150–8): see especially the Münster Faculty Album. An especially rich resource is K. Barth, *How I Changed My Mind* (Richmond, VA: John Knox, 1966).

6. See, for example, from the 1950s, 'Evangelical Theology in the Nineteenth Century' and 'The Humanity of God' in *The Humanity of God* (London: Collins, 1961), pp. 9–33, 35–65, and, from the 1960s, 'A Thank-You and a Bow – Kierkegaard's Reveille. Speech on being

awarded the Sonning Prize', in *Fragments Grave and Gay*, pp. 95–101, and 'Concluding Unscientific Postscript on Schleiermacher' in *The Theology of Schleiermacher* (Edinburgh: T. & T. Clark, 1982), pp. 261–79.

7. Münster Faculty Album, p. 151.

8. Ibid., p. 157.

9. Ibid., p. 152.

10. Ibid.

11. 'Concluding Unscientific Postscript', p. 262.

12. Münster Faculty Album, p. 152.

13. Ibid., p. 153.

14. Ibid.

15. Ibid.

16. Ibid., p. 154.

17. Ibid.

18. Ibid.

19. 'Concluding Unscientific Postscript', p. 264.

20. Münster Faculty Album, p. 154.

21. 'Concluding Unscientific Postscript', p. 265.

22. *Der Römerbrief* (Bern: Bäschlin, 1919). The English translation, *The Epistle to the Romans* (London: Oxford University Press, 1933) is from the thoroughly rewritten second edition of 1922.

23. London: Hodder and Stoughton, 1928.

24. 'The Christian's Place in Society' in *WGWM*, pp. 272–327.

25. Münster Faculty Album, p. 155.

26. Ibid., p. 156. See also Barth's Foreword to H. Heppe, *Reformed Dogmatics* (London: George Allen and Unwin, 1950), pp. v–vii.

27. Münster Faculty Album, p. 156.

28. Two of the projected three volumes have so far appeared in German (*Unterricht in der christlichen Religion* I and II (Zürich: Theologischer Verlag, 1985, 1990), translated in one volume as *The Göttingen Dogmatics. Instruction in the Christian Religion I* (Edinburgh: T & T Clark, 1990).

29. The lectures are published as *The Theology of Schleiermacher*.

30. London: SCM, 1962.

31. K. Barth, *Ethics* (Edinburgh: T. & T. Clark, 1981).

32. *How I Changed My Mind*, p. 41.

33. *Anselm. Fides Quaerens Intellectum* (London: SCM, 1960), p. 26.

34. *How I Changed My Mind*, pp. 42f.

35. Ibid., pp. 43f.

36. 'No! Answer to Emil Brunner', in K. Barth and E. Brunner, *Natural Theology* (London: Bles, 1946), pp. 67–128.

37. *How I Changed My Mind*, p. 45.

38. London: Hodder, 1933.

39. Article 1 of the Barmen Theological Declaration in A. C. Cochrane, *The Church's Confession Under Hitler* (Philadelphia: Westminster, 1962), p. 239.

40. 'Eightieth Birthday Celebrations', pp. 115f.

41. *CD* II/2, p. ix.

42. Ibid.

43. *CD* III/1, p. x.

44. *CD* IV/4, p. xii.

45. *Evangelical Theology. An Introduction* (London: Weidenfeld and Nicholson, 1963).

46. *Letters 1961–1968*, p. 295.

47. Ibid., p. 254.

48. Grand Rapids: Eerdmans, 1977.

49. 'Liberal Theology – An Interview', in *Final Testimonies*, pp. 34f.

50. D. Ritschl, 'How to Be Most Grateful to Karl Barth without Remaining a Barthian' in D. McKim (ed.), *How Karl Barth Changed My Mind* (Grand Rapids: Eerdmans, 1986), p. 87.

51. *A Late Friendship*, pp. 69–71.

52. *How I Changed My Mind*, p. 51.

53. *CD* I/1, I/2 and II/1 appeared in German in 1932, 1939 and 1940 respectively, from Chr Kaiser Verlag, Munich.

54. Munich: Kaiser, 1931.

55. *Credo* (London: Hodder and Stoughton, 1936) was published under the same title in German in 1935 (Munich: Kaiser).

56. *The Faith of the Church* (London: Collins, 1960) was originally published in French as *La Confession de la Foi de L'Eglise* (Paris: Delachaux et Niestlé, 1940).

57. London: Hodder and Stoughton, 1938: the original, *Gotteserkenntnis und Gottesdienst*, was published in the same year by Evangelischer Verlag, Zürich.

58. *God's Search for Man* (Edinburgh: T. & T. Clark, 1935) was published in German as *Die grosse Barmherzigkeit* (Munich: Kaiser, 1935).

59. *Letters 1961–1968*, p. 167.

60. *CD* IV/2, p. ix.

61. *How I Changed My Mind*, p. 39.

62. H. Frei, 'Eberhard Busch's Biography of Karl Barth' in *Types of Christian Theology* (New Haven: Yale University Press, 1992), p. 150.

63. 'The "Un-Mozartean" Swiss' in *Fragments Grave and Gay*, pp. 52f.

64. Münster Faculty Album, p. 151.

65. *How I Changed My Mind*, p. 41.

66. P. Tillich, *Systematic Theology* III (Chicago: University of Chicago Press, 1963), p. 186.

67. *A Late Friendship*, p. 3.

68. 'Evangelical Theology in the Nineteenth Century', p. 12.

2

'The deep secret YES'

By 1916 a number of us of the younger theological generation had hesitantly set out to introduce a theology better than that of the nineteenth century and of the turn of the century – better in the sense that in it, God, in his unique position over against man, and especially religious man, might be clearly given the honour we found him to have in the Bible.[1]

Barth's words as he reviewed his early years in a late speech identify two key factors in understanding the first fifteen years or so of his theological development – that it involved him in a fundamental change of direction, and that the change consisted in an astonished realization of the deity of God. Although towards the end of his life Barth sometimes took a calmer attitude towards the nineteenth-century theology which he had earlier rejected with vigorous, at times ruthless, intensity, his work was permanently stamped by the experience of feeling the need to reinvent the discipline of Christian theology. The process of reinvention involved Barth in a two-fold task of ground clearing and construction. The ground clearing consisted in establishing a critical account of the history of Protestant theology since Friedrich Schleiermacher (in whom its previous change of direction had taken place), exposing to the severest judgement the dogmatics, ethics, biblical exegesis and cultural theory of the traditions in which Barth himself had been thoroughly schooled. The construction consisted in rebuilding Christian theology from the ground up, somewhat clumsily at first as Barth found himself largely lacking in the resources needed to convert his instincts into arguments, and then with increasing confidence, weight and precision as he acquainted himself with and rearticulated traditions of Christian thought and language which in the nineteenth century had been almost entirely eclipsed. Ground clearing and construction went on alongside each other all the time, of course, as Barth found himself having to say 'no' in order to create a space for the affirmations which he wished to make. Yet it is crucial that the polemic should not be construed in such a way that Barth is made to appear a purely destructive thinker. Beneath the repudiations, the rhetorical struggle to bring the whole cultural and intellectual edifice of liberal Protestantism crashing to the ground, there is a fundamentally creative aim. 'The devastating negation under which we stand has a positive, obverse side'[2] – namely, the rediscovery that, precisely because God is sovereign, other, utterly beyond any cultural or religious project, God is the one in whom alone is found salvation and flourishing.

Barth's work up to the period of the beginning of the *Church Dogmatics* has been subject to intensive scrutiny in recent years for a couple of reasons. First, a great deal more material is now available, filling out the picture we have of Barth and pressing for the revision of accounts of him which were based on a narrower range of texts. Readers of Barth now have two of his early lecture cycles on the work of other theologians, namely Calvin and Schleiermacher (from 1922 and 1923/4 respectively); a lecture course on the Reformed confessional writings; a set of lectures on parts of the Gospel of John from 1925/6; above all, Barth's first lectures on dogmatics and ethics are now available, and their significance for understanding Barth's theology both in this period and beyond can scarcely be over-emphasized. In effect, the all-important period between Barth's second commentary on Romans in 1922 and his first published prolegomena to dogmatics, the *Christliche Dogmatik* of 1927, can now be mapped much more effectively than it was previously, when all that was known of the Barth of that period was his occasional writings. Most importantly, the publication of the early lecture cycles means that questions of the development of Barth's work can now be handled with a good deal more precision, and our initial task in this chapter, before we examine Barth's earlier theology, will be to indicate the main genetic–historical questions which bear upon this phase of his work.

A second reason for contemporary interest in Barth's early theological writings is that their content and rhetoric has been found companionable to some of the preoccupations which cluster around the word 'postmodernism'. Barth's rejection of nineteenth-century liberalism involved discarding any idea that God is a given presence in human religious culture, and this (if not the grand narratives of the *Church Dogmatics*) has made him appear to some readers as a postmodernist *avant la lettre* – though great care needs to be exercised if his work is not to be assimilated to modes of thought quite foreign to him. As we try to make sense of Barth's early writings, it will be important to set alongside the early apocalyptic writings (most of all, the second Romans commentary) the lecture texts from the 1920s whose positivity is much less easy to identify as a precursor to postmodernism.

Is there an early Barth?

Until fairly recently, it has been a stock-in-trade of interpretation of Barth's development to propose that, after his decisive turn from liberal theology during the First World War, his theology falls into two phases: a period dominated by 'dialectic' (by which is meant, roughly, polarized account of God and created humanity), and a period governed by 'analogy' (by which is meant a God-created and God-sustained correspondence between God and humanity). This account of Barth was first advanced in systematic form in the early 1950s by the Swiss Roman Catholic theologian Hans Urs von Balthasar, who deeply admired Barth; Barth expressed the highest praise of von Balthasar's book on himself.[3] After von Balthasar, the idea that Barth's development from his early years to the Christology of the *Church Dogmatics* is one 'from dialectic to analogy' enjoyed considerable authority and, indeed, some measure of endorsement from Barth himself. An important part of von Balthasar's reading of Barth, for example, was his suggestion that Barth's 1931 book on Anselm provided the key to the theological method of the *Church Dogmatics* and thus formed the hinge of the turn from dialectic to analogy – a view which Barth himself reinforced in the preface to the second edition of the Anselm book.[4] More generally, in later life Barth sometimes gave the impression that as he worked his way more deeply into the ideas of Christology, he left behind an eschatological way of thinking (with its heavy investment in polemic) and moved to a way of thinking at once more affirmative and less oppositional. In terms of the content of Barth's thinking, this has often led to the portrayal of his earlier work as built upon a sheerly abstract polarity of God and humanity, only later corrected by his espousal of the christological covenant as the theme of dogmatic reflection on Christian faith.

Three factors tell against this account of Barth's development, however, at least in its less sophisticated versions. First, it is very important that Barth's work before the *Church Dogmatics* is not simply represented by the Romans commentary and collections of occasional writings such as *The Word of God and the Word of Man* and *Theology and Church*. The lecture cycles, and especially the Göttingen dogmatics lectures and the *Ethics*, are at least as important as the commentaries and essays which Barth published at the time. Indeed, from the early 1920s onwards, when Barth moved into theological teaching, the centre of gravity of his work was his attempt to draw out the positive content of his theological convictions, a positive content which emerges less clearly in his published writings but which was expounded in considerable depth before his student audiences in Göttingen and Münster. Once the lecture cycles are factored into our account of Barth, then, the picture of him as simply negative cannot be sustained; from the beginning of his teaching career he demonstrated himself to be a serious constructive thinker.

Second, the 1920s lecture cycles are often in striking continuity with the later *Church Dogmatics*. The tying together of the doctrines of Trinity and revelation which will form Barth's basic approach to theological prolegomena in the first volume of the *Church Dogmatics* in 1932 is already firmly in place in 1924. Or again, material from the 1928/9 lectures on ethics finds its way, sometimes only quite lightly revised, into the *Church Dogmatics*. It is also noteworthy that the very early lectures on Calvin already articulate an account of that ethical character of Reformed dogmatics which so decisively determined the structure of the *Church Dogmatics*. This means that some (not all, of course) of Barth's primary theological decisions which would shape the rest of his dogmatic work were made in the first period of his professorate.

Third, even the writings which some judge to be extreme in their 'dialectical' contrasting of God and humanity are – as we shall see later in this chapter – by no means devoid of positive affirmations about human history and action on the basis of what is said about God. It is not only in his later work that Barth articulates correspondences or analogies between God and God's human covenant partners. The later phases of Barth's work involve, therefore, not so much a decisive turn from what has come earlier but the giving of a greater profile to and a massive amplification of the affirmations which Barth's earlier rhetoric sometimes obscures from less careful readers.

Lest the question of the relation of early and late Barth be thought a mere technical point of scholarship, it is worth keeping in mind its wide significance for making sense of Barth's works as a whole. One effect of reading Barth through the developmental pattern of 'dialectic to analogy' has been to de-emphasize the permanent importance of the so-called 'dialectical' writings, making them into a transient stage whose vision of the Christian faith was largely abandoned as a result of the Christocentrism of the *Church Dogmatics*. But this easily misconstrues both Barth's early and later writings. The misconstrual of the early writings is to read them as pure negativity, exercises in rhetorical demolition in which Barth allows for no relation between the utterly transcendent God and the contingent human world. The misconstrual of the later writings is to think that their affirmation of the covenant between God and humanity involves a retraction of the sharp sense of their difference.

In effect, a more complex picture of Barth's early development is required than one which assimilates it to one simple motif (dialectic). Barth certainly spent much energy in these years wresting himself free of liberal Protestant theology and the culture of which it formed part; certainly he found tools for doing so in highly contrastive understandings of God's relation to the world which will later strike him as abstract in tone and lacking in dogmatic (particularly trinitarian and christological) nuance. But much else is happening in the same period. Barth is, for example, trying to reinvent to his own satisfaction the genre of the dogmatic treatise, and steadily assembling the vast arsenal of resources (biblical, patristic, medieval, Reformation and modern) which he will later deploy in the *Church Dogmatics*. And, as we shall see, even Barth's most stinging criticisms of the prevailing orthodoxy are, at heart, an attempt to think his way towards the understanding of God's freedom in which he will later root his convictions about God's humanity. From the beginning Barth says 'no' in order to learn how to say 'yes'.

Breaking with liberalism

Though it is difficult to date the beginning of the process with any precision, it is clear that by the middle years of the First World War

Barth had come to see his task as the re-envisaging of the Christian faith and reorienting the work of ministry and theology in ways which broke with the dominant traditions of churchly and academic practice. Making the break involved him in identifying the basic assumptions of his cultural and theological heritage and submitting them to the most pressing critical scrutiny. What were those basic assumptions?

On Barth's view, the Protestant theological tradition since Schleiermacher had been characterized by an account of God's relation to humanity which he came to judge as fundamentally disturbed. Liberal theology and culture were built around an affirmation of God's immanence. That is, relation to God was considered to constitute a given factor of human history, culture and religion; that relation was an ingredient within human being and experience and therefore became something which could be described and, indeed, cultivated, without immediate reference to the gracious, intervening activity of God himself. Barth came to think that this notion of 'a given relationality between the human and the divine' was theologically ruinous.[5] Why?

For Barth, envisaging God's relation to humanity in this way undermined the sheer originality of God. That is, it worked against everything that is summed up by the tautology 'God is God' and threatened to convert God into a mere function of the creaturely realm. 'Beyond, *trans*: that is the crux of the situation.'[6] All through his early writings, Barth struggled to express an idea of God's transcendence as more than mere comparative superiority, more than some observable, exalted aspect of creaturely existence. 'God,' he wrote, 'is pure negation.'[7]

> God, the pure and absolute boundary and beginning of all that we are and have and do; God who is distinguished qualitatively from men and from everything human, and must never be identified with anything which we name, or experience, or conceive, or worship, as God ... God, the Lord, the Creator, the Redeemer: this is the Living God ... Above and beyond the apparently infinite series of possibilities and visibilities in this world there breaks forth, like a flash of lightning, impossibility and invisibility.[8]

What Barth found in Paul's letter to the Romans was a world suffused with a sense of God as distinct, qualitatively and infinitely. Divine transcendence is not to be thought of non-radically, 'merely as improved worldliness',[9] for God is 'that which lies upon the other side'[10] – the image of spatial removal, visual inaccessibility, was frequently used by the early Barth to make the point that God is not to be conceived out of his relation to the temporal and mundane. If there is such a thing as proper thought about God (and Barth sometimes appeared at this stage to doubt its possibility), it must proceed only by setting aside any sense of a 'relative relation between God and man'.[11] And it was just this which, on Barth's reading, liberalism – whether of the nineteenth-century tradition as a whole or, more proximately, of Barth's teachers – had failed to grasp by replacing a radical account of God's connection to humanity with a merely relational one.

Barth was tireless in exposing the substitution in all manner of forms. Most obviously, it took shape as a certain cultural and religious idiom in which God was drawn within the immanent world of human achievement. Thus in a 1922 lecture on 'The Problem of Ethics Today', Barth criticized the representatives of liberal high culture (what he called 'the generation of 1914'[12] – those whose support for the Kaiser's war policy had demonstrated their theological bankruptcy) for their confidence that

> here was a human culture building itself up in orderly fashion in politics, economics, and science, theoretical and applied, progressing steadily along its whole front, interpreted and ennobled by art, and through its religion and morality reaching well beyond itself toward yet better days.[13]

Or an earlier address on 'The Righteousness of God', delivered in 1916 while Barth was still in the pastorate, suggested that at the hands of 'the happy gentleman of culture who today drives up so briskly in his little car of progress and so cheerfully displays the pennants of his various ideals',[14] 'the longing for a new world ... has become the joy of development'.[15] Morality, the state and law, religion – the basic building blocks of what Barth later called ' "liberal", "positive" cultural Protestantism'[16] – are nothing less than self-wrought human righteousness, an evasion of the sheerly critical, utterly different, will of God. 'His will is not a corrected continuation of our own. It approaches us as a Wholly Other.'[17]

Put slightly differently, Barth pointed to the absence of a pervasive sense of divine grace in the tradition from which he was seeking to extricate himself: precisely because of its solid cultural authority, Protestantism in its liberal guise had eliminated the destabilizing potential of contingency upon divine action which grace brings with it. Towards the end of the 1920s, in a lecture surveying the fate of 'The Word of God in Theology from Schleiermacher to Ritschl', Barth argued that 'the grace, which the theologians of the time described so beautifully as free, did not remain free for them. They claimed it as a right, a certainty, a possession of the Christian, the so-called believing Christian.'[18] This domestication of grace occurs wherever God is made internal to any religious or moral project, or any pattern of speech or thought. Over against this, Barth frequently urged that God is 'KRISIS', an absolute judgement which, because it cannot be assigned a place in any contingent set of arrangements, simply shatters our attempts to make it a manageable feature of 'our' world:

> It is not against faith that we are warned, but against OUR faith; not against the place that has become visible where men can stand and live, but against OUR taking up a position there and proceeding to live out our lives there; not against freedom and detachment, but against their ambiguous appearance in OUR lives, against the certainty with which WE advance in freedom and detachment. The warning is uttered against any position or manner of life or endeavour that WE think to be satisfactory and justifiable, as though WE were able in some way or other to escape the KRISIS of God.[19]

What Barth was repulsing in these early pieces was an assemblage of cultural, religious and theological values which he believed had forgotten the non-given, non-possessable, irreversible character of God's presence to the world. Barth was not rejecting any and all ideas of God's relation to us – although he is often misread in this way, as if he sought to effect some eschatological erasure of the world. Rather, what Barth was rejecting was one dominant account of God and humanity, according to which God's relation to us can be discovered within us and our undertakings, when in fact that relation is constituted solely by the free, disorienting action of God. Thus Barth sought to deny that God's relation to us is inherent in human nature and activity, especially in its noblest forms; but he sought to preserve the relation itself, though grounded in and thereby chastened by the sheer gratuity of God. This irreversibility of God's relation to us does not, however, entail a purely abstract understanding of divine transcendence, even though there were occasions when Barth sounded as if he were close to such ideas.

Human life and history are not so much rejected as relativized by God the 'Primal Origin'.[20]

Why was Barth's reaction to liberal Protestantism so strong? There are, doubtless, biographical and cultural factors in play: Barth's lifelong tendency to think in terms of contrasts rather than correlations, and his place in the rather fevered intellectual world of Germany in the 1920s.[21] But there is more here than a religious thinker registering the 'reeling, rocking, and ruin'[22] of the bourgeois certainties of the imperialist era, and more than the nihilist cultural prophecy or garish expressionism which was common enough in the 1920s. Certainly, Barth's break with liberalism involved a turning away from an entire culture, from a whole set of understandings of the nature and purposes of human persons, history and institutions. But the source of the protest is theological. Again, it is doubtless true that the culture from which Barth was turning was a culture by which he had himself been deeply formed, morally, intellectually and professionally. The jagged, ceaselessly interrogative rhetoric to which he was given in those days betokens someone trying to extricate himself from something which he once found authoritative and persuasive, and which had once held out the promise of both an orderly account of the world and a stable professional role. But it was Scripture and theology which meant that Barth could no longer continue with liberalism. When it began to dawn on him that the gospel as he now saw it could not support liberalism's understanding of self and world, he not only faced the personal need to reconfigure his own theological views, but also set himself a much more overwhelming task: to explain (to himself and others), criticize and construct alternatives to what had once presented itself to him with the calm dignity of established tradition. As we turn to look in greater detail at three areas of Barth's work in this period – his interpretation of Scripture, his readings in the theological tradition and his work in dogmatics – we shall see something of how Barth went about explanation, critique and construction.

Scripture

In the summer of 1916, Barth sat down to study Paul's letter to the Romans, reading it, as he later remembered, 'as I had never read it before'.[23] The result was his commentary on *The Epistle to the Romans*, first published in 1919 and then completely rewritten for a second edition in 1922. The stance which Barth adopted towards the dominant models of exegetical practice, and especially his attitude to the historical–critical method, constituted a central aspect of the history of the reception of Barth's book. Jülicher, who had taught Barth in Marburg back in 1908, wrote in his review: 'Barth forced me point blank to make a decision about the question of practical exegesis of Scripture compared to strictly scientific exegesis';[24] others muted Barth's challenge by refusing to see his work as other than a piece of homiletic or spiritualistic excess. In effect, *Romans* is, as Gadamer noted, 'a kind of hermeneutical manifesto'.[25] Barth's departure from accepted interpretative practice and his refusal to let the task of exegesis be dominated by the task of historical reconstruction of the text's origins were spin-offs from a larger theological purpose. In part, that purpose was to rehabilitate the biblical world of discourse as authoritative and substantial in its own right. Barth had an overwhelmingly powerful sense of the otherness of the biblical world, and feared that scientific methods end up by taming the text, going through it or underneath it in order to account for the text in terms of the historical conditions which spawned it. If the finely developed techniques of his erstwhile teachers failed for Barth, it was in part because they were reductionist, proving themselves incapable of rendering an account of the biblical material as having its own substance and integrity. However, Barth was not simply trying to rehabilitate 'textuality',[26] as one might try to rescue a literary work from critics seeking to 'explain' it by establishing its background. It was not the Bible as text but the Bible as testimony to divine speech which for Barth was crucial in calling into question the hegemony of 'scientific exegesis'. In an early lecture on 'The Strange New World Within the Bible', given at his friend Thurneysen's church in 1916, Barth told his hearers: 'Within the Bible there is a strange new world, the world of God.' And he went on:

> When God enters, history for a while ceases to be, and there is nothing more to ask; for something wholly different and new begins – a history with its own distinct grounds, possibilities and hypotheses ... The paramount question is whether we have understanding for this different, new world, or good will enough to meditate and enter upon it inwardly.[27]

This sense that the biblical texts set before their readers 'the world of God' lay at the heart of Barth's attempts to move beyond critical methods of scriptural interpretation. The preface to the first edition of *Romans* begins:

Paul, as a child of his age, addressed his contemporaries. It is, however, far more important that, as Prophet and Apostle of the Kingdom of God, he veritably speaks to all men of every age. The differences between then and now, there and here, no doubt require careful investigation and consideration. But the purpose of such investigation can only be to demonstrate that these differences are, in fact, purely trivial.[28]

Barth goes on to acknowledge that his handling of Scripture is governed by something close to the 'venerable doctrine of inspiration'.[29] In pointing out the similarity, Barth was not countering the historical–critical method by counselling a return to pre-critical objectification of the privileged status of the text. He was simply affirming that a proper hermeneutic is underpinned by the principle that God is known through God. If Scripture is read on the basis of this principle, then the text and its authors such as Paul are best understood, not simply as objects for historical investigation, but in all their contingent, historical character as prophetic, apostolic realities through which divine revelation takes place. Barth's quarrel with historical criticism did not dispute its value as 'prolegomenon to ... understanding';[30] as such it is 'both necessary and justified'.[31] What Barth objected to was not certain methods, but their use in contexts and for ends that are incompatible with understanding the text as an instrument of divine speech. As he wrote to Harnack in the early 1920s, 'the point is not to keep the historical–critical method of biblical and historical research ... away from the work of theology, but rather to fit that method ... into that work in a meaningful way'.[32] Partly, then, Barth is pressing for recognition of the limits of historical–critical work, an admission that 'genuine understanding and interpretation' must move beyond this 'preliminary work'.[33] Or as he put it in another early lecture, 'intelligent and fruitful discussion of the Bible begins where the judgement as to its human, its historical and psychological character has been made and *put behind us*'.[34] Barth's *Romans*, like his other earlier attempts to wrestle with biblical texts, emerged out of a reformulation of the question: 'What is exegesis?'[35] Reformulating the question meant envisaging the practice of exegesis as involving the attempt to listen to the text as apostolic testimony to divine address. In the context of such hearing, linguistic comment and historical observation are subservient to the end of encountering that to which the text bears prophetic witness. 'When an investigation is rightly conducted,' Barth proposed, 'boulders composed of fortuitous or incidental or merely historical conceptions ought to disappear almost entirely. The Word ought to be exposed in the words.'[36]

It is important to realize that the confidence with which Barth could relativize historical criticism was not only born of a decision about the nature and function of the biblical texts as media for divine speaking. It was also something which Barth took from the *content* of Scripture. For Barth, that content, however widely spread, has a unifying centre in the affirmation of God, God's utter subjectivity as the one who manifests himself in grace. Barth's commentary on 1 Corinthians 15, *The Resurrection of the Dead*, first published in 1924, is an example of how this unified content governs exegesis. The 'secret nerve' of the whole letter, Barth argued, is Paul's phrase 'from God' (1 Cor 4.5, etc.). Not only does this mean that – unlike many interpreters – Barth does not consider the treatment of the resurrection in 1 Corinthians 15 as unrelated to the rest of the letter, but views it as the letter's core. It also means that the message of the letter revolves around 'the understanding or the failure to understand the three words *apo tou theou* (from God)'.[37] In Jesus' resurrection we face the sheer miracle of God's creative action, utterly 'original' and therefore in no sense capable of assimilation, whether in thought or in speech. Even Paul's own apostolic language is an attempt to do what cannot be done: 'Can we draw the bird on the wing? . . . Undoubtedly the attempt is made here [by Paul], the attempt to utter the *impossible*, and to that extent a wholly impossible attempt.'[38] Crucially, this content determines the exegete's task. 'How tempting it is,' Barth wrote, for example, 'to read [1 Cor 15.3–11] . . . with the eyes of historical intelligence',[39] handling it as if it were a piece of evidentialist apologetics, and using it as a basis for reconstruction of the fact of Jesus' resurrection from the dead. For Barth, approaching the text through the category of contingent history means handling it as if

> this 'positive' manner of asserting the resurrection of Jesus were not in fact the secret denial of the very thing that we would fain assert, the resurrection as the deed *of God*, whom no eye has seen nor ear heard, who has entered no human heart, neither outwardly nor inwardly, not subjective and not objective, not mystical nor spiritistic nor flatly objective, but as a historical divine fact, which as such is only to be grasped in the category of revelation and in no other.[40]

If methods of exegesis are thus shaped by the divine act of revelation which is Scripture's content, then a drastic redirection of the reader's task follows. Barth offered some clues here in the introduction to his Münster lectures on the early chapters of the Gospel of John from 1925/6. Taking his direction from Augustine's *Homilies on the Gospel of John* (it is, of course, significant that it should be a pre-modern commentator to whom he turned for help), Barth tries to steer the reader to a different place from that which he or she customarily occupies when the reader's situation is dominated by the questions of scientific exegesis. As Barth presents matters, it is all-important to grasp 'the concrete specificity of the situation in which we find ourselves regarding the Gospel'.[41] The most important aspect of orienting ourselves in this situation is that we should read the gospel as gospel, as something 'new and unheard of, truth that challenges all our other knowledge'. Thus 'we hear (and understand) the Gospel only when we do not ignore that relation between it and us, when we do not ignore the actuality or reality with which it does not so much stand over against us as encounter us'.[42] Barth's point was not merely a refusal to consider the text as 'simply the monument of no more than a historical entity'.[43] Nor was it an assertion of the necessary 'self-involving' character of interpretation as having an inescapable subjective component: far from it. The reader of the gospel faces a demand for faith. But this demand is not 'some so-called subjective presupposition',[44] but the objective grasp of the situation in which the reader has been placed as one who is addressed by God. Above all, the reader's situation is truly described in theological terms, invoking language about God, revelation, faith; to be a reader of the text is to be (and not merely to think of oneself as) accosted by the gospel.

> If we want to be truly objective readers and expositors of John's Gospel ... we will not want to free ourselves from the fact that we are baptized, that for us, then, John's Gospel is part of the canonical scripture of the Christian church. It was not written and does not exist as anything other. Canonical scripture, however, means scripture to which we stand in that relation from the very first, a Word that is spoken to us from the very first in the name of God and with the claim that it is saying something radically new, a Word which even before we could hear it has opened a dialogue with us, a dialogue which, because it is conducted in the name of God, we cannot escape.[45]

For Barth, we cannot transcend this relation which the text establishes with us. Nor do we have to consider our situation as something 'that we have to suspend or suppress ... for the sake of scientific interrogation of the matter ... as though we stood in some better relation to the Gospel ... e.g., by way of our own observation, reflection, or experience'.[46]

As a result of this reorientation, the role of the reader becomes primarily passive. The text addresses us as a demand for faith. Faith, however, is no natural capacity but that which is worked in the reader by God. 'What is faith if not the illumination without which we cannot perceive the light of scripture? And what is this illumination if not the inscrutable and uncontrollable work of God upon us for which we can only pray?'[47] What is required above all of the reader is thus

> sincere and earnest desire to read and expound the Gospel, not as teachers but as students, not as those who know but as those who do not know, as those who let ourselves be told what the Gospel, and through it the divine wisdom, is seeking to tell us, holding ourselves free for it as for a message that we have never heard before.[48]

Looking back at *Romans* in 1932, Barth summed up the book thus: 'My sole aim was to interpret Scripture',[49] and in one sense all his work finds its centre in that one basic preoccupation. To do the job, however, Barth felt it necessary to reinvent a way of reading the Bible which he believed historical scholarship had all but obliterated, a way of reading which he felt compelled to adopt in face of the character of the scriptural texts as testimony to the event of divine self-manifestation. What prompted Barth's discovery of the centrality of *Deus dixit* for biblical interpretation was, of course, the problem of preaching. He read Scripture with the urgency, perplexity and helplessness of the preacher:

> it simply came about that the familiar situation of the minister on Saturday at his desk and on Sunday in his pulpit crystallized in my case into a marginal note to all theology, which finally assumed the voluminous form of a complete commentary upon the Epistle to the Romans ... What else can theology be but the truest possible expression of this quest and questioning on the part of the minister, the description of this embarrassment into which a man falls when he ventures upon this task and out of which he cannot find his way – a cry for rescue arising from great need and great hope?[50]

If part of Barth's answer to the preacher's questioning was a renewed theological depiction of what it means to interpret the

Bible, another part was the re-establishment of dogmatics in relation to the task of proclamation. Before turning to consider Barth's early dogmatic materials, however, we need to look briefly at his reading in the work of other theologians, through which he oriented himself to the dogmatic task.

Reading theologians

'What do I do? I study', wrote Barth to Thurneysen from his first teaching position in Göttingen early in 1922.[51] At the beginning of his teaching career, Barth immersed himself in reading classical and modern theology, envious of and intimidated by the prodigious learning of colleagues like Hirsch. At the same time, he adopted the habit in both lectures and seminars of discussing theological ideas by careful scrutiny of the great texts of the tradition. Whether the texts provoked agreement or disagreement, Barth read and taught them with a kind of vividness and intensity which expressed deep respect. From the record of such reading and teaching, we look at two examples from the 1920s, his lectures on Calvin and Schleiermacher.

Calvin

Barth's 1922 Göttingen lectures on Calvin are a rough document, produced in great haste in the midst of trying to master a great deal of material. Of all Barth's treatments of magisterial theological thinkers from the past, the lecture cycle is the least successful as a piece of textual analysis, frequently drifting from its theme into biographical or historical asides. Yet there is something permanently significant here. The lectures constitute very early testimony to Barth's lifelong conviction that theology in the Reformed tradition is concerned with dogmatics *and* ethics, divine *and* human action.

In the lectures, Barth offers an interpretation of the second-generation continental Reformers which pictures them as taking up again a theme in both medieval Christianity and modernity: the problem of ethics, though on the basis of a restructuring of the question effected by Luther's doctrine of justification by faith. Barth writes thus:

> We obviously turn to the horizontal line of human thought and action in time that is so sharply broken by the vertical line of the

knowledge of God in Christ. The problem of human life and striving as the Middle Ages unbrokenly pursued it cannot be simply cut off by being put under the shadow of its finitude, that is, in the light of its origin. What does the attack of the vertical mean for what takes place horizontally? What becomes of all that we will and work here below on the line of death that is suddenly made visible, that we have to will and work because as people in time we are always here below on that line of death? ... The Middle Ages died with Luther's discovery, but their problem, the problem of the active life, of ethics in the broadest sense, did not die with them.[52]

From this problem emerged Barth's account of the difference between Luther and Calvin. For Luther, he suggested, morality is a *second* thought. Because Luther 'takes so seriously the need to ground action in transcendental freedom',[53] then:

The whole relation of the vertical to the horizontal, or rather the outworking of this relation, was for him, strongly though he emphasized it, of secondary and not primary importance. We often detect indeed how he gives himself a push to turn back from faith, his real concern, to works, which were not in the full sense his concern. We also detect at this point a deficiency.[54]

In the Calvin of the Geneva Catechism, on the other hand, we find 'what it looks like when a theologian really addresses and unites both parts, when the fight for works of the Spirit is also self-evident and a heart's concern'.[55] 'This relating to the horizontal, this unity of faith and life, dogmatics and ethics, this attempt to answer the question of human striving and willing that Luther's discovery had for a moment pushed into the background, was distinctive, natural, and original to the Reformed.'[56] Barth was aware that there is a threat on both sides – a threat which he himself no doubt felt acutely in these early years as he sought to state his protest against the ethicizing of Christianity without losing sight of the reality of historical action.

If the Calvinistic thought might yield to the view that our seeking of perfection in this world in time is in itself the goal of our existence and a fulfilment of the will of God, we might infer from the Lutheran thought that our action in the world is hermetically sealed off against God.[57]

Barth was particularly concerned with the potential weakness of Calvin's position. 'Calvin', he wrote, 'became a moralist.'[58] This difficulty Barth traced to an aspect of Calvin's doctrine of God. Calvin's account of divine sovereignty is such that it pushes him to think of the relation of God and humanity in terms of ethical agency, and so 'even the proclamation of grace wears a moral garb ... for Calvin, divine service was a parade ground on which imperatives held sway in every relation'.[59] The picture of Calvin as moralist is, however, qualified somewhat as Barth tries to draw Calvin into line with the 'eschatological' interrogation of ethics which, as we have seen, formed a basic component of his critique of liberal Protestantism. Barth is, for example, eager to deny the charge of legalism brought against the Reformed, and lays some stress on Calvin's sense that all willing and striving stand 'under the shadow of the relativity of all things human'.[60]

This rather shifting picture of Calvin expressed the ambivalence of Barth's own thinking as he moved to articulate in the different context and literary style of academia the reality of both grace and human agency. But the qualifications notwithstanding, Barth's sympathies were evidently with Calvin, 'the creator of a new Christian sociology'.[61] From the beginning, even when he urged an eschatological disjunction of grace and morals, Barth was concerned not to lose sight of human action in history. What the Calvin lecture cycle enabled Barth to develop was at least the beginning of a theological ethics in which human action would not simply be rather precariously incorporated within a dominant eschatological structure, but would be seen to be doctrinally important, though in a way fundamentally at variance with liberal Protestant dogmatics. In the Calvin lecture cycle, Barth very quickly formed some of the basic lines of his mature ethical thinking, which we shall explore later in more detail: the picture of God and humanity as agents in relation; the irreversibility of gospel and law; and the coinherence of dogmatics and ethics.

Schleiermacher

Schleiermacher was for Barth modern Protestant theologian *par excellence*, the finest (and therefore the most problematic) example of its most deeply held commitments, 'the most brilliant representative not only of a theology past but also of the theology present'.[62] Schleiermacher was a constant dialogue partner in Barth's writing from the beginning of his academic career to its close. Above all, this was because Barth considered him a contemporary. 'Schleiermacher,' he told his students,

> is not dead for us and his theology has not been transcended. If anyone still speaks today in Protestant theology as though he were still among us, it is Schleiermacher. We *study* Paul and the reformers, but we *see* with the eyes of Schleiermacher and think along the same lines as he did. This is true even when we criticize or reject the most important of his theologoumena or even all of them.[63]

Schleiermacher was the voice of a tradition of Christian theology about which Barth had the deepest reservations but which at the same time fascinated (even threatened) him and often helped to determine the way he formulated theological questions. Barth's articulation of a theological position usually involved him in re-reading Schleiermacher and reformulating his relation to what he found there. And hence Barth frequently found himself unravelling Schleiermacher's arguments or inverting Schleiermacher's terms, never wholly shaking himself free of his influence, precisely because they had so much in common. A christological emphasis, a churchly orientation, a vision of Christian faith as humane: all these can be found in both figures, though the content of Christ, church and humanness differs widely in both thinkers, as it is arrived at by such very different routes.

The complexity of Barth's relation to Schleiermacher has not always been recognized. Supporters and detractors have often reduced Barth's interpretation of the great master to a few sloganized antitheses (objective v. subjective; revelation v. religion; God v. humanity). Barth was not wholly innocent of making bold summaries of the contrast between his own work and that of Schleiermacher; but behind them lay long, complex and, above all, respectful analysis of the texts. That respectful reading began very early, and by 1923/4, when Barth lectured on Schleiermacher, he was already able to present what was in many ways a well-developed and nuanced '*immanent* debate with the subject',[64] notably in his handling of Schleiermacher as preacher. A taste of what Barth has to say can be gained from looking at his reflections on Schleiermacher's christological festival sermons.

Barth was troubled by what he found in these sermons, and the worry was focused on the way in which they seemed to approach the christological mysteries (Christmas, Good Friday and Easter) from the standpoint of the subjective conditions under which we make sense of them, rather than from the standpoint of their sheer intrusive originality as free acts of God. As he preaches on the nativity, for example, Schleiermacher's theme is the 'reception of the Christmas message'.[65] 'The Christmas message thus runs into the question on man's side: What is that to *us*?'[66] One effect of this is the moralization of Christology. Barth summed up the basic components of Schleiermacher's underlying theology thus: 'Christ, a specific outlook as his legacy, the need to maintain and quicken this, his gift to humanity, and the final imperative, let us act with the same mind.'[67] What Barth feared here is a running together of Christology and anthropology, as a result of which the specificity of Jesus Christ – his existence as *this* one, unique, irreplaceable – is lost as he becomes only a modification of a general realm of religious emotion. Perhaps the best material in the lectures is the account of Schleiermacher's exquisite Christmas Eve dialogue, an imaginary set of conversations among a German family gathered to celebrate Christmas. Barth tried to suggest that the heart of 'the Christmas aspect of Christianity'[68] in Schleiermacher's rendering is the natural relation of mother and child; Mary and Jesus symbolize a relation illustrated in greater depth in the mother and child of the family circle in which the dialogue is set. And so Barth asks:

> is not Christmas as the feast of Christ's birth again pushed out on to the periphery ... Does it really have to be Mary and Christ that we celebrate? Could not another divine mother and another divine son take their place, with no essential change, if the upshot of it all is that in Mary and Christ we recognize in the best sense ourselves? Are Mary and Jesus merely an accidental paradigm ... of the mother–child relationship, of exalted humanity?[69]

Similar apprehensions are expressed over Schleiermacher's treatment of the passion and the resurrection, which furnish analogies for events in the spiritual life of the church. 'Is this Christ really *Christ*, the revelation of *God*? This member of a series even though his significance for the whole series is strongly emphasized? ... This *symbol*, no matter how attentively we listen when we are told that this symbol is also power?'[70] Many of the keynotes of Barth's later Christology are already present here: his insistence on the radically interceptive character of God's revelation in Christ, his insistence that the nature of Jesus' identity must have priority over questions of how he is real to us, his deep unease at any idea of Jesus as symbol. Yet what made Barth's criticism all the more forceful was the fact that he found it impossible to deny that – despite everything – Christology remains insistently present in Schleiermacher, an irritant to the system which had tried to absorb it:

> the stone of stumbling in Christianity, the problem of contingent revelation, was still present and caused difficulties in spite of this very sincere and brilliant attempt at modernization ... And what rocks he, the great leader of theology, has left in the path of his successors simply because nothing could wash away the fact that his was a real Christology.[71]

Schleiermacher's Christology is 'the incurable wound in his system. It is so by its very presence. It is the point where the system involuntarily breaks up. When we see it from this standpoint, thanks to its own fragility we cannot part from Schleiermacher implacably even at this point.'[72]

In light of this, to call Barth's early interpretation of Schleiermacher a 'monologue' or 'a flurry of sweeping accusations and condemnations' hardly does justice to the tone of his text.[73] Certainly he told his students at the beginning of the lectures:

> I have indeed no reason to conceal the fact that I view with mistrust both Schleiermacher and all that Protestant theology essentially became under his influence, that in Christian matters I do *not* regard the decision that was made in that intellectually and culturally significant age as a happy one, that the result of my study of Schleiermacher thus far may be summed up in that saying of Goethe: 'Lo, his spirit calls to thee from the cave: Be a man and do *not* follow me'.[74]

However, he also urged them to grasp Schleiermacher as 'a classical figure', and aimed in his teaching 'to see and know and learn to understand him with you, not to induce the arrogant view that you can become a match for him but to handle him modestly, not to condemn him but to comprehend him as what he was and obviously had to be'.[75] The very fact that Barth could write in these terms so soon after completing the second edition of his apocalyptic commentary on Romans tells us much about the complexity of his work in this period.

The *Göttingen Dogmatics*

Barth's first set of lectures on dogmatics is important for a number of reasons. In terms of tracing the development of his thinking, the texts offer remarkable testimony that many of the theological decisions about the shape of Christian doctrine which found final expression in the *Church Dogmatics* had already been made in the mid-1920s. The relating of dogmatics to the event of proclamation; the exposition of the doctrine of Trinity and the concept of revelation; the departure from Lutheran teaching on justification; the rejection of double predestination; and many other apparently 'later' themes are expounded at some length in the *Göttingen Dogmatics*. Not only does this make Barth's development look rather different; it also shows that the 'early' Barth was by no means simply preoccupied with the eschatological criticism of all things. At the doctrinal level, the lectures offer a vivid account of what Christian doctrine looks like when shaped by a deep sense of 'divine *autousia* ... God's subjectivity'.[76] Lacking the magisterial tone of the *Church Dogmatics*, they are able to set their ideas before their readers with a kind of animation and candour which makes them much more than merely a draft of what Barth would later achieve.

Rather than surveying the doctrinal content of the lectures as a whole, we shall look at the distinctively theological reorientation of the task of dogmatics, in which Barth drew upon and developed the redefinition of the task of interpreting Scripture upon which we have already touched. 'Dogmatics as a work that praises its master flourishes against a specific background.'[77] What is the specific background of dogmatics? And if the end of dogmatics is the 'praise of its master', what kind of person should the dogmatic theologian be?

Theology operates in the sphere of the church and its proclamation. The sphere or region of its operation, from which it draws its rationale and to which its efforts are directed, is a particular activity undertaken by particular people – the speaking of Christians and, in particular, the speech about God which occurs as Christian preaching. Dogmatics is not inquiry into general religious or cultural or historical phenomena; it does not (as Barth put it a little later) do its job 'in the empty space above the churches'.[78] It asks a very specific question about a very specific human undertaking: 'To what extent is the address that takes place in Christian preaching identical with the address that took place through the prophets and apostles, with the revelation that gave rise to the prophetic and apostolic kerygma? To what extent is it the *Word of God*?'[79] By making this the key question for dogmatics, Barth was reintegrating theology back into the life of the Christian community, since that community is the place where human testimony to revelation is borne. In this particular sphere of life, dogmatics has a specific task: it is the critical measuring of the church's speech against God's own Word of self-communication. This critical measure is needed precisely because preaching is a human act and therefore needs to be set against its transcendent origin. Dogmatics thus has a regulative function with regard to the church's speech. It is not inquiry into the human conditions of possibility for Christian speech (such as might be established by anthropology, religious psychology or the history of religions). Working from the assumption that in the sphere of the church speech about God is both possible and actual, dogmatics measures that speech against the given revelation of God. What is most important here is to grasp how radically Barth revised the whole shape of the theological enterprise: no longer concerned with universal reason, morals or experience, the theologian is set firmly within the church, alongside the preacher who has been disturbed by the imperious summons to pass on in human words the *Deus dixit* of revelation.

Within this sphere, the person of the theologian is redefined. Here we may once again contrast Barth with the great liberal historian Harnack. In a lecture at a conference in 1920 at which Barth also spoke, Harnack envisaged the theologian as historian, that is, as one who through profound study has acquired a transcendent grasp of the problems of humanity which enables an expanded vision of human life. He appealed to his youthful audience to seize upon the moral value of such study: 'To broaden oneself inwardly through history does not only belong to education, *it is education.*'[80] Above all, this is because this process 'connects itself harmoniously to the inner life of the spirit',[81] for 'history seeks to change people mired in their elemental drives and in sadness into pure and courageous ones'.[82] The address as a whole shows that Harnack was poignantly aware that the ideal was already waning.[83] Barth himself gave it little credence. Partly this was because its sphere was that of bourgeois self-cultivation rather than the struggle of the Christian community to speak about God. Partly it was because Barth was thoroughly disenchanted about Harnack's confidence that a comprehensive historical grasp of human affairs would yield the right sort of moral knowledge. Partly it was because of the serenity of the ideal, the absence from it of a sense that thinking about God is a threat. For Harnack, Barth became a 'despiser of academic theology', as he called him in what was to become a famous exchange of open letters in 1923. For Barth, the tradition of Harnack failed to grasp what is involved in talking of God: properly understood, Christian theology is a 'mortally dangerous undertaking'.[84] To do theology, therefore, requires that the theologian be a certain kind of person – a person seriously confronted by the questions: *What* are you going to say about God? What are *you* going to say about God?

> The questions put a pistol at the breast of theologians ... If these questions are right, it [dogmatics] is not just a matter of the so-called religions and religious personalities of distant times and countries which we can keep at a distance, knowing either nothing or not much about them. In our own midst a commission has been given whereby certain people have to speak, and they have to speak, mark you, about *God*. And it is not a matter of indifference, or of chance or caprice, what they say. This 'what' is an unsettling question, a sword of Damocles that hangs over them and, obviously, therefore, over all of us ... How rightly do those sigh who honestly take up the matter, and how right they are again to sigh about the results of their exertions![85]

That passage contains a whole world of differences from the intellectual culture which Harnack represented. What lay behind the differences was a particular understanding of revelation. Over against what he saw as its near-total eclipse in the immanentism of the liberal Protestant tradition, Barth understood revelation as the utterly intrusive action of God. Crucially, revelation does not make God available; in unveiling himself, God remains hidden:

> We must always understand revelation as God's revelation. In revelation, God is always, not quantitatively (for what is gigantic or infinite does not make God God), but qualitatively different from us, not spatially, but occupying a totally different place according to the mode of space. In his deity, for which no picture or likeness or symbol is appropriate (for, strictly, symbols apply only to gods and not to God), and in which he can never in any way be an object for us, all comprehension fails us, all such statements as 'thou art' or 'he is'. 'I am who I am' (Exod. 3:14). God is only in the first person.[86]

In face of such a revelation we may indeed only 'sigh' in perplexity and longing. But God's hiddenness is not the opposite of his self-manifestation, but rather God's utter freedom. 'God is hidden ... because he is the living God who reveals himself as he is, the triune God, inexhaustibly living, immutably the subject, from himself and not from us, ... the one who, because he is God, can never be object.'[87]

This awed sense of the subjectivity of God informed every topic which Barth touched in the *Göttingen Dogmatics*. It surfaced in his rejection of Protestant scholastic definitions of Scripture, which threaten to make revelation into a direct given, without any sense of divine hiddenness. It lay behind his oft-repeated refusal to place weight on any natural human capacity for revelation. Most tellingly, it shaped his Christology, where he laid considerable emphasis on the 'indirectness' of God's self-manifestation in Christ (a theme he takes up from Kierkegaard).[88]

> Christology, set face to face with the fact of Jesus Christ, is an effort to understand that the objective possibility of God's revelation involves ... the 'irremovable mystery' of God in his indirect communication, but also the mystery of God which has entered time and history, which has become palpable and actual, in God's encounter with us, by virtue of the incarnation.[89]

As we shall see, Barth's later Christology will add a good deal more by way of nuance to this treatment of incarnation, especially as the rather formal categories are filled out through close attention to the gospel story. What Barth will not abandon is his insistence that the 'givenness' of God's revelation in Christ is always miracle, never convertible into some worldly state of affairs. The same affirmation lay behind his account of the nature and tasks of theology in the *Göttingen Dogmatics*, and its development in those lectures is an important part of the legacy of his early work.

Conclusion

Barth was never a purely critical thinker, and he came early to the conviction that a well-ordered theology will be a theology of the Word of God and therefore one which accords due weight to both God and humanity. If, in writings like the second Romans commentary and elsewhere Barth felt constrained to develop a 'necessary atheology',[90] this was only because his reading of the nineteenth-century tradition convinced him that fundamental distortions had been introduced into Christian intellectual and moral culture which could be corrected only by the strongest of affirmations of God's free subjectivity. As Barth strove to recover God's entire originality over against human nostrification of the divine, the threat of dualism certainly loomed over him. But there is more than enough in what he had to say at this stage in his theological career to suggest that 'what looks like dualism may rather be a strategy for defending difference'.[91]

In later years, of course, Barth criticized himself for failing in these earlier writings to discern that 'the *deity* of the *living* God . . . found its meaning and its power only in the context of His history and of His dialogue with *man*, and thus in His togetherness with man'.[92] Because God is essentially *pro nobis*, Christian proclamation and theology cannot simply negate:

> even if it is the case that by reason of their negativity, negative conceptions are fitted to express God's being in Himself, this method is suspicious by the fact that . . . God's freedom is not identical with God's being over against the world, but is just as operative in His relation to the world as in His being in Himself, and therefore is by no means to be exhaustively described in negative concepts – not even if we can rightly attribute to the latter a special appropriateness to describe the transcendent God. God is the One who is free even in His being for us, in which He is certainly not to be apprehended only by means of negative concepts.[93]

But as we shall see as we turn to look at the *Church Dogmatics*, the continuity of Barth's later work with his negatives in the second two decades of the century should not be ignored. For, on the one hand, even the late Barth, searching for ways to describe the Christian life as a human undertaking, can also write that God's friendship with humanity 'is a matter of *God's* sovereign togetherness with man, a togetherness grounded in Him and determined, delimited, and ordered through Him alone'.[94] And, on the other hand, even the Barth of the 1920s can insist that the negatives are only a ground-clearing exercise. 'Nothing less than *all* depends on the exact and thorough determination of the positive point which is here in question', he wrote in response to Tillich in 1923.[95] That positive point, 'the "deep secret YES under and above the No" ', is, as Barth notes in *Romans*, 'the Kingdom and Dominion of God'.[96] Barth's *Church Dogmatics*, to which we now turn, is one long explication of that Kingdom and Dominion in its turning to humanity in mercy and love.

Notes

1. 'A Thank-You and a Bow – Kierkegaard's Reveille. Speech on being awarded the Sonning Prize', in *Fragments Grave and Gay* (London: Collins, 1971), p. 97.

2. 'The Problem of Ethics Today', *WGWM*, p. 169.

3. H. U. von Balthasar, *The Theology of Karl Barth. Exposition and Interpretation* (San Francisco: Ignatius, 1992). For Barth's praise of the book, see *CD* IV/1, p. 768. On these developmental questions, see now B. McCormack, *Karl Barth's Critically Realistic Dialectical Theology* (Oxford: Clarendon Press, 1995).

4. *FQI*, p. 11.

5. R. E. Willis, *The Ethics of Karl Barth* (Leiden: Brill, 1971), p. 7.

6. 'The Christian's Place in Society', *WGWM*, p. 321.

7. *Romans*, p. 141.

8. Ibid., pp. 330f.

9. Ibid., p. 108.

10. Ibid., p. 120.

11. Ibid., p. 108.

12. 'The Problem of Ethics Today', *WGWM*, p. 144.

13. Ibid., p. 145.

14. 'The Righteousness of God', *WGWM*, p. 17.

15. Ibid., p. 16.

16. 'Church and Culture', *ThCh*, p. 354.

17. 'The Righteousness of God', *WGWM*, p. 24.

18. 'The Word in Theology from Schleiermacher to Ritschl', *ThCh*, p. 216.

19. *Romans*, p. 504.

20. Ibid., p. 461.

21. For helpful general background, see P. Gay, *Weimar Culture. The Outsider as Insider* (New York: Harper and Row, 1968).

22. 'The Problem of Ethics Today', *WGWM*, p. 146.

23. 'Concluding Unscientific Postscript', p. 264.

24. A. Jülicher, 'A Modern Interpreter of Paul', in J. M. Robinson (ed.), *The Beginnings of Dialectical Theology* (Richmond: John Knox Press, 1968), p. 73. This volume reprints a number of responses to Barth: see pp. 61–130.

25. H.-G. Gadamer, *Truth and Method* (London: Sheed and Ward, 1979), p. 463.

26. See here G. Lindbeck, 'Barth and Textuality', *Theology Today* 43 (1986), pp. 361–76.

27. 'The Strange New World Within the Bible', *WGWM*, pp. 33, 37.

28. *Romans*, p. 1.

29. Ibid.; cf. p. 18.

30. Ibid., p. 7.

31. Ibid., p. 6.

32. The exchange from which the quotation is taken is available in H. M. Rumscheidt (ed.), *Adolf von Harnack. Liberal Theology at its Height* (London: Collins, 1988), pp. 85–106; see p. 96.

33. *Romans*, p. 7.

34. 'Biblical Questions, Insights and Vistas', *WGWM*, pp. 60f.

35. *Romans*, p. ix.

36. Ibid., p. 8.

37. *The Resurrection of the Dead* (London: Hodder and Stoughton, 1933), pp. 18f.

38. Ibid., p. 116.

39. Ibid.

40. Ibid., pp. 145f.

41. *Witness to the Word. A Commentary on John I* (Grand Rapids: Eerdmans, 1986), p. 5.

42. Ibid., pp. 3f.

43. Ibid., p. 4.

44. Ibid.

45. Ibid., pp. 4f.

46. Ibid., p. 5.

47. Ibid., p. 8.

48. Ibid., p. 9.

49. *Romans*, p. ix.

50. 'The Need and Promise of Christian Preaching', *WGWM*, p. 101.

51. J. D. Smart (ed.), *Revolutionary Theology in the Making. Barth–Thurneysen Correspondence, 1914–1925* (London: Epworth, 1964), p. 81.

52. *The Theology of Calvin* (Edinburgh: T. & T. Clark, 1992), p. 49.

53. Ibid., p. 76.

54. Ibid., p. 75.

55. Ibid., p. 76.

56. Ibid., p. 77.
57. Ibid., p. 78.
58. Ibid., p. 121.
59. Ibid., p. 122.
60. Ibid, p. 207.
61. Ibid., p. 90.
62. *The Theology of Schleiermacher* (Edinburgh: T. & T. Clark, 1982), p. xv.
63. Ibid., p. xiii.
64. Ibid., p. xvi.
65. Ibid., p. 52.
66. Ibid., p. 54.
67. Ibid., p. 55.
68. Ibid., p. 61.
69. Ibid., p. 62.
70. Ibid., p. 103.
71. Ibid., pp. 104f.
72. Ibid., p. 107.
73. J. E. Thiel, 'Barth's Early Interpretation of Schleiermacher', in J. O. Duke, R. F. Streetman (eds), *Barth and Schleiermacher: Beyond the Impasse?* (Philadelphia: Fortress Press, 1988), p. 11.
74. *The Theology of Schleiermacher*, pp. xvf.
75. Ibid., p. xvi.
76. *GD*, p. 89.
77. Ibid., p. 4.
78. 'Fate and Idea in Theology', in H.-M. Rumscheidt (ed.), *The Way of Theology in Karl Barth* (Allison Park: Pickwick, 1986), p. 26.
79. Ibid., p. 24.
80. A. von Harnack, 'What Has History to Offer as Certain Knowledge Concerning the Meaning of World Events?', in H-.M. Rumscheidt (ed.), *Adolf von Harnack*, p. 57.
81. Ibid.
82. Ibid., p. 62.
83. For useful background here, see F. Ringer, *The Decline of the German Mandarins. The German Academic Community, 1890–1933* (Cambridge, MA: Harvard University Press, 1969).
84. *GD*, p. 3.
85. Ibid., p. 6.
86. Ibid., pp. 134f.

87. Ibid., p. 135.

88. S. Kierkegaard, *Training in Christianity* (Princeton, NJ: Princeton University Press, 1944), pp. 96–104.

89. *GD*, pp. 152f.

90. R. H. Roberts, *A Theology on its Way?* (Edinburgh: T. & T. Clark, 1991), p. 197.

91. W. Lowe, *Theology and Difference. The Wound of Reason* (Bloomington: Indiana University Press, 1991), p. 45. Lowe's treatment of Barth on pp. 33–47 is highly instructive in this respect.

92. 'The Humanity of God', p. 45.

93. *CD* II/1, p. 347.

94. 'The Humanity of God', p. 45.

95. K. Barth, 'The Paradoxical Nature of the "Positive Paradox". Answers and Questions to Paul Tillich', in J. M. Robinson (ed.), *The Beginnings of Dialectical Theology*, p. 143.

96. *Romans*, p. 295.

3

The Word of God and theology

Reading *Church Dogmatics*

Barth's *Church Dogmatics* is a vast and complex work, and not without reason many would-be readers are daunted by the project of exploring it at any depth. What deters the reader is often not simply the sheer scale of the work, nor the fact that its 8,000 or so pages assume close familiarity with the text of Scripture and more than passing acquaintance with the history of Christian thought. More than anything else, it is Barth's rhetoric which so often proves baffling at first encounter, particularly when he is read in transla-tion. Barth's rhetoric – his overall strategy of communication – makes some particular and very heavy demands on his readers. This is not particularly a matter of vocabulary: in fact, Barth's prose is largely free of technical jargon, apart from a fairly small number of well-used classical theological terms. Nor is it Barth's legendary prolixity alone, though that is a very important element in his strategy. It is more that many features of Barth's way of writing – sentence structure, frequent duplication or triplication of words, modes of address and appeal to the reader, patterns of argument, use of irony, humour or interrogation, adducing of evidence from authorities – all conspire together to position writer and reader in such a way that a particular kind of encounter is generated. For many readers, it is a novel and disconcerting experience. If we take to the *Church Dogmatics* the kind of expectations we might take to a scholarly monograph, we shall be disappointed from the begin-ning. Modern scholarly prose has, by and large, become the standardized expression of a certain understanding of intellectual inquiry in which the implied reader is appealed to by the author as an impartial tribunal, hearing the case which the book makes, weighing the evidence it brings forward and then reaching a judgement. When Barth broke with the liberal historicist scholarship of his teachers, one of the things which was jettisoned was this ideal of disinterested inquiry and its embodiment in the literary form of the scholarly treatise. In its place, Barth slowly created a literary art whose persuasiveness is closely akin to the form of speech which he first used to articulate his discovery of the freedom of God: preaching. Two features of this literary art – its inordinate length and the context which it creates for itself – are worth exploring by way of orientation to the task of reading Barth's *magnum opus*.

Why is the *Church Dogmatics* so long, even in its unfinished state? Partly it is because Barth was a fluent writer who was never stuck for words. Partly it is because so much is happening in the *Church Dogmatics* – not only lengthy discussions of doctrinal themes, but also biblical exegesis, historical theology, ethics, occasional polemic and a certain amount of spiritual exhortation. Partly it is because – as Hans Frei has pointed out – Barth was reinstating a theological language which had fallen into disrepair, and doing so by *using* the language in a lengthy and leisurely fashion.[1] But more than anything else, Barth's particular method of exposition made for the expansiveness of the *Church Dogmatics*. His way of arguing was not so much linear or sequential as cumulative. He built up his account of whatever topic he had to hand by producing an extensive set of variations on a few basic themes. The 'argument' (if such it be) proceeds less by pursuing a sequence of logical stages and more by repetition and elaboration or layering, reiterating a train of thought or transposing it into another key and making the fullest possible use of recapitulation and rephrasing. The force of the 'argument' gradually accumulates, swelling towards a conclusion rather than reaching it by taking measured steps.

The bulk of the *Church Dogmatics* is thus a function of its rhetorical design. As a consequence, the work has to be read at considerable length in order to acquire a sense of the argument as a whole, especially since Barth was acutely conscious of the many strands which connected all the different doctrines together. For all its variety of subject matter and genre, the *Church Dogmatics* is one cohesive argument, and no single stage within the argument is definitive for the whole (a warning to readers who extract one piece of the argument as if it could stand in isolation from the rest, and then proceed to criticize it for failing to say what can in fact be found elsewhere in the work as a whole). In the end, then, there is no substitute for the exhausting business of studying the argument in its (unfinished) entirety. Only in this way can we properly catch the rhythm of Barth's thinking and come to see how his peculiar rhetoric is intrinsic to what he has to say. It is crucial, therefore, that we take very seriously 'the inner connection of Barth's language with his "subject matter" '.[2]

What is the context in which the *Church Dogmatics* places itself? Although the material first saw the light of day as university lectures, it is a work of *church* dogmatics, written from and to the church and only as such addressed to other localities. Commenting on the use of the word 'church' in the title at the beginning of the first volume, Barth noted that dogmatics as he understood it 'is bound to the sphere of the Church, where alone it is possible and meaningful'.[3] Once again, this is of considerable importance in orienting ourselves to the rhetoric of the text, for two reasons.

First, as *church* dogmatics Barth's work differs sharply from a dominant mode of modern theology, which can be termed apologetic or foundationalist because it understands theology as critical, transcendental inquiry into the possibility of Christian belief. Barth's concern, by contrast, is not with the possibility of 'church', but with describing how things look once one is inside the region or culture of the church. This conviction about theology's task had, of course, been gathering momentum in Barth from his first years as a theological teacher, but was stated with especial precision in his study *Anselm*, a book which is best read in conjunction with the *Church Dogmatics* as a formal account of what the latter will set out to achieve. Barth found in Anselm a theology which proceeds from consent to the 'Credo', that is, the church's confession of God's revealing Word. Far from considering itself critical inquiry into the church and its confession, theology on Anselm's model is 'an extension and explication of that acceptance of the Credo of the Church which faith itself already implied'.[4] This decision about the church as the field of theology's operation can be seen very clearly in the sources and norms of which Barth makes use in the *Church Dogmatics*. His appeal is to Scripture and derivatively to the classical texts of the Christian tradition. Appeals to non-theological disciplines – especially philosophy – or to general human experience do not carry anything like the same weight. Other disciplines may function as conversation partners, but they do not provide more universal, less context-specific norms. General human experience, whilst it may enter the discussion as a low-level, commonsense factor, is not theorized into an anthropological foundation for theology, and is frequently corrected by reference to norms available only in the church's confession of the gospel.

Secondly, this striking emphasis on the church as the region of theological activities deeply affects the understanding of his intended reader which Barth implies throughout the *Church Dogmatics*. Figuring out who Barth has in mind as his audience is often complex, but vitally important if we are not to misunderstand what he is trying to achieve. Barth has various audiences in mind, sometimes addressing several at once. What is consistent, however, is Barth's implicit conviction that the reader to whom he addresses himself is, like every human being, already within the sphere of the realities which Barth is describing. Face to face with his reader, Barth considers it his task as writer to instruct the reader in the sheer magnitude, worth and surpassing significance of these realities. All the genres and rhetorical ploys which the reader comes across in the *Church Dogmatics* are subservient to the controlling end, which is instruction in the absorbing and utterly compelling reality of God.

For some readers, such instruction, undertaken so single-mindedly and with such rhetorical energy, makes Barth impossible, even oppressive, to read. To some, his writing appears to be an attempt to create a world of theological reality by sheer power of language, convincing by overwhelming rather than demonstrating. To others, it seems an act of wilful defiance of modernity – doing at inordinate length what the Enlightenment had disallowed: talking of God with fluency and delight. To others, again, the cumulative power of Barth's writing can seem an exercise in unbridled – male – forcefulness, its repetitious and boundless energy wearing down the reader into submission. At the very least, Barth rarely seems to invite the kind of considered, critical reading which the canons of rational discourse prescribe.

Readers must decide for themselves about these matters. But a couple of anticipatory hints may be offered at this stage. First, reading Barth with profit and sympathy involves taking seriously the unconventionality of his way of arguing. Barth's *Church Dogmatics* breaks the conventions of the modern academy, refusing to follow Aristotle in thinking that rhetoric is the counterpart of dialectic[5] – refusing, that is, to consider that intellectual language serves logical thought about facts and should not be bent to mere persuasion. Unlike Aristotle and his modern heirs, Barth's rhetoric seeks to influence the reader's judgement, move the reader's emotions and engage the reader's will. (In this, he is closer to much feminist writing than to the – apparently – apolitical language of the scholarly text.) Second, the vigour of Barth's writing goes hand-in-hand with a certain humility and irony about himself and his work. Intellectual humility and irony sometimes take the form of constant subverting of any conclusions. In Barth's case, however, they are expressed as a passion to allow the inherent potency of theology's object – God – to declare itself through the essentially inadequate medium of human speech. Such a theology may still have massive rhetorical strength, but the strength will be understood as an indication of its object, not an attempt to eclipse it. The power of Barth's writing is very often what we might call 'the power of indication'. Read in this way, the *Church Dogmatics* is not an authoritarian final expression of some truth about God, but a work of celebration, a work which tries to put into words what happens when we are caught up in and transformed by a movement, by a living, speaking event and gift.

The doctrine of the Word of God

The two part-volumes of *Church Dogmatics* I, *The Doctrine of the Word of God*, which appeared in 1932 and 1938, trace a long circle of argument. They begin and end with considerations of the nature and functions of dogmatics, rooting these considerations in extensive discussions of revelation and the being and activity of the triune God. In effect, Barth makes the doctrine of the self-revealing Trinity do the jobs which in many other dogmatic works are undertaken by independent accounts of theological prolegomena (that is, accounts of the methods, norms and sources of theology). Tracing why he does this will take us to the heart of the volume and help us identify what have often been considered its most basic problems.

Because Barth begins by firmly placing theology within the church, he steers away from conceptions of the discipline as some sort of rational act in which we transcend the life of the church or try to place that life on a better foundation. Dogmatics is the church's evaluation of its own utterance by its own given norm of revelation. 'Hence [dogmatics] does not have to begin by finding or inventing the standard by which it measures. It sees and recognises that this is given with the Church' (*CD* I/1, p. 12). Set thus within the sphere of the church, dogmatics is undertaken with the same dispositions as any other activity in that sphere. It is an act of faith, stemming from that 'determination of human action by the being of the Church and therefore by Jesus Christ, by the gracious address of God to man' (I/1, p. 17) and closely allied to prayer, 'the attitude without which there can be no dogmatic work' (I/1, p. 23). Out of this context, Barth makes his approach to dogmatic prolegomena. Prolegomenal discussion often seeks to construct a platform from which theology can be launched, establishing the possibility of talk of God by showing from outside the sphere of faith and church that, on the basis of general principles of knowledge, metaphysics or experience, there is some readiness for revelation on the part of humanity. Why does Barth refuse to travel this path? His refusal has often been read as signalling theology's withdrawal into a closed, isolated world – into what Barth himself rather troublingly called its 'self-enclosed circle' into which 'there can be no entering ... from without' (I/1, p. 42). But the charge of isolationism does not catch the force of Barth's objection, which proceeds along two lines. First, the search for apologetic prolegomena presupposes that there is some point of contact between God's revelation and the recipient of revelation other than that which revelation itself establishes by its occurrence. As soon as we begin to search for some anthropological datum as the contact between God's Word and the hearers, we have already set aside the reality of such a contact by inquiring into its possibility. Second, apologetic prolegomena work with the assumption that 'the Church and faith are to be understood as links in a greater nexus of being' (I/1, p. 36). The sphere of the church and its speech, thought and action, rather than being miracle, are reduced to mere contingent historical realities which can then be discussed through some general theory of knowledge or ontology. In effect, both these objections continue to counter what Barth had already found it necessary to repudiate in theological liberalism, namely, the exchange whereby revelation became religious history and experience, grounded not in the freedom of God but in the wider human context of its occurrence. In place of this, Barth sets out an understanding of dogmatics which derives its principles at all points from the active, speaking reality of the being of God. What establishes the viability of dogmatics is not axioms drawn from the worlds of history, religion, experience or disciplined inquiry, but the sheer miracle of God's self-communicative presence. The effect of this on the shape of Christian doctrine is nothing short of revolutionary, for it means that dogmatics starts, not with preliminaries, but at the heart of the matter: God's revelation as Father, Son and Holy Spirit.

Like the *Göttingen Dogmatics*, the *Church Dogmatics* sees

its task as critical examination of the church's proclamation. Proclamation is poised between, on the one hand, its divine commission to be human speech through which God 'speaks like a king through the mouth of his herald' (I/1, p. 52) and, on the other, its ineradicable humanity. Because there is no automatic connection between divine revelation and human speech, proclamation always faces the question of its own authenticity: Is it responsible to its own commission? Dogmatics attempts an answer. 'What is said about God in the Church seeks, as proclamation, to be God's Word. It is measured by its own specific criterion in dogmatics' (I/1, p. 77). But if the church is to undertake this self-examination, it can do so only by appealing to the divine act of communication (the Word of God) which generates both the church and its speech. Barth's first major assignment in the *Church Dogmatics* is therefore to sketch a theology of the Word of God. He does so by offering two different yet complementary maps of the territory. The first is a rather more formal depiction of what he calls the 'three-fold form of the Word of God' (paragraphs 4–6); the second is a much more massive discussion of Trinity, incarnation and the outpouring of the Spirit (paragraphs 8–18).

The Word of God

For Barth, God's Word is never available in a straightforward way. It is not a deposit of truth upon which the church can draw, or a set of statements which can be consulted. The Word of God is an act which God undertakes. God's Word is that complex but unitary event in which God has spoken, speaks and will speak, an event which encounters us through the human means of Scripture and its proclamation in the church. The one event of the one Word of God thus has three forms: the act of revelation itself, its attestation in the prophetic and apostolic words, and the preaching of that testimony in the community. Describing this differentiated event involves a gradual progress through three concentric circles. The innermost circle is the Word of God in its pure form as divine speech-act; but it is surrounded by and only approachable through the human speech-acts of Scripture and proclamation which are appointed by God to be its bearers and witnesses, so becoming themselves God's Word by derivation.

The Word of God is the Word preached: that is, human proclamation, when it is true to its divine calling, is an event of divine speech. Being true to the divine calling involves allowing the Word of God to be the commission, the theme and the criterion of proclamation. But more than anything else, it means grasping that preaching is, very simply, a miracle. When proclamation truly happens, then in and with 'the willing and doing of the proclaimer' (I/1, p. 94: translation altered), there is 'the divine willing and doing' (ibid.). The Word of God is the Word written: that is, the canon of Holy Scripture is God's Word. In the same way that proclamation is the herald of divine speech, so also Scripture is an instrument of divine communication, attesting to and recollecting the fact that the Word has already been spoken by God. Crucially for Barth this means that the Bible is a field of divine activity: to talk of Scripture as God's Word is to offer 'a description of God's action in the Bible' (I/1, p. 110). Hence, in a key phrase, he proposes that 'Revelation engenders the Scripture which attests it' (I/1, p. 115). What is most important about Scripture is the stance or movement of the biblical witnesses as they point away from themselves to that which generates their testimony: 'they speak and write ... about that other' (I/1, p. 112).

The 'other' of which Scripture and proclamation speak and which lies at their heart is the reality of God's free act of revelation which Barth calls 'The Word of God Revealed'. Proclamation and Scripture cannot 'bring [the Word of God] on the scene themselves' (I/1, p. 120); both are functions of the fundamental reality: *Deus dixit*. Barth's deep sense of the 'original' character of the Word of God (already, as we have seen, the great lever which he used to dislodge theological immanentism) evokes an intense and captivated meditation on the nature of God's Word. Barth is clearly enchanted by the thought of the unfettered liberty of God in his self-manifestation. As he spirals round this theme, he offers a series of depictions of the Word's liberty: its spirituality (that is, the impossibility of reducing it to some material or historical condition); its personal reality as the self-presentation of God's own subjectivity; its purposiveness; its majestic power to rule in which the hearer is claimed and commanded; above all, its mystery. The whole meditation has its centre in a single affirmation: 'God is Lord in the wording of his Word' (I/1, p. 139) – that is, as God's self-utterance makes itself heard as human speech, it does so in its full dignity, spontaneity and aseity (self-existence) as the Word of the Lord.

From here the discussion moves naturally to consider the human hearers of revelation in a treatment of 'The Knowability of the Word of God'. This section contains an early example of a pattern of argument which will be developed many times in the *Church*

Dogmatics. Barth wants to make two affirmations about the human reception of revelation. First, he wants to stress that we cannot think about the event of revelation 'without remembering at once the man who hears and knows it' (I/1, p. 191). There is a necessary anthropological dimension to our talk about the Word of God. Yet, second, that dimension is not free-standing, nor something contributed by the human hearer independent of the event of the Word. Rather, revelation itself creates its own hearers, so (and only so) placing the hearer firmly in the picture. It is because of the directedness of the Word, the fact that God is and acts and speaks *thus*, that talk of God must of necessity include talk of humanity. Later sketches of the *Church Dogmatics* will root this very deeply in the covenantal character of God's dealings with his creatures, and in turn root the covenant in the being of Jesus Christ, divine and human. The argument in one shape or another will, moreover, be crucial to such diverse areas as Barth's anthropology, sacramental theology and ethics. At this early stage in the work, it enables him to hold together both the utter sovereignty of God through which we are determined as hearers of the Word and the real and self-determining character of our hearing and response.

The triune God

Barth rescued the doctrine of the Trinity from the obscurity in which it had languished in modern Protestant dogmatics. Schleiermacher had famously relegated discussion of the Trinity to the conclusion of *The Christian Faith*, whereas the doctrine is massively present throughout the *Church Dogmatics*. Barth approaches all aspects of Christian doctrine with trinitarian teaching in mind. Where the material in hand most naturally gravitates towards one of the three trinitarian persons (the doctrine of salvation to the Son, for example, or the doctrine of the church to the Spirit), Barth is almost always scrupulous in preventing any eclipse of the other persons. The effect of this is that the architecture of the *Church Dogmatics* itself reinforces the mutuality of the three persons in the godhead. Any full account of what Barth has to say about trinitarian theology would, then, need to look at the *Church Dogmatics* as a whole. The shape of the doctrine is, however, expounded in the first volume at the beginning of Barth's account of Christian theology.

The placement is very important indeed. By making it the starting-point of dogmatics, Barth indicated both that the Christian doctrine of God is the doctrine of the Trinity, and also that the Christian doctrine of God, understood in trinitarian fashion, is the only secure basis for theology. What Barth has to say about the doctrine of the Trinity is thus inseparable from what he has to say about the doctrine of revelation, since revelation (itself the foundation of dogmatics) is nothing other than the self-revelation of Father, Son and Spirit. Revelation is not the manifestation by God of realities other than God: as self-revelation, it is trinitarian in character, since God is God's self as Trinity. As Barth puts it:

> If we really want to understand revelation in terms of its subject, i.e., God, then the first thing we have to realise is that this subject, God, the Revealer, is identical with His act in revelation and also identical with its effect. It is from this fact ... that we learn that we must begin the doctrine of revelation with the doctrine of the triune God. (I/1, p. 296)

From this binding together of Trinity and revelation, two things follow. One (to which we will presently turn) is that 'revelation' furnishes the basic conceptuality through which Barth expounds the being of God as Father, Son and Spirit in this first treatment of the topic. The other is that the doctrine of revelation itself is dramatically reshaped. It is no longer what it had often been in the hands of post-Reformation theologians, a theory of theological knowledge in which revelation served as a warrant for Christian belief. Rather, revelation is in Barth's hands simply the doctrine of God in its cognitive effect. This, of course, is in line with the entire approach to dogmatics which we have already seen him to be adopting – an approach which does not start from the question, 'How do we know God?' but from the question, 'Who is this God who effects knowledge of himself?' The first question elicits epistemology; the second question a doctrine of the self-revealing triune God. This is why Barth can sum up the doctrine of the Trinity with the phrase: 'God reveals Himself as the Lord' (I/1, p. 306). Revelation is the gift to us of the communicative presence of Father, Son and Spirit in the utter liberty which is God's alone.

How does this linking of the doctrines of Trinity and revelation shape the content of trinitarian theology? As we will see at the end of this chapter, Barth's handling of this theme has come under heavy fire (not all of which hits the target). The vital nerve of his presentation is undoubtedly his account of the unity of God. The opening proposition of Barth's account of 'The Triunity of God' begins: 'The God who reveals Himself according to Scripture is

One in three distinctive modes of being subsisting in their mutual relations: Father, Son and Holy Spirit' (I/1, p. 348). From the beginning, Barth is insistent that the Trinity is one subject. Thus, the doctrine of the Trinity is 'an explanatory confirmation' of God's name, a name which is 'the name of a single being, of the one and only willer and doer whom the Bible calls God' (ibid.). Unlike some more recent accounts of the Trinity as a community of persons, Barth is very heavily invested in the simplicity and singularity of God's triune being. Indeed, he argues that the doctrine of the Trinity is a guard against tritheism, a means by which the church defends 'the recognition of God's unity, and therefore monotheism' (I/1, p. 351). A key role here is played by the idea of 'repetition' as a way of talking of the unity-in-plurality of the Godhead. 'The name [note the singular] of Father, Son and Spirit means that God is the one God in threefold repetition' (I/1, p. 350); and so 'As the doctrine of the repetition of eternity in eternity the doctrine of the Trinity confirms the knowledge of the unity of God' (I/1, p. 353). On a casual reading, the concept of 'repetition' may seem to de-emphasize differentiation and stress sameness in a way that makes the reader begin to wonder whether Barth has simply collapsed the differences of Father, Son and Spirit by making them three identical realities. As the discussion moves on, however, it becomes clear that what is being rejected is not distinctions *per se*, but the wrong kind of distinctions, distinctions which imperil God's unity. Establishing the right kind of distinctions, moreover, means rejecting the wrong kind of divine unity – numerical or monadic unity with no internal relations. And so, Barth writes, 'The concept of the revealed unity of the revealed God ... does not exclude but rather includes a distinction ... or order ... in the essence of God' (I/1, p. 355).

This 'distinction' within God's essence is what the term 'person' is straining after in a trinitarian context. Yet Barth is very uneasy about the term and not convinced that it is a serviceable designation of what makes Father, Son and Spirit into what they are. Partly this is because of its proximity to what has been expounded through the term 'personality', so that talk of trinitarian 'persons' quickly suggests a group of individuals identified and defined in terms of unique characteristics. When harnessed to philosophical idealism, moreover, 'person' acquires overtones of 'consciousness', reinforcing its centrifugal force as it comes to signify that which individuates. Because Barth does not see 'person' as a term of relation but a term of distinction, and because he is keen to eschew what he regards as the wrong kind of distinction in trinitarian theology, he canvasses the term 'mode (or way) of being': 'God is One in those ways of being ... in the mode of the Father, in the mode of the Son, and in the mode of the Holy Ghost' (I/1, p. 359). This term, Barth hopes, will state the unity-in-distinction of the Godhead without tritheistic or monadic concepts of God. The difference is real, for

> This one God is God three times in different ways, so different that it is only in this threefold difference that He is God, so different that this difference, this being in these three modes of being, is absolutely essential to Him. (I/1, p. 360)

Yet even here Barth presses the topic of unity by introducing the action of the *perichoresis* (mutual interpenetration) of the triune modes of being: 'each of the Three only with the other Two' (I/1, p. 370).

In the rest of *Church Dogmatics* I/1, Barth gives himself over to a description of the work of revelation which is proper to each mode of God's being. As Father, God reveals himself to be the Creator, the 'Lord of our existence' (I/1, p. 384) who is the Father as the Father of the Son. As Son, God reveals himself to be the Reconciler, that is, as 'the Lord in the midst of our enmity towards Himself' (I/1, p. 399), mighty in overcoming sin and uniting us to God as the Son of the Father. As Spirit, God reveals himself to be the Redeemer, the 'Lord who sets us free' (I/1, p. 448), making real our reconciliation to God as the love of the Father and the Son.[6] The self-revealing God is this one, Creator, Reconciler and Redeemer, and is so antecedently, independent of our apprehension of him and therefore in absolute autonomy. Crucially, of course, that autonomy is not the dark freedom of a self-enclosed life, but actual as the gift of divine presence and grace, the gift of revelation. Barth's next task, as we turn to the second part-volume of *The Doctrine of the Word of God*, is to both retrace and further his argument by looking at the grace of God in incarnation and the giving of the Spirit.

Incarnation and Spirit

How is God real to us? The answers given to that question by many modern theologians, however varied their forms, tend to work with an assumption that the question concerns two distinct spheres of reality: the reality of God and our own reality. These two spheres of reality are not only distinct, they are distant, and so need to be brought into relation. Moreover, such answers tend to assume that it is our human reality which is stable, well-grounded and axiomatic, and that the reality of God has in some fashion to become 'meaningful' in terms of that well-established human realm. Our realm – the worlds of human history, culture and experience, ideas and language, modes of inquiry – sets the conditions under which we may say that God is real to us. Responsible theology will seek to demonstrate how it is that God may be present to us as the people we are. One way of setting about this task is to shift certain doctrines to centre stage in Christian theology. Most frequently, it is anthropology which comes to the fore, since it is commonly supposed that it is in the doctrine of the human person that Christian theology elaborates an account of the possible ways of God's presence to us. Another variant is to look to non-theological disciplines (philosophies of human subjectivity, for example, or of history) to supply an account of the a priori conditions under which God can be real. The gap between God's reality and ours is not closed by talking about God but by talking about ourselves as those to whom God is to be present.

Barth simply discards this entire tradition (and thereby earns the wrath of some of its most sophisticated modern representatives). God is real because God is God. And God is real to us because God makes himself real in the incarnation of the Word and the outpouring of the Holy Spirit. In pressing this argument at considerable length in *Church Dogmatics* I/2, Barth is pushing more deeply into the doctrine of the Trinity which he has already expounded, expanding the claim that revelation is from start to finish the work of the triune God and not some co-operative venture between God and his creatures. Furthermore, in taking this route he is offering a strictly doctrinal depiction of an issue which in modern theology is routinely handled in other ways: by theories of human experience, hermeneutics, or analysis of the historicity of understanding. Barth departs from this tradition above all, then, because his understanding of God as Lord will not permit the thought that human reality is some relatively independent sphere within the terms of which God must appear. As always for Barth, theology must follow the primary rule according to which the 'order of knowing corresponds to the order of being in which God is the Lord but in which man is God's creature and servant' (I/2, p. 7). There could hardly be a more complete dissent from the intellectual conventions of modernity.

Giving an account of these matters involves Barth in a lengthy exposition of Christology and pneumatology in paragraphs 15 and 16, which are the first truly great piece of writing in the *Church Dogmatics*, attaining a level of sustained conceptual and rhetorical grandeur equal to anything else Barth wrote. There is an intense delight in and amazement before the matter, a sense of its infinite profundity (Hans Frei was surely correct to speak of Barth's 'God-in-Christ intoxicated imagination'[7]). Closely allied to the sheer descriptive depth of the writing is Barth's evident sense of the impossibility of any kind of comprehensiveness in presenting the matter to which he felt so powerfully attracted. Theology is not to be conceived of as a way of grasping hold of the Credo by concepts or language, or of transcending it in thought. The object of the Credo – the infinite self-giving movement of the triune God – is irreducible. That object will not yield to inspection, giving up its secrets to those who seek to explain it in terms of some more comprehensive reality. God simply *is*, and can only be indicated as such. At key points in Barth's presentation, the long, swooping dives of the argument are pulled up short and he can do nothing other than explain: 'He and not I! He and not we! He, the Lord! He for us! He in our stead ... It is He, He who is the reality' (I/2, p. 368). At other times, Barth's procedure is not to attempt a conceptual translation of the language of faith, but simply to offer a reflective expansion of a biblical or credal phrase – precisely because dogmatics is not an *enhancement* of faith's primary ways of speaking about God, but merely a discursive repetition whose aim is nothing more than saying what has already been said.[8]

The overarching aim of the exposition is to propound that in the work of Jesus Christ and the Holy Spirit, God is both the objective and subjective reality and possibility of revelation. Revelation and its reception proceed alike from the triune God, and so coming to understand how God is known involves nothing more than following the path which is already indicated by the doctrine of the Trinity. Barth moves towards his aim along two interrelated lines.

The first, christological, line ponders the objective aspect of revelation: its intrinsic givenness as the act of God in Christ. Following this line involves Barth developing an almost ruthless particularity, a concentration of the imagination on one point and one point only: the name of Jesus, his absolute specificity as 'this one', the first and the last and the most simple thing. 'The fact that this first and last thing according to the New Testament is precisely the name of Jesus, reminds us that the reality in which the New

Testament sees God's revelation taking place is utterly *simple*, the simple reality of God' (I/2, p. 11). Jesus' name thus indicates that which in its divine objectivity is constitutive of all reality. All talk of God, creation, humanity, salvation and glory can in one sense be only a repetition or drawing out of this name. The 'christological concentration' of the *Church Dogmatics* – the fact that it is 'christologically determined as a whole and in all its parts' (I/2, p. 123) – is here given its first extended statement.

Out of this christological concentration, Barth develops another principle which will surface frequently in the *Church Dogmatics*, namely the priority of actuality over possibility. The thrust of this rather formal-sounding principle is to insist on the precedence of what God actually is and does over questions of how it is possible for God to be and act. In the discussion of Jesus Christ as the objective reality, this means that theology does not first work out the antecedent conditions under which a revelation from God might be possible, and only subsequently present Jesus Christ as the actual fulfilment of this possibility. Following this latter route would involve starting from something other than God's actual self-definition, working towards God as if God had not in fact become manifest, and so undermining God's axiomatic reality. For Barth, by contrast, we do not move from what God might do to what God does; rather, what God does, God *can* do. Barth's treatment of the relation of revelation to history is a case in point.[9] Much post-Enlightenment theology is predicated on the axiomatic character of our temporal experience; our 'historicity', the fact that we are self-consciously temporal beings, is the given on the basis of which all else must proceed. Revelation, therefore, if it is to be revelation to us, must enter within the sphere of our history. Barth once again cheerfully breaks the rule. 'Theologically,' he writes, 'the only sensible way of putting and answering the question as to the time of ... revelation is to assume the special concept of this special time' (I/2, p. 45). Revelation is not constituted by our historical awareness of ourselves; quite the contrary, our history is constituted by God's revealing presence to us, by 'God's time' which is 'real time' (I/2, p. 49). This divine time, actual and present with its own potency, does not wait for us to establish its possibility before it can be. It simply is, simply makes itself into our present, and so shows that in Christ revelation is objectively real and possible.

The second, pneumatological, line of reflection ponders the subjective reality of revelation. As we have already seen, Barth pursues the startling claim that in order to talk of revelation's subjective aspect (its presence to and reception by particular people), we do not retire language about God and replace it with language about ourselves, but rather talk of the third mode of God's being as Holy Spirit. Despite what is sometimes said about him, Barth is as keen as any neo-Protestant theologian to emphasize the importance of the human reality to which revelation occurs: 'Not God alone, but God and man together constitute the content of the Word of God' (I/2, p. 207). The basis of this, however, is not some quasi-independent subjective realm of experience, but the divinity of the Spirit. 'Spirit' and, derivatively, 'church' as the Spirit-generated community do for Barth the work which in other theologies is undertaken by anthropology, history and such like. All that is needed to get matters straight is to follow 'objective revelation through its whole unified movement from God to man' (I/2, p. 239).

The attention which Barth devotes to the subjective side of revelation takes away much of the force of the common criticism that his theology is (in Austin Farrer's woefully ill-informed judgement) simply the 'mighty thumping of the transcendentalist drum'.[10] Those who interpret Barth in this way tend to seize upon his negations (such as the refusal of any anthropological conditions for the occurrence of revelation), extracting them from their context and making them stand alone. Barth's treatment of 'The Revelation of God as the *Aufhebung* of Religion' (I/2, pp. 280–361) is unfairly maligned along these lines. This is partly because the translation of *Aufhebung* as 'Abolition' catches only half of the German term, which means both abrogation and preservation. Partly it is because the real object of Barth's attack is not 'other religions' but the whole human (and Christian) enterprise of religious self-justification. Partly, again, it is because Barth's lengthy and positive treatment of 'true religion' (I/2, pp. 325–61) is almost never taken into account. But above all the criticism is miscalculated because it neglects the overall structure of Barth's argument as a whole in *Church Dogmatics* I/2, whose aim is to demonstrate that objective and subjective are inseparable precisely because of the directedness of revelation to human being and action. If 'religion' is 'abolished', it is only in order to secure on a firmly pneumatological basis 'the life of the children of God' in action, love and praise (I/2, pp. 362–454). Because of (not despite) the fact that the self-revealing triune God is all in all, humanity is liberated to be truly itself.

Holy Scripture

The final turn of the argument before Barth goes back to the nature of dogmatics is his treatment of Holy Scripture as the third form of the Word of God. What Barth has to say in the nearly three hundred pages he devotes to this theme ranges over much more than simply questions of the nature and authority of the Bible. He offers a doctrine of Scripture, a hermeneutics and an ecclesiology of the Word. This involves him in viewing the Bible from two perspectives. First, he considers it in terms of God's use of Scripture – from the viewpoint of the commissioning of the human word of the Bible to be a witness to God's self-revealing activity. Second, he considers it in terms of the church's use of the Bible – from the viewpoint of the attitudes and practices which ought to characterize the members of the community which is addressed by God's Word through Scripture. Handling these two issues together, Barth is in effect suggesting that our perception of the nature and authority of Scripture is bound up with a certain way of being a reader. That way of being a reader is characterized (at the individual level) by obedient receptivity and (at the communal level) by a complex process of mutual deference and free responsibility in the interpretation and application of Scripture. The task here is thinking through 'the confession in which the Church clarifies that perception which corresponds to a right and necessary attitude of obedience to the witness of revelation' (I/2, p. 460).

Barth is presenting a more extended and architectonic version of the understanding of the Bible and its interpretation with which he had worked in the biblical commentaries he began writing twenty years before. As with those earlier treatments, the claim from which everything else radiates concerns the relation between Scripture and revelation. For Barth, that relation is best described by talking of 'Scripture as a Witness to Divine Revelation' (I/2, pp. 457–72). The language of witness has a double purpose: it gives full weight to the function of Scripture as the bearer of revelation, and it does so without taking away from the fact that the Bible is a collection of human texts. With the notion of witness,

> we distinguish the Bible as such from revelation. A witness is not absolutely identical with that to which it witnesses ... In the Bible we meet with human words written in human speech, and in these words, and therefore by means of them, we hear of the lordship of the triune God. Therefore when we have to do with the Bible, we have to do primarily with this means, with these

words, with the witness which as such is not itself revelation, but only . . . the witness to it. (I/2, p. 463)

However, within this limitation,

> the Bible is not distinguished from revelation. It is simply revelation as it comes to us, mediating and therefore accommodating itself to us . . . Yet it is for us revelation by means of the words of the prophets and apostles written in the Bible, in which they are still alive for us as the immediate and direct recipients of revelation, and by which they speak to us. A real witness is not identical with that to which it witnesses, but it sets it before us. (Ibid.)

Barth is attempting to reintegrate what had become, over the course of one hundred and fifty years, sharply opposed ways of reading the Bible: on the one hand, an ahistorical treatment of the Bible as a divine word to the church, and on the other hand, a purely natural or historical account of it as 'like any other book'. Barth's way of breaking the deadlock between the two views is to turn the argument on its head. Far from undermining Scripture's relation to revelation, a true understanding of the Bible and its humanity ought to highlight its function as testimony to God's self-manifestation. Taking the human word of Scripture seriously (which is what Barth means by reading it 'historically', that is, as a human historical product) does not mean turning the Bible into an example of a general category of, for example, ancient religious texts. What is of greatest importance for Barth is not the Bible's formal similarity to other literature but its specific content as *this* text. We have therefore to read the biblical material as 'the human speech uttered by specific men at specific times in a specific situation, in a specific language and with a specific intention' (I/2, p. 464). The content of this specific speech, by which our understanding of it is to be led, is that, as a genuinely human word, 'it points away from itself, that as a word it points toward a fact, and object' (ibid.). The fact or object which Scripture indicates is revelation.

Barth, then, cheerfully affirms – though on distinctly theological grounds – the importance of 'historical' interpretation of the Bible. But 'historical' interpretation does not mean resolving the specific character of the biblical texts into their context. It means alertness to what the texts say, taking their content seriously without envisaging that content as simply a means of access for historical reconstruction. The rule Barth enunciates here is devastatingly simple: 'We have to listen to what it [Scripture] says to us as a human word. We have to understand it as a human word in the light of what it says' (I/2, p. 466). Viewing the Bible as a revelatory text is thus not imposing an alien category on it, but merely letting its 'concrete humanity' (I/2, p. 464) guide our reading.

From here, Barth moves to consider the kinds of skills needed by readers of Scripture. The account of Scripture which he has so far presented emphasizes its 'historical definiteness' – that is, the fact that as *this* text it addresses us as a witness to God's speech. Corresponding to this particular character of the text, Barth recommends a particular attitude for readers to adopt to the event of God's Word in the scriptural text. In spelling out this attitude, Barth is concerned to identify something much deeper than simple exegetical technique. What is required of readers is that they be shaped at the most fundamental level by the miracle of divine speech which encounters us through the text. To be a true reader of Scripture is to be governed by 'the mystery of the sovereign freedom of the substance' (I/2, p. 470) which Scripture denotes. This 'substance' in all its spiritual power presses the reader to be a particular kind of person.

> We have to know the mystery of the substance if we are really to meet it, if we are really to be open and ready, really to give ourselves to it, when we are told it, that it may really meet us as the substance. And when it is a matter of understanding, the knowledge of this mystery will create in us a peculiar fear and reserve which is not at all usual to us. We will then know that in the face of this subject-matter there can be no question of our achieving, as we do in others, the confident approach which masters and subdues the matter. It is rather a question of being gripped by the subject-matter ... really gripped, so that it is only as those who are mastered by the subject-matter, who are subdued by it, that we can investigate the humanity of the word by which it is told us. (Ibid.)

Claimed by God's Word in this way, and responding to the claim by abandoning that 'self-assured mastery' which so afflicts the practice of exegesis, '[w]e shall be at least restrained in our evil domination of the text' (I/2, pp. 470f.).

Such a hermeneutic is radical indeed: it replaces suspicion by consent; it makes historical reconstruction a mere preliminary; it requires spiritual skills of the interpreter. Once again, Barth cannot be understood unless we see how drastically he is revising the task of Christian theology, by trying to depict its job in relation to a Christian way of life and thought organized around the event of the Word of God. As *Church Dogmatics* I/2 draws to a close, Barth turns once again to consider the dogmatic task in the light of what has been said about God, Christ, Spirit, revelation, Scripture and church.

Dogmatics

Though the complexity and grandeur of the *Church Dogmatics* may at first belie it, Barth's conception of the theological task is at heart simple and modest. Dogmatics is called to perform the simple task of being the place where the church evaluates its own proclamation against its given norm, revelation. But the dogmatics by which this job is undertaken is essentially a modest activity. It is not some sort of tribunal before which those directly charged with church proclamation must appear; quite the opposite. Dogmatics is simply the church standing beneath revelation, exemplifying that openness to correction which is the hallmark of the true hearer of God's Word. The dogmatician does not work with the confidence that – unlike others in the church – he or she has already heard what revelation has to say. If dogmatics corrects and criticizes, it does so by correcting and criticizing itself.

Barth's way of explaining this is to suggest that dogmatics relates to two fundamental modes of the life of the church: its hearing of God's Word and its teaching of it. Dogmatics is part of the life of the 'hearing church' in so far as it 'adopts the attitude' (I/2, p. 797) of the church by attentiveness to the Word, demonstrating subjection to the primacy of God's revelatory speech. In 'complete solidarity', dogmatics 'reminds the Church (and itself first of all), that there exists prior to and above and after every *ego dico* and *ecclesia dicit a haec dixit Dominus*' (I/2, p. 801). Therefore 'the formal task of dogmatics in regard to Church proclamation consists in confronting it with its own law in all its transcendence, in reminding it that it is the Word of God because Jesus Christ and He alone speaks in the prophetic and apostolic witness' (I/2, p. 802). Dogmatics can only perform this task, however, as it is itself subject to transcendent authority, 'theonomy' (I/2, p. 815). No reader of Barth can miss the pervasiveness of this attitude in many of the features of his work: its restlessness; its unwillingness to invest too heavily in any one concept or method; above all, its demonstration of the 'readiness that its whole life should be assailed, convulsed, revolutionised and reshaped' (I/2, p. 804) – a readiness which ought to characterize all that is said and done in the church. More specifically, the 'theonomy' of the church is expressed in three characteristics of theological work. It must have a 'biblical character' (I/2, p. 816). That is to say, dogmatics must adopt the attitude of the biblical witnesses as the prototype of renouncing intellectual autonomy, and instead be 'exclusively controlled by the realities' which theology must simply 'indicate and confirm' (I/2, p. 817). This does not mean that dogmatics is simply exegesis, or that it is not free to take up questions from elsewhere. But whatever its agenda, dogmatics 'takes the form of its thought from its submission to the biblical *Deus dixit*' (I/2, p. 822). Second, dogmatics has a 'confessional attitude' (ibid.): in its particular church context, dogmatics has to take seriously its relative determination by confessional allegiance. Third, dogmatics is required to demonstrate a 'church attitude' (I/2, p. 840), in solidarity with the church which now must proclaim the Word of God. What Barth is seeking to articulate is an account of theology that is not governed either by the demand that it establish the grounds on which Christian faith is possible, or by the demand that all viewpoints be summoned before the bar of universal reason. Both demands were (and remain) deeply engrained in the practice of mainstream Western academic theology. But: 'the Word of God did not found an academy but a Church' (I/2, p. 841). It is in that context and under the norms by which that context operates that theology does its job.

Only out of this attitude of hearing is dogmatics undertaken as part of the 'teaching' church and commissioned not only to be a means of the church's self-critique but also a summons to proclamation. Such proclamation does not run ahead of the Word of God, as it were, anticipating it or speaking instead of God. It is simply a following of 'the way which God has taken, takes, and will take with man in the person of Jesus Christ and through the operation of the Holy Spirit. The method of church proclamation consists, and can only consist, in a treading of this way' (I/2, pp. 856f.). Out of this, Barth develops some thoughts about the structure of dogmatics, a topic which he frequently pondered and about which he was highly self-conscious in the *Church Dogmatics*. If dogmatics is about the business of tracing the path which God's Word takes, then it must be oriented to the movement which it follows. No system, no organizing principle, no critical theory and certainly no methodological prescription can be allowed to have the upper hand. The 'method' of dogmatics is, in fact, quite unmethodical, consisting in

> unceasing and ready vigilance to see that the object is able to speak for itself, and that its effect on human thinking and speaking is not disturbed. It implies the confidence that these effects will come, and come with regal power, that the object can do this, and that what it can do it will actually do. Therefore it presupposes the operation of the object itself, to which is to be ascribed the awakening of this very confidence. (I/2, p. 867)

This presupposition – 'the operation of the object itself ' – is nothing less than the key to everything Barth wants to say about theology. That object is, of course, subject, the majestic subject Father, Son and Holy Spirit, who in speaking his Word creates the church within which theology has its unassuming role to play.

Conclusion

Barth's early doctrine of the Trinity was one of the great fruits of his remarkable powers as a constructive dogmatician, and the conceptual daring it demonstrated in the interweaving of the doctrines of divine revelation and divine triunity has made it a benchmark for later discussion. The renewal of trinitarian theology over the last twenty-five years, particularly in English-language systematic theology, is scarcely thinkable without the example of Barth's confidence in setting forth a trinitarian structure to the Christian doctrine of God. For all this, his account of the matter is often judged as flawed, introducing distortions into the shape of Christian doctrine which can be discerned throughout his dogmatics. Indeed, many of the major disagreements with Barth in a wide variety of areas (theological anthropology, the doctrine of creation, ecclesiology and sacraments, for example) crystallize around one or other aspect of his trinitarian teaching.

The core of the problem, on some accounts, is the proximity of the doctrines of Trinity and revelation. By expounding them together, Barth seems to lock himself into a conception of God as a single, self-revealing subject, thereby making it acutely difficult to talk of the triune plurality of God. At the very least, there seems some sort of tension between Barth's insistence that the Christian doctrine of God is the doctrine of the Trinity, and his exposition of

Father, Son and Spirit through the idiom of self-manifestation. That idiom appears to push Barth into expounding the doctrine of the Trinity by tracing the logic of a single, self-manifesting 'I', a 'singular subject'.[11] The effects of this on the doctrine of the Trinity are manifold. At one level it means that, despite explicit statements to the contrary, Barth is constrained to give divine unity priority over divine triunity. The divine essence is God's singularity as Lord, the 'I' who encounters us in self-communication. As a consequence, Barth has a weak sense of the relations between the divine persons, the fellowship or mutuality of encounter between Father, Son and Spirit. Here, it is suggested, Barth fails to see that 'relation' is not something only to be predicated of God as a (singular) communicative subject encountering humanity in the act of revelation; it describes that which characterizes the essence of God. Father, Son and Spirit are not merely modes of God's self-manifestation conceived in linear terms, but ways of talking of the communion which God is. 'What Barth's conception of unity fails to take due cognizance of is the extent to which the New Testament accounts make it difficult to avoid affirming that God is a Thou to himself and an I in relation to himself.'[12] All this is signalled by Barth's worries about the term 'person' and is, furthermore, bound up with his assertion of divine sovereignty which forms the backcloth to the entire discussion and which critics such as Moltmann believe to be dominated by a monarchical motif whose monotheism sits uneasily with trinitarian affirmations.[13] Some consider that these problems are to be traced to Barth's (perhaps unconscious) dependence on philosophical notions of subjectivity developed in the German idealist tradition (Hegel and Fichte are the usual candidates), notions which, at least at this stage in Barth's development, are uncorrected by christological or pneumatological considerations and which reinforce the monistic or modalistic tendency of his conception.[14] Others locate the difficulty in Barth's preoccupation with epistemological issues, which lead him to construe the Christian faith in terms of the question: 'How do we know God?' When the doctrine of the Trinity is expounded as an answer to this question, then the divine economy is no longer seen as a fellowship of mutual interactions into which the history of the world is drawn into saving communion, but as the cognitive self-bestowal of the Revealer.[15]

On the other hand, criticism of Barth often proceeds by expecting him to do and say things he does not wish to do and say, and then finding him wanting. Thus the force of some of these assessments of Barth will to some extent depend on whether the reader is persuaded of the necessity, fruitfulness and coherence of one or other version of the 'social trinitarianism' which has acquired considerable prestige in contemporary theology. But there are other factors, too: not the least, how one reads the texts from Barth. Partly this is a matter of interpreting the trinitarian sections of *Church Dogmatics* I. Does Barth's rather narrow account of the history of the term 'person' make him too cautious about its possibilities in a trinitarian context? Does he exploit as fully as he might the significance of the begetting of the Son and the procession of the Spirit for discussion of the divine essence? Or is the force of his emphasis on revelation simply a means of securing the all-important fact that it really is *God* who encounters us in revelation? Answers to such questions will themselves depend on how one places *Church Dogmatics* I with respect to the argument of the work as a whole. Some critics concede that the later volumes, especially the rich and comprehensive Christology and pneumatology of the doctrine of reconciliation in volume IV, heavily qualify the apparently monarchical tone of the earlier trinitarian material. At the very least, this means that Barth's trinitarian thinking evolved after the 1930s. Much more, however, it means that what Barth has to say on the doctrine of the Trinity is not simply to be sought in those passages where he is explicitly treating the theme. In one very important sense, the whole of the *Church Dogmatics* is a doctrine of the Trinity, both in its architectural conception and its specific content, and criticisms of his explicit exposition of the divine triunity sometimes need to be set in the light of what happens elsewhere. Thus, the suggestion that Barth is dominated by epistemological issues may be questionable, not only because it rests on a partial reading of *Church Dogmatics* I, but also because it underestimates how crucial is the theme of God and humanity as agents in covenant relation (a theme which acquires increasing prominence from *Church Dogmatics* II onwards, though it is by no means absent from volume I). Or again, the contrast of a trinitarian conception expounded via revelation and one oriented to the inner-divine communion can hardly be sustained from what Barth will go on to say about the doctrine of God in volume II or the treatment of the mission of the Son in volume IV. The *Church Dogmatics* is both comprehensive and integrated, and reading Barth well involves bearing in mind the fact that apparently unrelated, even divergent, tracts of argument have a coherence which can usually only be seen in the scope of the whole. In terms of the doctrine of the Trinity, this means that if *Church Dogmatics* I reflects on the question 'How is

God *God* for us?', it is the task of what follows to ask the same question with a different emphasis: 'How is God God *for us*?'

Notes

1. H. Frei, 'Eberhard Busch's Biography of Karl Barth' in *Types of Christian Theology* (New Haven: Yale University Press, 1992), pp. 158f.
2. E. Jüngel, 'Introduction', in *Karl Barth. A Theological Legacy* (Philadelphia: Westminster Press, 1986), p. 12.
3. *CD* I/1, p. xiii. Subsequent page references are given in the main text.
4. *FQI*, pp. 26f.
5. Aristotle, *Rhetoric* 1354a.
6. The trinitarian pattern – Creator, Reconciler, Redeemer – into which Barth's thinking about the total shape of Christian doctrine had been falling for a number of years, remained the basic structure of the *Church Dogmatics*, although the doctrine of redemption was never written.
7. H. Frei, 'Karl Barth: Theologian', in *Theology and Narrative. Selected Essays* (Oxford: Oxford University Press, 1993), p. 171.
8. The best example of this in *CD* I/2 is the lengthy exposition of John 1.14 as the organizing principle for and substance of the treatment of 'Very God and Very Man', pp. 132–71.
9. *CD* I/2, pp. 45–121.
10. A. Farrer, *Interpretation and Belief* (London: SPCK, 1976), p. 50. Farrer's encounter with Barth in 1931 is recounted in P. Curtis, *A Hawk Among Sparrows. A Biography of Austin Farrer* (London: SPCK, 1985), pp. 96f.
11. A. Torrance, *Persons in Communion. An Essay in Trinitarian Description and Human Participation, with Special Reference to Volume One of Karl Barth's* Church Dogmatics (Edinburgh: T. & T. Clark, 1996), p. 241.
12. Ibid., p. 220.
13. J. Moltmann, *The Trinity and the Kingdom of God* (London: SCM, 1981). See also C. LaCugna, *God For Us. The Trinity and the Christian Life* (San Francisco: Harper and Row, 1991), p. 254.
14. See T. Rendtorff, *Theories des Christentums. Historisch-theologische Studien zu seiner neuzeitlichen Verfassung* (Gütersloh: Mohn, 1972) for an argument that Barth transfers on to the Christian doctrine of God ideas of autonomy derived from modern anthropology. More detailed trinitarian material can be found in W. Pannenberg, *Grundfragen systematischer Theologie. Gesammelte Aufsätze* II (Göttingen: Vandenhoeck und Ruprecht, 1980), pp. 80–128.

15. One of the best accounts of this criticism is the careful reading of Barth by R. Williams, 'Barth on the Triune God', in S. W. Sykes (ed.), *Karl Barth. Studies of His Theological Method* (Oxford: Clarendon Press, 1979), pp. 147–93.

4

God

In the preface to the very first volume of the *Church Dogmatics* in 1932, Barth concluded his account of the plan of the work with a quotation from the letter of James: 'If the Lord will, and we live'. Looking back ten years later, as he wrote the preface to *Church Dogmatics* II/2, he commented:

> I did not then suspect how very appropriate it was to speak in that way. A year later we were plunged into the Third Reich and the German Church-conflict. From that time the affairs of Europe and finally of the whole world hurtled with ever-increasing violence into the crisis which still engulfs us. By the very nature of things I have not been able to devote the last ten years solely to dogmatics ... Yet dogmatics has been ever with me, giving me a constant awareness of what should be my central and basic theme as a thinker.[1]

Although it is possible to read what Barth has to say in these two volumes as a colossal exercise in conceptual dramatics in which the devastations of modern European history scarcely register, such an interpretation hardly does justice to Barth's intense awareness of his political and cultural context, or to his profound involvement in that context as a church leader. It is certainly true that Barth proceeds with the doctrine of God 'as if nothing had happened': that is, he does not consider that the brutalities of Germany in the 1930s require him to reinvent the theological task. But he took that view, not because he did not know or care that something had indeed happened: he knew it all too well and cared deeply. But he did not consider that what had happened – however appalling – could somehow cancel out the church's task of careful, critical reflection upon its speech of God. Indeed, faced with the remarkably swift capitulation of much of German Protestantism in face of the Nazi ideology, Barth came to consider the dogmatic task all the more important, offering precisely the kind of critical safeguard against the nostrification of God which lay at the heart of the collapse of German church life and thought. Barth's insistence on the priority of theology was thus deliberate, a calculated and far-sighted attempt to steer the church back to its proper calling and thereby to strengthen its capacity to resist.

In approaching this section of the *Church Dogmatics*, three things need to be borne in mind. First, as we have already seen, this is not the first treatment of the doctrine of God: volume I has already devoted a great deal of space to the doctrine of the Trinity. It is crucial, therefore, to appreciate that what Barth offers in volume II is an extension or deepening of what has already been said in the first volume: the 'God' of whom he now comes to speak is none other than the Father, the Son and the Spirit. Nowhere does Barth suggest that there is any other Christian construal of the term 'God' than a trinitarian one; accordingly, there is no change of subject when we move from talk of the Trinity to talk of God. Second, Barth has almost no interest here in general questions of the existence of God, still less in questions of the existence or character of 'a' god. At this point, he breaks with a strong convention of much philosophical theology, which proceeds to the discussion of the divine nature only after securing the existence of God by a process of demonstration. Barth's unease with this procedure is partly driven by his deep commitment to the self-existence (aseity) of God, which is in principle undemonstrable. Partly, again, it arises out of his particularism, his vigilance to ensure that talk of God is talk of *this one*, one whose nature is determined by attention to the sequence of the acts in which that nature is manifest. Prior (usually abstract) definitions of the nature of God are disallowed by Barth, who both starts from and ends with the reality of God as God is actually known through self-demonstration. Third, therefore, consistent attention to this particular divine reality, made known in Jesus Christ the God-man, shows that talk of God is inseparable from talk of the extraordinary mercy with which God elects, creates, rescues and glorifies human covenant partners for himself. Barth's doctrine of God is thus at one and the same time a classic treatment of divine sovereignty and also an unparalleled essay in

Christian humanism. Indeed, it is the humane character of Barth's presentation of the nature of God which is one of the most important things it had to say to the distress and inhumanity which faced Barth everywhere he looked as he doggedly put together his text.

The text of the doctrine of God falls into four sections: the knowledge of God (paragraphs 25–7); the reality of God (paragraphs 28–31); the election of God (paragraphs 32–5), and the command of God (paragraphs 36–9).

The knowledge of God

The problem of the relation between the objective reality of God and the knowing human subject had been a major preoccupation of Christian theology since Kant, whose deep-seated agnosticism concerning the possibility of such a relation was mediated to Barth in his student years by later neo-Kantian philosophers from Marburg. Like his near-contemporary Bultmann, Barth was deeply impressed with the gravity of the issue. But, unlike Bultmann, he did not try to solve it by developing a theology focused on human existence and a severely ascetic repudiation of divine objectivity (Bultmann's severity is itself reminiscent of Kant's negative theology). Barth took another road: that of attempting to spell out a properly Christian sense of the objectivity of God, with the aim not so much of meeting the Kantian challenge head-on as of subverting it by refusing to be trapped within its categories. Thus in *Church Dogmatics* II, Barth begins his account of the knowledge of God by announcing that the central issue is that of characterizing 'the particular and utterly unique objectivity of God' (*CD* II/1, p. 14). Making such a characterization leads Barth to distinguish between the primary objectivity of God and his secondary objectivity. God's primary objectivity is God as objectively immediate to himself, in the self-knowledge which is intrinsic to the triune life. God's secondary objectivity is God as mediately objective to the human knower. This initially somewhat obscure distinction is worth pausing over.

First, Barth's stress that God is primarily objective to himself (and not just objective in so far as he is an object of human cognition) is an attempt to shift the epistemological centre of gravity away from the projective activities of human knowing and on to divine action. 'Only because God posits Himself as the object is man posited as the knower of Gods' he writes (II/1, p. 22); or again: 'God is known through God and through God alone' (II/1, p. 44). A theological epistemology must in no way contravene the first principle of all theology, namely the majesty and freedom of the prevenient God in which he is utterly distinct, ineffably prior to all human attempts to make him into one more object of cognizance. God *is*, and is of himself objective to himself: Kant's negative theology is not so much argued against as simply repudiated from the beginning, because of its incompatibility with basic Christian convictions about the nature of God.

However, Barth's assertion of the primary objectivity of God should not be read as an exercise in theological realism of an unsophisticated kind: no less than Kant, Barth is clear that such divine objectivity is not available to human creatures. If God is indeed an object to our minds, if God is known – as indeed God is – then it is in God's secondary objectivity. With this term, Barth specifies the mode of God's presence to the human knower. God's objectivity to us is what he calls a 'clothed objectivity' (II/1, p. 18), an objectivity which is real but nevertheless mediate or indirect, and hence appropriately designated 'sacramental'. This objectivity is that of the incarnation: in Jesus, 'the first sacrament', and then by derivation in other creaturely realities which God selects and elevates to be testimonies to his self-declaration. This kind of objectivity is secondary or sacramental in that there God's manifestation is indirect, though real. As Barth puts it: 'Knowing Him in His revelation we know Him in this His attestation for us and therefore *ad extra* and therefore in this otherness: that is, in such a way that, by His being revealed to us as He and as Thou, He remains hidden from us as I and therefore in the being and essence of His Godhead' (II/1, p. 58). As 'I', as one who is inexhaustibly subject and object to himself, God is other; as 'Thou', as one who bestows himself in his secondary objectivity, God is known and therefore knowable. What Barth is moving towards with these various concepts is a notion of a real but mysterious presence of God as object, and a divine objectivity which is to be characterized as the event of gift rather than as possession. This is why throughout his discussion of the knowledge of God as object, he insists that faith is the mode of human knowledge of God, since faith is that human attitude which conforms to the specific character of God's self-bestowal:

> knowledge of God as knowledge of faith is in itself and of essential necessity obedience. It is an act of human decision

corresponding to the act of divine decision; corresponding to the act of the divine being as the living Lord; corresponding to the act of grace in which faith is grounded and continually grounded again in God. In this act God posits Himself as our object and ourselves as those who know Him. But the fact that He does so means that our knowing can consist only in our following this act, in ourselves becoming a correspondence of this act, in ourselves and our whole existence and therefore our conceiving and considering becoming the human act of corresponding to the divine act. This is obedience, the obedience of faith. (II/1, p. 26)

If we stand back a little from the details of Barth's account, two features are of especial importance. First, he does not start from the critical question of whether knowledge of God is possible, but from what he calls the knowledge of God in its 'fulfilment' (*Vollzug*), in terms of the actuality of its performance rather than in terms of its transcendental conditions. Thereby, second, he is moving in a contrary direction from an entire tradition in modern Christian theology in which the study of questions of theological epistemology had been conducted largely without reference to divine action, or at least with a very restricted account of divine action as scarcely operative in the field of human knowledge. But for Barth, our knowledge of God is not only what we do; it is our active conformity to the self-knowledge of God in which we participate in a dependent fashion through creaturely signs. Such is the confidence afforded by Barth's doctrine of revelation that he could pursue at great length an argument which he sums up as follows: 'God speaks to man in His Word. Thereby He gives Himself to be known by him; therein He is known by him' (II/1, p. 44).

Once Barth has treated the actuality of knowledge of God, he moves on in the section on 'The Knowability of God' to investigate the possibility which is presupposed and manifest in this actuality. Once again, he finds himself countering the instincts of those strands of the Christian tradition (on his reading of the matter, chiefly liberal Protestant and Roman Catholic) which have addressed this topic by appealing in the wrong way to a doctrine of human capacity. It is – emphatically – not that Barth wants to deny any and all such capacity, however frequently he is misread as asserting this. His point is simply that in talking of human capacity (he prefers the more active term 'readiness'), we must not fail to make reference to the being and action of God by whom such capacity is given, and in whose hands it always lies:

the readiness of man cannot be independent. It is a readiness which cannot finally be grounded in itself, i.e., in the nature and activity of man, so that between it and the readiness of God there is a relationship of mutual conditioning, the readiness of man meeting the readiness of God halfway, so to speak, God in His readiness having to wait, as it were, for the readiness of man in order that together they may constitute the knowability of God which establishes the knowledge of God ... If there is this readiness on the side of man, it can have only a borrowed, mediated and subsequent independence. It can be communicated to man only as a capacity and willingness for gratitude and obedience. It can be opened and apportioned to man only from the source of all readiness – the readiness of God Himself. (II/1, pp. 65f.)

There is certainly a denial here, as can quickly be seen in Barth's criticisms of certain kinds of natural theology in II/1: less fiery, probably, than his dispute with Brunner earlier in the decade, but no less decisive a rejection. But the negation is a function of a positive assertion, namely that theology does proper justice to human readiness only when we shift the location of that readiness from a quasi-independent anthropology to Christology.

In Christian doctrine, and therefore in the doctrine of the knowledge and knowability of God, we have always to take in blind seriousness the basic Pauline perception of Colossians 3.3 which is that of all Scripture – that our life is our life hid with Christ in God. With Christ: never at all apart from Him, never at all independently of Him, never at all in and for itself. (II/1, p. 149)

Throughout the discussion of the knowledge of God, therefore, Barth looks to christological doctrine to do the work which might more conventionally be undertaken by accounts of the dynamics of human subjectivity. Thus, for example, he asks how it can be that there is a link between the objectivity of God and human subjectivity, such that we may truly speak of a human readiness for God. In his answer, he employs the notion of Christ's fraternity with us as the one who assumed our flesh, thereby in our place abolishing enmity with God. More specifically, Barth appeals to the doctrine of Christ's high priestly office (in which, as the ascended and enthroned Lord, he intercedes for us and distributes the merits won by his saving work) and the doctrine of the Holy Spirit who works in us the 'temporal form' of our reconciliation to God, which is 'the form of faith' (II/1, p. 159). Our knowledge of God is thus not a function of any cognitive capacities which we may possess, but of the fact that, in Christ, we have peace with God:

> When we speak of this peace, and therefore of the man ready for God to whom God is knowable, we are speaking of Jesus Christ, of the reconciliation of man with God that took place and is eternal in Him the Son of God. It is in this way, and only in this way, that we speak genuinely and really about ourselves, because in the reality of Jesus Christ everything is accomplished for us that must and can be accomplished; because in eternity He intercedes for us; and because in the Holy Spirit the unity of the Father and the Son becomes effectual among and in us too in the twofold form of faith and the Church. (II/1, p. 161)

The final turn of Barth's argument concerning the knowledge of God is to examine its limits. As so often in the *Church Dogmatics*, the new section both extends and recapitulates the argument of what has gone before. He revisits the notion of God's hiddenness, which he had earlier used in talking of the primary objectivity in which God is known only to himself, and here underlines that the notion disables any potentiality to which our cognitive projects might pretend. Our 'views and concepts' – the whole enterprise of constructing knowledge by perceptual images and critical reflection – are 'not at all capable of grasping God' (II/1, p. 182), for

> The assertion of God's hiddenness ... tells us that God does not belong to the objects which we can always subjugate to the process of our viewing, conceiving and expressing and therefore our spiritual oversight and control. In contrast to that of all other objects, His nature is not one which in this sense lies in the sphere of our control. God is inapprehensible. (II/1, p. 187)

Readers of Barth who are disposed to find similarities between him and varieties of postmodern thought make much of such passages, which seem to echo the exposure of the mythology of 'givenness' which is one of the basic features of much postmodernism. But, once again, Barth is never a purely negative theologian; even if, of ourselves, 'we do not really know what we are saying when we say "God" ' (II/1, p. 189), nevertheless, on the basis of God's address of us, we are both permitted and commanded to know and speak about God. 'Knowing the true God in His revelation, we apprehend Him in His hiddenness' (II/1, p, 194).

There is a critical edge to Barth's realism. He has no hesitation in stating that all human language about God – even scriptural language – stands 'under the crisis of the hiddenness of God' (II/1, p. 195). But where postmodern theology halts and falls into silence or arbitrary linguistic play, Barth presses ahead to speak of the miracle of grace in which knowledge of the hidden God occurs despite the essential unsuitability of human media.

> The nature of His revelation ... is that it is grace. That is, it is a bestowal which utterly transcends all our capacity, being and existence as such, but does not destroy us, does not consume and break our being and existence. On the contrary ... it is present to us to our salvation, and it can be affirmed and grasped by us in faith, to become a determination of our being and existence. (II/1, pp. 197f.)

And, again, the basis of this is christological: in the Word made flesh, we are given 'the first, original and controlling sign of all signs' (II/1, p. 199), which disallows any fundamental scepticism. There is, even for a *theologia viatorum*, a proper veracity of human thought and speech about God as they are 'taken up by the grace of God and determined to participation in the veracity of the revelation of God' (II/1, p. 213).

Such, then, in brief compass, is Barth's presentation of the knowledge of God. It is sometimes suggested that Barth's dogmatics is excessively preoccupied with epistemological questions, such that all theological topics (especially soteriology) are transposed into questions of the knowledge of God. What one makes of that critique depends to a large extent on how one places Barth with respect to modernity, and the degree to which one believes him to be trapped within the cage against which his theology crashes time and again. But at the exegetical level, it is at least worth noting that careful inspection of Barth's texts, especially in *Church Dogmatics* II/1, does not easily bear out the interpretation of Barth as one who effected the transposition of all doctrine into epistemology. Quite the opposite: Barth handles epistemological questions by engaging in leisurely exposition of trinitarian, incarnational and pneumatological doctrine, and, far from being pressed into an epistemological mould, those doctrines are themselves exploited to reach ends which might otherwise be gained by an epistemological route. It is not so much that doctrines are transposed into epistemology as that epistemology is transposed into doctrine – as it should be, Barth would argue, in a well-ordered and Christianly conscientious dogmatics.

The reality of God

'God is' (II/1, p. 257). With this utterly minimal statement, Barth announces what he regards as *the* preoccupation of Christian dogmatics. In developing and explaining that statement in the pages which follow, Barth's concern is not the possibility of divine existence but its character. And, moreover, that character can only properly be discerned by laying aside what we believe ourselves to know of deity, and instead learning from God who God is. Thereby, Christian dogmatics demonstrates its adherence to the principle which Barth laid down at the very beginning of *Church Dogmatics* II/1, namely that 'In the doctrine of God we have to learn what we are saying when we say "God". In the doctrine of God we have to learn to say "God" in the correct sense' (II/1, p. 3). To expound the doctrine of God out of the simple statement 'God is' is thus not only to presuppose the veracity of the church's talk of God but also, more importantly, to orient theological inquiry towards the description of the content of that statement. Barth has no confidence in the theological strategy which handles the term 'God' as if it could be understood without reference to a particular identity (that enacted in the drama of creation and reconciliation summed up in Jesus Christ). What theology seeks to unearth is thus the sheer 'this-ness', the irreducible specificity, of the one indicated in the Christian confession.

Accordingly, Barth proceeds immediately to a discussion of the works of God, that is, the divine actions which are the manifestation of the divine identity. 'God is who He is in His works ... in His works He is Himself revealed as the One He is' (II/1, p. 260). In making this move, Barth is evidently trying to prevent the absorption of the doctrine of God into a general ontology or metaphysics of first principles. But he is aware that this puts him rather easily in the neighbourhood of that species of Christian theology which refuses to address questions of the 'being' or 'essence' of God, believing them to be purely speculative and of no salvific or moral utility. In the early Protestant tradition, the anxiety was voiced by Melanchthon, for whom reflection on the benefits of Christ's saving work set the limits to legitimate theological inquiry; by the end of the nineteenth century, hostility towards so-called metaphysical discussion of the being of God had become a basic principle of Ritschlian theology. Barth's point is rather different: what he rejects is not the legitimacy of theological talk of God's being, but the assertion that theological talk of God's being is to be governed by general ontological principles rather than by attention to the acts of God in which he presents himself to the world: 'What God is as God, the divine individuality and characteristics, the *essentia* or "essence" of God, is something which we shall encounter either at the place where God deals with us as Lord and Saviour or not at all' (II/1, p. 261). This is why Barth turns to the category of 'event' in order to achieve his main purpose in this treatment of the divine reality, that is, a conceptual transcription of the statement 'God is', for,

> with regard to the being of God, the word 'event' or 'act' is *final*, and cannot be surpassed or compromised. To its very deepest depths God's Godhead consists in the fact that it is an event – not any event, not events in general, but the event of His action, in which we have a share in God's revelation. (II/1, p. 263)

Even here, however, the particularity of God remains a critical principle. As event or act, God is *actus purus et singularis*, pure and singular act: 'pure', because uncaused, free and sheerly self-sufficient; 'singular', because utterly distinct from all other acts and events. In short: 'God exists in His act. God is His own decision. God lives from and by Himself' (II/1, p. 272).

These rather formal preliminaries serve as the frame for the substantive discussion which follows, which is directed towards the questions: What is the act of God? How does God live? How is the life-act of God nameable? The answer which Barth expounds is that the 'essence of God which is seen in His revealed name is His being and therefore His act as Father, Son and Holy Spirit' (II/1, p. 273). Crucially, this act in which God has his being is an act which is directed towards us, creating and sustaining relation:

> As it is revealed to us as the definition of that which confronts us in His revelation, this name definitely has this primary and decisive thing to say to us in all its constituents – that God is He who, without having to do so, seeks and creates fellowship between Himself and us. He does not have to do it, because in Himself without us, and therefore without this, He has that

which He seeks and creates between Himself and us. It implies so to speak an overflow of His essence that He turns to us. (Ibid.)

To say that God is, so goes the flow of Barth's argument, is to say that God's essence is known in his revealed name, that is, in his acts as Father, Son and Spirit; those acts are acts whose end is the engendering of fellowship with us; and therefore God's Godhead 'consists in the fact that He loves' (II/1, p. 275).

From Barth's presentation it becomes immediately clear how wide of the mark it is to view his work as tied to the logic of divine aseity in such a way that humanity is an imperilled theme in dogmatics, or to interpret his doctrine of the Trinity as monistic and closed. His argument throughout the *Church Dogmatics* (and in earlier work) pulls in a quite different direction – not away from but towards the creature whom God reconciles and redeems. If 'love' is fundamental to the being of God, then the charge of hostility to the human realm simply falls. Of course, Barth is not unaware that what he has to say at this point (especially in its implications for divine 'personality') may put him uncomfortably close to the region of the anthropomorphism of the nineteenth-century liberal tradition, and he therefore takes great pains to uphold the principles of purity and singularity, even while insisting that God in his inmost being is one who establishes fellowship with us. In part, he protects himself by insisting that love is defined by God's acts and not vice versa; partly, again, by stressing that talk of God as person does not receive its impulse from considerations of the nature of human personality but from the antecedent life of the divine Trinity: 'Not we but God is I' (II/1, p. 284). But the most important presentation of these issues is found in the section on the freedom of God (paragraph 28.3), a section which is crucial in laying out some of the primary features of Barth's doctrine of God, not the least its humane quality.

What, Barth asks, is the 'characteristic depth' (II/1, p. 299) of the being of God? His answer is freedom: 'God's being as He who lives and loves is being in freedom' (II/1, p. 301). This simple statement opens out into a fundamental theological principle which informs the rest of the account of the doctrine of God, above all its treatment of election. The principle is that in the case of God freedom cannot be defined simply and formally as independence or unconstrainedness; divine freedom is 'the freedom proper to and characteristic of Him' (II/1, p. 304). Its material content is therefore discovered not by unpacking the concept of freedom, but by attending to the actual identity of the one of whom we speak, an identity exhibited in its execution in the history of Jesus. 'The legitimacy of every theory concerning the relationship of God and man or God and the world can be tested by considering whether it can be understood also as an interpretation of the relationship and fellowship created and sustained in Jesus Christ' (II/1, p. 320). To be sure, the freedom of God is God's utter freedom from origination or conditioning from outside by what is not himself. But the corollary of this is not God's unrelatedness to that which is other than himself, but rather the fact that God's self-determination is exercised in being with and for humanity:

> Now that it [created existence] has originated in His will and subsists by His will, He does not detach Himself from it in an alien aloofness, but is present as the being of its being with the eternal faithfulness of which no creature is capable towards another. God can allow this other which is so utterly distinct from Himself to live and move and have its being within Himself. He can grant and leave it its own special being distinct from His own, and yet even in this way, and therefore in this its creaturely freedom, sustain, uphold and govern it by His own divine being, thus being its beginning, centre and end. (II/1, p. 314)

Throughout the section – constructed with his characteristic layering of themes – Barth is trying to indicate the inseparability of divine freedom and divine love. Divine freedom, because it is not abstract but takes form in the acts of creation, reconciliation and redemption, is the freedom in which God loves. Freedom is not anterior to God's love but its divine depth; divine love is the actuality (not the surrender or compromise) of divine sovereignty.

These decisions shape the presentation of the divine 'perfections' (Barth prefers this term to the more usual one of 'attributes'). The coinherence of freedom and love, God *a se* and God *pro nobis*, is reflected in both the form and the content of Barth's discussion of the nature of God. The inseparability of love and freedom is expressed in the way in which he arranges his presentation. The divine perfections are set out first under the rubric of the perfections of divine loving (paragraph 30), and then under the perfections of divine freedom (paragraph 31). Then, within this arrangement, the perfections are paired, one of the pair giving greater (but not exclusive) profile to the divine loving, and the other similarly emphasizing the divine freedom: grace and holiness, mercy and righteousness, patience and wisdom as the perfections of divine loving, and unity and omnipresence, constancy and omnipotence, and eternity and glory as the perfections of the divine freedom. What is most important about the rather complex way in which Barth builds up his account is that it is mobile: the 'point' of the argument lies in its entire movement and in the intricate sets of echoes, backward and forward references, recapitulations and variations by which that movement is carried.

In terms of the content of the divine perfections, the inseparability of love and freedom is intrinsic to what Barth has to say about each of the paired concepts. We can merely hint at one example, that of the patience and wisdom of God. Divine patience is the particular manifestation of divine love, because it is the establishment of the creature's own substance. 'Patience exists where space and time are given with a definite intention, where freedom is allowed in expectation of a response. God acts in this way. He makes this purposeful concession of space and time. He allows this freedom of expectancy' (II/1, p. 408). This 'concession', this granting of being to another by God, is such that God 'does not suspend and destroy it as this other but accompanies and sustains it and allows it to develop in freedom' (II/1, pp. 409f.): even when God's patience issues in 'radical judgment' of the creature, it does not mean the creature's 'violent end' (II/1, p. 411), but an intervention for the sake of its 'independent life' (ibid.). Yet in this perfection God's freedom is manifest under its aspect of utter correctness and truthfulness:

> The wisdom of God is the inner truth and clarity with which the divine life in its self-fulfilment and its works justifies and confirms itself and in which it is the source and sum and criterion of all that is clear and true. It is in this inner truth and clarity that God loves, and this is the source of the dignity with which He is free in His love. In it He also demonstrates the legitimacy, necessity and the sufficiency of His divine existence and action. God is glorious in His wisdom. He attests Himself as God by attesting His wisdom. (II/1, p. 426)

At the heart of the discussion both of the knowledge of God and of the divine perfections is thus a conviction expressed at the beginning of the second part-volume of the doctrine of God: 'We should still not have learned to say "God" correctly ... if we thought it enough simply to say "God"' (II/2, p. 5). The same conviction stands at the head of the doctrine of divine election, to which we now turn.

The election of God

The doctrine of election forms the centrepiece of the doctrine of God; indeed, it is one of the most crucial chapters in the *Church Dogmatics* as a whole, summing up much of what Barth has had to say so far and pointing forward to essential features of the doctrines of creation and reconciliation. It is arguably the classic instance in the *Church Dogmatics* of Barth working out his conviction that the church's talk of Jesus Christ is to furnish the ground and content of all theological doctrine. Moreover, in writing this section of the *Church Dogmatics* Barth felt largely alone, lacking in intellectual precedents and at odds even with the Reformed tradition in which the doctrine of election had played such a large role in explicating the soteriological and anthropological consequences of the doctrine of divine sovereignty.

These factors may offer some explanation of why Barth is more than usually explicit in laying out the conditions of success for an account of divine election (a parallel passage can be found in the treatment of Christian baptism right at the end of the *Church Dogmatics*, where Barth finds himself similarly in dispute with the mainstream Reformed tradition and so particularly vigorous in canvassing the criteria by which he wishes to be judged).[2] Here in II/2, the criteria are a mixture of formal and material conditions. Formally, the doctrine of election is not to be dominated by church tradition, by considerations of the doctrine's practical utility, or by experience – all of which conspire to undermine the reference of the doctrine to the Word of God. Barth is painfully aware that the doctrine of election is both vital and vulnerable: vital, because it forms the intersection-point of theology, soteriology, anthropology and much else; vulnerable, because it appears to be especially receptive to external influences which undermine or compromise its strictly biblical character. And so here more than anywhere Barth insists on 'the basic rule of all Church dogmatics', namely that

> no single item of Christian doctrine is legitimately grounded, or rightly developed and expounded, unless it can of itself be understood and explained as part of the responsibility laid upon

the hearing and teaching Church towards the self-revelation of God attested in Holy Scripture. Thus the doctrine of election cannot be legitimately understood or represented except in the form of an exposition of what God Himself has said and still says concerning Himself. (II/2, p. 35)

Behind this formal move, however, lies a material principle: the particularity of God, which is at all costs to be respected in the construction of a doctrine of election. There is a danger, Barth notes, that we may start from a 'concept of God as omnipotent Will, governing and irresistibly directing each and every creature according to His own law' (II/2, p. 44). What is being objected to here is not so much the underlying notion of divine sovereignty, but the indeterminateness of such a concept of deity. The error which Barth feels it so necessary to censure is that of 'supposing that God is irresistibly efficacious *in abstracto*, naked freedom and sovereignty' (ibid.). And within the error lies that against which the entire *Church Dogmatics* is directed: 'God in general' (II/2, p. 49), uncorrected and undisciplined by the name of Jesus, and therefore an open field for the exercise of the speculative arts. But, Barth protests, for Christian theology things must not be so:

When Holy Scripture speaks of God it concentrates our attention and thoughts upon one single point and what is to be known at that point. And what is to be known there is quite simple ... [God] does the general for the sake of the particular. Or to put it another way, He does the general through the particular, and in and with it. That is God according to His self-revelation. (II/2, pp. 52f.)

More closely, this means that in matters concerning predestination, theology's attention is to be directed not to abstract questions of choice, causality, freedom and the like – as if these questions could be asked and answered without appeal to any specifically Christian content – but to 'the name of Jesus' (II/2, p. 53). This name, and the sequence of salvation history at whose centre it lies, is to be the lodestone of any discussion of election. Such a discussion therefore takes its form from a repetition of that saving drama rather than from the refinement of a priori concepts:

in this name we may now confirm the divine decision as an event in human history and therefore as the substance of all the preceding history of Israel and the hope of all the succeeding history of the Church. What happened was this, that under this name God Himself became man, that He became this particular man, and as such the Representative of the whole people that hastens towards this man and derives from Him ... According to Scripture the One who bears this name is the One who in His own 'I' introduces the concept of sovereignty and every perfection. When the bearer of this name becomes the object of our attention and thoughts, when they are directed to Jesus Christ, then we see God, and our thoughts are fixed on Him. (II/2, pp. 53f.)

As it proceeds with a descriptive expansion of the name of Jesus, Barth's doctrine of election insists from the beginning that the theme of election is not simply God but also humanity. Because election is governed by the name (that is, the lived identity) of Jesus 'in matter and substance', then it cannot be expounded as if its effective centre were simply the divine will or rule, without any real consideration of the human realities to which that will and rule direct themselves. The theme of election is covenant, 'the primal history which is played out between God and this one man [Jesus] and His people' (II/2, p. 8). Certainly, Barth agrees, the doctrine of election serves to underline that the grace with which God establishes the covenant is free (not rendered ineffective by creaturely resistance), mysterious (inscrutable under any conditions other than itself), and righteous (not subject to creaturely norms of judgement). But election – precisely *in* its freedom, mystery and righteousness, not despite them – is 'the sum of the Gospel' (II/2, p. 24). If Barth can say this, it is because in the earlier sections of his doctrine of God he has already devoted much labour to explaining that, as the one whose freedom is freedom to love, God is 'God for us' (II/2, p. 25). Divine election is no exception, but rather the confirmation of the sheer depth of God's love: 'That God wills neither to be without the world nor against it can never be stated more clearly than when we speak of His election' (II/2, p. 26). Election is no mere formal assertion of divine absoluteness; still less is it a means of inserting a hidden divine will behind the merciful acts of God. It is simply an indication that in God *for us* we really have to do with *God* for us, and therefore with the entirely effective mercy of God whose love is undefeated.

The theme of election is thus at one and the same time singular and two-fold. It is singular in that talk of divine election is focused on the irreplaceable, non-symbolic reality of Jesus Christ. It is two-fold because Jesus Christ is both 'electing and elected', the

God-man to whom are ascribed both 'the active determination of election' and 'the passive determination of election' (II/2, p. 103). In this striking move, Barth appeals to the doctrine of Christ's two natures in order to effect a radical reshaping of the notion of 'double predestination'. In Barth's hands, the term comes to refer, not to a decision of God in which the human race is divided into the elect and the reprobate, but to God's self-election and God's election of humanity, both actual in Jesus Christ. 'Primarily,' he proposes, 'God elected or predestinated Himself' (II/2, p. 162); and, in fulfilment of the divine self-election, 'God elected man, this man' (ibid.). We take each side in turn.

First, in Jesus Christ we are to discern election as divine self-election. Barth, we have already noted, is insistent that we exclude any sense of arbitrary divine omnipotence or pure indeterminacy from an account of the eternal will of God, since what matters is the specificity of that will. God elects to be this God, God in this man, God known in and as Jesus Christ. Put simply: 'In the beginning with God was this One, Jesus Christ. And that is predestination' (II/2, p. 145). In considering divine self-election, we are reflecting on the capacity which is actual in the particular ways and works of God; formal characteristics such as liberty of foreordination can only be understood in connection with patient tracing of these particular works and ways. Thus God's self-election is his determination of himself to be gracious; and that 'grace' is not merely one modulation of an absolute will which could be directed in other ways, for other ends. In divine self-election we do not face unfocused autonomy but a determination for identity.

Second, in Jesus Christ we are to discern election as the election of humanity. Once again, Barth maximizes the christological element. The dominance of the notion of the divine decree in parts of the earlier Reformed tradition sometimes gave the impression that the doctrine of election could be expounded largely without reference to the incarnation – as if election concerned a relation between God and humanity to which Jesus Christ was largely incidental, or as if the line from the will of God to the elect did not traverse the history of Jesus. Barth simply refuses to follow the tradition here, insisting that whatever anthropological entailments the doctrine of election may have, they are to be christologically determined. This entails not only that the agent of election is none other than Jesus Christ himself (not some 'unknown God' (II/2, p. 147)) and that the means of election is Christ's sharing of our humanity in the incarnation. It also involves an affirmation that election is to that form of human life which Jesus Christ himself establishes. Election is election to participate in the covenant which is secured in Jesus Christ, in which humanity is 'enriched and saved and glorified in the living fellowship of that covenant' (II/2, p. 168).

The result of these christological corrections is thus an account of electing God and elect humanity in which election is not fate but form. Election and ethics are thus inseparable, since humanity is elect not simply to a state but a way of life. Election is purposive determination, determination to blessedness, gratitude and service as witness. It is for this reason that Barth moves from his discussion of election to a lengthy consideration of the moral aspects of the doctrine of God in the final chapter of volume II/2. Treatment of the details of his ethics will be held over for a later chapter. But it is important at this stage simply to note why Barth devotes so much space to morals within his treatment of the doctrine of God. He does not do so in qualification of strict adherence to divine sovereignty, but precisely as a consequence of such strict adherence. Because God is sovereign in this way, as the one who elects to covenant, then the indicative becomes an imperative:

> [God] does not exist in His divine being and perfections without Jesus Christ, in whom He is both very God and very man. He does not exist, therefore, without the covenant with man which was made and executed in this name. God is not known completely – and therefore not known at all – if He is not known as the maker and Lord of this covenant between Himself and man. The Christian doctrine of God cannot have 'only' God for its content, but since its object is *this* God it must also have man, to the extent that in Jesus Christ man is made a partner in the covenant decreed and founded by God. (II/2, p. 509)

But a partner is an agent; and therefore: 'Ruling grace is commanding grace' (II/2, p. 511).

Conclusion

As Barth lectured on the doctrine of God in the late 1930s and early 1940s – towards the end of the lecture cycle, with Allied war planes roaring 'unceremoniously over our heads'[3] – and turned his texts into the pages of *Church Dogmatics* II, he found himself drawing together and extending lines of thought which had been present to him since the previous great European conflict. Twenty years previously, he had written with all the astonishment of one who was stumbling into a new world of words and thoughts of almost unimaginable persuasiveness; now he could write with more composure, though still with extraordinary intellectual and spiritual vitality, and with a range, perceptiveness and authority which are classical in stature, most of all in the handling of predestination. Von Balthasar's judgement that Barth's treatment of election is 'the most magnificent, unified and well-grounded section' of the *Church Dogmatics*, 'the heartbeat of his whole theology',[4] was reached before Barth had begun to publish on the doctrine of reconciliation; but he is not wide of the mark. If the doctrine of election was a topic which drew from Barth some of his very best writing, it was because in digging deep into its history and dogmatic structure, he was able to articulate with greater assurance his most basic conception of Christianity. Near to the heart of that conception lay what von Balthasar calls the 'binary reciprocity' of God and humanity which forms 'the basic theme and leitmotiv of the whole of salvation history'.[5] In revelation, election and command, God is not a blankly autonomous force but the one who is free to love; in knowing, being determined and obeying, the creature is free because loved by this God. This conception – utterly preoccupying, offering an endless vista for spiritual and theological meditation – was now firmly established as the chief business of Barth's life. Even though by the time he reached the end of *Church Dogmatics* II/2 Barth was in his mid-fifties, he was only a third of the way through the undertaking which would engross him for another two decades before finally running into the sand. Thus in the summer semester of 1942, he took up the doctrine of creation, not without a measure of apprehension and a sense that here he was starting out rather less in command of the material than he might wish.

Notes

1. *CD* II/2, p. ix. Subsequent page references to the *Church Dogmatics* are in the main body of the text.
2. See *CD* IV/4, pp. 169–76.
3. E. Busch, *Karl Barth*, p. 301.
4. H. U. von Balthasar, *The Theology of Karl Barth*, p. 174.
5. Ibid., p. 177.

5

Creation and humanity

Part of what makes Barth's account of creation and humanity in *Church Dogmatics* III rather difficult of access is that both the content and the function of what he has to say about these topics diverge quite markedly from the more characteristic treatments which they have received at the hands of modern theologians. Barth was strongly persuaded of the necessity to demarcate what Christian theology says about creation and humanity from what might be said about them in other fields of human experience and inquiry. He was, accordingly, very reluctant to follow modern conventions and allow these doctrines to perform the pre-theological task of providing the foundations for a Christian understanding of God. Instead, he expounds them as derivative, not prolegomenal, matters, presupposing already-established truths about the triune God of the Christian confession. More, perhaps, than any other modern Protestant thinker, Barth consistently urged that in a Christian account of creation and in Christian anthropology, we are already within dogmatics, not simply in its outer courts; and so he saw the re-christianizing of these doctrines as one of his major tasks here.

In making these moves in handling topics in the theology of creation, Barth offered resistance to the gradual metamorphosis of the Christian doctrine of creation into an account of the origins of reality which lacked much by way of Christian specificity. The atrophy of the particularities of Christian theological conviction has been an especially striking feature of those theologies of creation which have assumed that the co-ordination of theology and natural science requires the suspension of positive dogmatics in favour of more acceptable generic concepts – perhaps the most favoured of which is the notion of 'cause'. There is a very long history here: the eliding of dogmatics is not only a modern phenomenon, the result of over-anxious theologians conceding territory to colonizing natural scientists. The roots are much earlier, at the beginnings of the modern period which saw the invention of a conceptual apparatus to describe the relations of creator and creation that owed less to Christian beliefs about Father, Son and Spirit and more to abstract ideas of causality.[1] The results of this development continue to be felt, however, most of all in accounts of creation which devote little space to what Barth regarded as the central issues, namely the identity of the creator as the triune God, out of which alone theology can proceed to depict the character of the creator's action and relation to the world.

Making these issues his focus in the doctrine of creation also involves Barth in restructuring theological anthropology, which has registered many of the same developments as that doctrine. Rather than treating anthropology as a natural bridge between theology and human self-reflection, he treats it as a subordinate or consequential doctrine, for which a christological foundation must be provided. Here his clash with modernity is rather more evident than in the case of the doctrine of creation, for in the dogmatics of nineteenth-century Protestantism Barth had strong counter-examples to the procedure he considered to be theologically normative. 'As the man Jesus is Himself the revealing Word of God, He is the source of our knowledge of the nature of man as created by God':[2] that simple proposal at the beginning of Barth's account of 'The Creature' announces the reversal of an entire tradition of theology in which the self-reflective human subject and agent is considered to be axiomatic. Yet the reversal does not – despite much misinterpretation of Barth at this point – entail the repudiation of a robust sense of the human person as subject and agent, but rather the reintegration of anthropology into a teleological account of God and God's creatures in which to be human is to act out of gratitude for grace.

In this chapter we offer a sketch of some of the major features of Barth's account of creation (*CD* III/1), the human creature (*CD* III/2) and providence (*CD* III/3); discussion of the ethics of creation (*CD* III/4) will be held over for the chapter on Barth's moral theology.

Creation

On Barth's account of the matter, the Christian doctrine of creation is concerned with (as the title of paragraph 40 has it) 'Faith in God the Creator'; not simply an account of origins, the doctrine treats of God – that is, it talks of the creator's identity rather than of some opaque act undertaken by a nameless force. Like all Christian talk, talk of creation properly takes place in the sphere which is demarcated by the Credo. At the beginning, therefore, Barth makes a very deliberate choice to move straight to the centre of the doctrine, rather than lingering in its outer regions where it might be thought to border helpfully on other disciplines:

> the doctrine of the creation no less than the whole remaining content of Christian confession is an article of faith, i.e., the rendering of a knowledge which no man has procured for himself or ever will; which is neither native to him nor accessible to him by way of observation and logical thinking; for which he has no organ and no ability; which he can in fact achieve only in faith; but which is actually consummated in faith, i.e., in the reception of and response to the divine witness. (*CD* III/1, p. 3)

Why does Barth adopt this line, seemingly isolating Christian theology at a point where it might most naturally expect to find congenial conversation partners? He advances three main reasons.

First, for Christian theology the assertion that there truly is a reality distinct from God can only be an assertion of faith:

> if we are of the bold opinion that we ourselves, and with us the so-called world, are and are not *not*, we have to realise that this is always an undemonstrable and contestable hypothesis ... unless we have accepted the divine self-witness and therefore confessed with the whole of Christendom that in the beginning God created the heaven and earth and ourselves and therefore gave to the world distinct from Himself a demonstrable and indisputable reality. (III/1, p. 5)

Barth's point here is that not only the existence of the creator but also the existence of the creature is a matter of faith, that is, a matter of which the knowledge is certain only in so far as it is derived from the self-manifestation of God. This already involves Barth in shifting the centre of gravity of the doctrine of creation and humanity – away from creaturely consciousness of existence as the supposed primary datum and towards the free, sovereign self-existence of the creator. That is why '[w]e know only in faith that the world is' (III/1, p. 6). Second, the character of the Christian doctrine of creation is such that it cannot be understood as a hypothesis, that is, a human attempt at self-explanation which proceeds by forming a conception of the order of the world and, ultimately, a conception of God. Although Barth believes this to be the trajectory of most Protestant accounts of creation since Schleiermacher, he proposes that the doctrine properly flows in a contrary direction: from faith's certainty of the creator to the affirmation of the creature, and not the other way round. Third, therefore, talk of God as creator of heaven and earth refers to the biblical witness and has to be filled out from Scripture rather than from extra-biblical sources. 'God' does not here mean some general 'principle which is superior to the world' (III/1, p. 12), but Father, Son and Spirit, made known in the purposive action of bringing the world into being out of 'the good-pleasure of the free omnipotence of the divine love' (III/1, p. 15). All along the line, in other words, Barth is concerned to clothe with specifically Christian content what have become bare metaphysical or cosmological concepts.

Alongside this, there is an epistemological point to be secured. Knowledge of God as creator of heaven and earth, and of heaven and earth as the creation of God, derives from knowledge of Jesus Christ. Barth is (to some, perversely) insistent on this point:

> From [the] revealed fact of the unity of God with man effected in Jesus Christ, the first truth that we learn is the simple one that God is not alone. He does not live His divine life only in His own space. There is a world-space in which He is the Lord of a being distinct from Himself, i.e., of man, this giving proof of its reality. (III/1, p. 25)

Barth thus roots the article on creation in the article on Christ. 'I believe in Jesus Christ, God's Son our Lord, in order to perceive and to understand that God the Almighty, the Father, is the Creator of heaven and earth. If I did not believe the former, I could not perceive and understand the latter' (III/1, p. 29). It should be noted immediately that this striking christological orientation of creation does not mean that Christology somehow absorbs creation into itself. Rather, what it does is give a distinctly teleological character to the doctrine of creation; the created order can be understood only in the light of God's purposes for creation enacted in Jesus Christ and made real in the power of the Holy Spirit. The creation *is* (and therefore is known as) that reality which God destines for fellowship with Jesus Christ. And, because of this, 'creation' and 'covenant' are correlative terms.

The intimate connection between creation and covenant is the theme of by far the longest section of *Church Dogmatics* III/1, much of which is given over to very lengthy exegetical accounts of the two creation stories in Gen. 1.1–2.4a and 2.4b–25. The whole discussion revolves around two propositions. First, creation is what Barth calls the external basis of the covenant; that is, God's works of creation 'have in view the institution, preservation, and execution of the covenant of grace, for partnership in which he has predestined and called man' (III/1, p. 43). Christian talk of creation is not pre-occupied with cosmological questions (such as the first cause of all things, or the nature of contingency) but with the history which is creation's purpose, for 'Creation sets the stage for the story of the covenant of grace' (III/1, p. 44). Second, covenant is the internal basis of creation – which is a way of saying the same thing in reverse. Covenant is not an accidental modulation of created reality, but the fulfilment of its essential nature as established by the creator. Taken together, these two propositions show Barth recontextualizing the doctrine of creation, extracting it from what have become its usual locations (either a cosmological account of origins or anthropological reflections on contingency) and reintroducing it into 'the sequence of events in which God concludes and executes this covenant with man' (III/1, p. 59). This, he hopes, prevents the de-christianization of the doctrine by maximizing its connections with other doctrines and ensuring that it is not left isolated, an erratic block of dogmatic material ripe for annexation by natural science or philosophy. Creation is 'first in the series of works of the triune God' (III/1, p. 42), and so most of all must be co-ordinated with the doctrine of the Trinity. Indeed, it is only a doctrine of the Trinity which can prevent us from thinking either that creation is a quasi-independent act of God unrelated to the work of salvation, or that salvation–history can be abstracted from the work of God in which the world and humanity are willed and brought into being. Creation, covenant and Trinity are indissolubly united in the church's confession.

The creature

For all its daring in restructuring the doctrine of creation, and for all that it contains many passages of undoubted intellectual power or sensitivity, in important respects the first part-volume of *Church Dogmatics* III lacks some of the assurance of other parts of the work. On occasions, the argument seems strained, especially in the exegetical sections, doggedly pressing a point beyond where it can usefully be taken and schematizing the material too tightly (usually a sign in Barth that he is ill-at-ease with the subject-matter and so trying to keep control of it). When he moves to Christian anthropology in the second part-volume, these problems largely fall away and the writing again takes on the kind of grand confidence which it had demonstrated in the treatment of election back in *Church Dogmatics* II. After an initial orientation to theological anthropology in paragraph 43, which indicates the major features of the exposition which is to follow, *CD* III/2 sets out four main blocks of material on the human person: as creature (paragraph 44); as covenant-partner (paragraph 45); as soul and body (paragraph 46); and as creature within time (paragraph 47). By now, readers of the *Church Dogmatics* have come to see that the argument is less sequential than cumulative, and the same approach is followed here also: a number of tracks are cut through the territory, each at a rather different angle, but all together constituting a unified dogmatic proposal. Both the scope and the complexity of the text are breathtaking. It is certainly the most architecturally intricate piece of writing in the *Church Dogmatics* so far (though on that score it is exceeded by the doctrine of reconciliation in volume IV), and it is consistently and boldly original in the way in which it conceives and organizes its matter; as a result, the rhetoric as well as the content make heavy demands of the reader.

In line with Barth's conviction that anthropology is a derivative, not a foundational, doctrine, the opening paragraph is largely occupied with stating the ontic and noetic priority of Christology over anthropology: 'Theological anthropology expounds the knowledge of man which is made possible by the fact that man stands in the light of the Word of God. The Word of God is thus its foundation' (*CD* III/2, p. 20). The argument is amplified throughout the volume in Barth's characteristic fashion, by descriptive expansion (dogmatic, biblical, historical) of the content of what he regards as a properly Christian anthropology, accompanied by polemical demarcation of Christian theology from non-theological alternatives. Barth evidently regards these non-theological anthropologies as 'a very persistent rival' (III/2, p. 21). He devotes space to a critique of 'speculative anthropology', which believes itself competent to discover unaided the essence of human being, to be 'both the teacher and the pupil of the truth' (III/2, p. 22); he is also critical (but less sharply so) of the 'exact sciences of man' (III/2, p. 23 – he has in mind physiology, biology, psychology and sociology), which, though they may provide useful data, cannot exceed their bounds and offer an 'axiomatic, dogmatic and speculative' world-view (III/2, p. 25). Later paragraphs in the volume fill out these polemic outlines in greater detail, as in the remarks in paragraph 44 on Portmann, Fichte and Jaspers, or the rather full reading of Nietzsche in paragraph 45. However, the creative energy resides in the dogmatic descriptions which precede and generate the polemic, and so we concentrate here on Barth's positive proposal, whose real character can best be appreciated by working in some detail through one sequence of argument which illustrates the major of the whole, the very rich section entitled 'Real Man', paragraph 44.3.

'The ontological determination of humanity is grounded in the fact that one man among all others is the man Jesus' (III/2, p. 132). From the outset, the comprehensive scope of Barth's proposal is evident. In his anthropology, he is not simply talking of the being of the Christian or of the religious person, but of humanity as such, for

> a decision has been made concerning the being and nature of every man by the mere fact that with him and among all other men He too has become a man. No matter who or what or where he may be, he cannot alter the fact that this One is also man. And because this One is also man, every man in his place and time is changed. (III/2, p. 133)

Thus, the alteration of human reality which is brought about by the fact that Jesus Christ has assumed human nature is not a state of affairs whose completion rests upon our attitude or consent; nor is Jesus Christ's relation to us a modification or modulation of some pre-existing humanness which we may have prior to his coming among us. Rather, 'every man as such is the fellow-man of Jesus' (III/2, p. 134). And so:

> Basically and comprehensively ... to be a man is to be with God. What a man is in this Counterpart is obviously the basic and

comprehensive determination of his true being. Whatever else he is, he is on the basis of the fact that he is with Jesus and therefore with God. (III/2, p. 135)

Already, then, Barth is pressing the point that 'being human' is a function of the relation borne to us by another, and a very particular other. Barth is not offering a general ontology of sociality or relationality, but making the very particular assertion that it is because Jesus Christ is Neighbour, Companion, Brother and Counterpart (cf. III/2, p. 134) that we are constituted as the beings that we are and knowable as such. Noetically and ontologically, human being is unthinkable apart from the fact that 'man is with God because he is with Jesus' (III/2, p. 136).

This twin concept of 'being with God' and 'being with Jesus' leads Barth to a further line of analysis, which he sums up in the statement that human being 'is a being which derives from God' (III/2, p. 140). 'Derivation', being *from* God as well as *with* God, means both that human being is distinct from God and that in that distinctiveness it is 'absolutely grounded' (ibid.) in him. Here we encounter a pattern of argument which is of fundamental significance for understanding not only Barth's anthropology but also his dogmatics as a whole, namely the conviction that as creator and creature God and humanity are neither identical nor absolutely unrelated but rather realities which exist in an ordered relation of giver and recipient of life and grace:

The present and active God confronts him in free and sovereign transcendence in the one man Jesus who is not at all identical with himself. He confronts him in this One as the Other indestructibly unlike for all His likeness. In this sphere the kingdom of God *comes* to man. What constitutes the being of man in this sphere is not a oneness of being but a genuine togetherness of being with God. Here, too, then, the being of man is his own being in contrast to that of God. But here God acts and rules and makes history ... The being of man in all its independence and particularity, in all its difference from the being of God, is the being which is acted upon in this action of God, ruled in this rule of God and drawn into this history inaugurated and controlled by God. (III/2, p. 141)

The concept of derivation, so crucial to making sense of the overall structure of Barth's thought, is traced in two directions.

First, derivation is closely associated with election. To be with God is to derive from God, and to derive from God is to rest upon God's election. Once more, the notion of election is not simply concerned with dividing the human race into chosen and reprobate; it is more a way of articulating the teleological aspect of created human nature: 'Election,' Barth writes, 'means a special decision with a special intention in relation to a special object' (III/2, p. 142). In the election of Jesus Christ, the election of all is secured, and thereby the purpose of God – God's 'yes' to creation, his unde-feated affirmation of what he has made – prevails over 'a whole monstrous kingdom' (III/2, p. 143) which seeks to hold in check the thrust of that purpose. In election, the will of God directs itself to the preservation of the human creature; and Jesus is 'the penetrat-ing spearhead' or the 'executive and revelatory spearhead' of that will (III/2, p. 144) – the utterly effective enactment of the divine purpose through which human being is. What the notion of election offers is thus not so much a theological equivalent of fate, but a means of talking about human being and activity in terms of the larger context of purposive divine action which encloses it and holds it in existence.

> Man as such, because he is the fellow of the man Jesus, is from the very first destined to share in the deliverance from evil effected in this one man, to participate in the conflict against the enemy of all creaturely being, to figure in the history of the victory over this enemy, to belong to the body of the Head in whom the triumph of the Creator has been achieved on behalf of the creature. (III/2, p. 146)

'Being human' and 'being elect', being chosen to live and act in the sphere of the covenantal mercy of God, are all ways of talking of a single reality.

One important consequence is that Barth is led to speak of sin as 'an impossible possibility' (III/2, p. 146) – if to be human is to be united to Christ, then sin cannot be definitive of human being. Barth's point is not that sin is not a real fact of our existence; it is that sin is a contradiction of the very constitution of human being. To decide for sin is not to decide for a possibility which, however dreadful it may be, is equally as real an actualization of human being as the life of obedience to God. To decide for sin is to negate what one inescapably is as a human being, and therefore to adopt an impossibility as if it were merely one more way of being a creature.

A second way of extending the concept of derivation is to say that human being 'consists in listening to the Word of God' (III/2, p. 147). The core of the statement, once again, is christological. 'The man Jesus ... is the sum of the divine address, the Word of God, to the created cosmos' (ibid.), and what he says is, simply, 'Himself' (III/2, p. 148); that is, he declares his existence to be the very presence of God the creator in which the being of humanity is upheld. To be addressed is to be summoned, to be called into being and thereby called to activity (for Barth, imperatives indicate not so much repressive commands as invitations to assume the status of agents). 'When the reality of human nature is in question, the word "real" is simply equivalent to the word "summoned"' (III/2, p. 150). And this is a further reason why Barth refuses to pursue the question of what human realities are antecedent to the call of God, for to inquire into such is, in the end, to deny that the presence and summons of Jesus Christ have the status of a divine act of *creatio ex nihilo*.

This very decided concentration on Christology often draws a good deal of fire: does it not threaten to dissolve humanity as a whole into Christ, and thus corrode our sense of ourselves as acting subjects? Barth's reply to the objection is not to meet it directly, but to offer a descriptive response. Alongside his talk of derivation, election and hearing the Word, he also undertakes a very long description of gratitude and responsibility as genuine human acts. This means that Barth chooses not to resolve the apparent anthropological reduction at a theoretical level, but to develop a further set of variations on his basic theme, which are intended to show how he can do justice to the demand for genuine, inalienable human activity, but within the terms of his operative theological principles. 'Gratitude' and 'responsibility' serve Barth's purpose here because both can be described as genuine human undertakings, without attributing to them absolute or unoriginated spontaneity. They are neither purely self-originating activities, nor do they proceed in an autonomous way; yet they remain modes of action in which human beings project themselves. All that Barth seeks to deny, therefore, is that only acts which are completely self-generated acts can properly be called modes of human self-realization. Thus he proposes that 'the being of man [is] his act in gratitude' (III/2, p. 166). Gratitude is action (not mere attitude); it is the form taken by human historical existence as it complements, answers and corresponds to the action of grace by which it is generated:

when we see [the human person] as the being responsive and complementary to the grace of God, as a being in gratitude, we see him for the first time ... in his own act. Seen here at its root, and understood as thanksgiving for the grace of God, this is the act in which he accepts the validity of the act which not he but God has wrought. But in this form it is his own act. He is the subject of his history as its divinely posited object. The grace of God demands that it should be accepted as such. It calls for gratitude. The fact that it finds gratitude, that the God who is gracious to His creature is honoured in the world of creation, is the being of man, and this being engaged in its characteristic activity. (III/2, p. 168)

Again, the activity which corresponds to grace and answers the divine summons can be talked of as responsibility:

the being of man is an answer, or more precisely, a being lived in the act of answering the Word of God, a being which in the creaturely sphere and as itself creaturely makes that address and return to God, to the God from whom it flows and in whose Word it is rooted. Called into life by the Word of God, it is not only a reception of His gift, but it fulfils the task of answering Him, and makes that address and return to Him ... To this extent it is an act of responsibility. Man is, and is human, as he performs this act of responsibility, offering himself as the response to the Word of God, and conducting, shaping and expressing himself as an answer to it. He is, and is man, as he does this. (III/2, p. 175)

As Barth expands this kind of description, what is most striking is the vigour with which he insists on the creative Word of God as establishing a task for humanity: 'the statement "I am," must be interpreted by the further statement: "I will" ' (III/2, p. 180); or again, ' "I am" ... means "I do" ' (III/2, p. 181). Gratitude and responsibility are thus modes of freedom – a freedom which is not, of course, absolute, pure self-positing, but rather that spontaneity which is itself the fruit of the only properly spontaneous act, that of the creator himself. In sum:

An object is something posited in its own being by another. Man is the creature of God, and therefore posited by God, known by Him, subjected to His law and judged by Him. Hence man is also object. But he is subject too. A subject is something which freely posits itself in its own being. Man is, as he is responsible before

God, as he knows and obeys and seeks after Him, and thus posits Himself. Hence he is also subject. Now these two are not two mutually inconsistent descriptions of man's being. In the very fact that man is the object of God, he is also human subject. Among all the objects posited by God it is the characteristic mode of this one to posit itself and therefore to be subject. Man is the one creature which God in creating calls to free personal responsibility before Him, and thus treats as a self, a free being. (III/2, p. 194)

Providence

The final dogmatic theme treated in volume III of the *Church Dogmatics* (before Barth embarks on his account of the ethics of creation) is the doctrine of providence. In many respects, what he undertakes here draws together and completes the discussions of the first two part-volumes. The doctrine of creation offered an identity description of the triune agent of creation who brings into being another reality and establishes a covenant relation with what he creates; the doctrine of the human creature sets out an account of creatureliness as that reality which in Jesus Christ is destined, equipped and established for fellowship with God. Both discussions, we note, give high profile to the temporal (or, perhaps better, the dramatic) character of the relation of creator and creature: God and the creature are properly described not abstractly but in their respective roles in the history of the covenant. It is, therefore, appropriate that Barth should move next to an account of providence as *continuatio creationis*, the ongoing history of creation, and state his summary of the doctrine thus: 'in the act of creation God the Creator as such has associated Himself with His creature as such as the Lord of its history, and is faithful to it as such' (*CD* III/3, p. 12).

The account of divine providence set out in *Church Dogmatics* III/3[3] is undergirded by the basic principle which Barth announced in *Church Dogmatics* II/1: 'The world has meaning as it acquires meaning from Him who alone has and is meaning' (II/1, p. 427). This statement occurs towards the end of Barth's discussion of the relation between divine patience and divine wisdom. God's wisdom, he argues, is God's self-attestation to the world, God's glorious self-demonstration, God himself as 'the truth and clarity which justifies, confirms and attests itself' (ibid.). It is God's 'holy and righteous, gracious and merciful meaning, to lead us to penitence, and therefore to make our own lives meaningful'

(II/1, p. 432). Meaning, we note, is not established so much as acquired; and, strictly speaking, it is not communicable (God alone, Barth tells us, has meaning). And so whilst God's wisdom is, indeed, 'the philosophy of the created universe and the philosophy of human life', nevertheless it is 'not to be derived from reflection upon the universe or the being of man. It can be appreciated only by the bearing of God's own Word which as such gives us the right philosophy of the universe and our own human life' (ibid.). At the outset, then, it is crucial to note Barth's separation of a true apprehension of the divine wisdom from the processes of inventing, schematizing or otherwise bestowing meaning upon the world. 'The divine wisdom', Barth says, correcting a statement from Schleiermacher, 'is the divine self-communication ordering and determining the world for itself' (II/1, p. 433).

It is this which lies behind two important themes in the presentation of providence in *Church Dogmatics* III/3. First, the content of providence is God's continuing, historical fellowship with the creation over which he is Lord. Second, belief in providence so defined is 'the practical recognition that things are as we have said'; that is to say 'it is the joy of the confidence and the willingness of the obedience grounded in this reality and its perception' (III/3, p. 14). From the very beginning, in other words, Barth refuses any kind of idealism in Christian talk of providence. We would simply not be talking of the providence of the God of Israel, nor of Christian belief in that providential God, if we thought that we were dealing with some projected historical totality. Barth clearly wants to ensure that the point does not elude his readers, and offers three 'sharp delimitations' of the nature of Christian belief in providence.

First, 'the Christian belief in providence is faith in the strict sense of the term, and this means ... that it is a hearing and receiving of the Word of God' (III/3, p. 15). Belief in providence is not consent to a narrative projection. It is not 'an opinion, postulate or hypothesis concerning God, the world, man, and other things, an attempt at interpretation, exposition and explanation based upon all kinds of impressions and needs, carried through in the form of a systematic construction' (III/3, p. 16). And it is not this because the movement which the doctrine states begins with God.

> We can and must understand that the knowledge of this lordship of God can be compared only to the category of axiomatic knowledge, and that even in relation to this knowledge it forms

a class apart ... It consists in a realisation of the possibility which God gives to man. (Ibid.)

In sum: belief in providence has nothing to do with 'a so called world view, even a Christian world view. For a world view is an opinion, postulate and hypothesis even when it pretends to be Christian' (III/3, p. 18).

Second, therefore, the content of belief in divine providence is strictly theological, depending 'on God and God alone' (III/3, p. 19). Crucially, this means that Barth distinguishes belief in providence from the unavoidable human activity of making sense of life by plotting a course of the cosmic process and one's own place in it. 'Man makes such conceptions. It is inevitable that he should do so, for otherwise he would not be capable of any practical orientation and decision' (III/3, p. 20). Barth's point is not that we can dispense with all and any such constructs, but that they should not be allowed to step beyond their limits, replacing the Word of God by some 'little booklet' of history (III/3, p. 22). Belief in providence 'is faith in God and his dominion and judgment to which all history, even that of the Spirit, even that of human conceptions of history, is wholly subject. It cannot, then, become belief in a human system of history invented by man' (III/3, p. 21). From the beginning, then, Barth takes some care to differentiate faith in providence from totalizing historical schemes. 'Our attempts to orientate ourselves in the dark, in the great movement of the masks of God which we call history, are necessary, right and good. But when it is a matter of receiving and having light in this darkness ... we are forced back upon the Word of God, and this alone is to be received' (III/3, pp. 23f.). This in turn entails Barth's rejection of any over-belief at this point. The fact that Christian knowledge of providence is 'true and thoughtful and courageous' does not exclude the fact that it is also 'relative, provisional and modest' (III/3, p. 23). Faith is not blind; but nor is it all-seeing; rather, it is a seeing which is given ever afresh by the Spirit.

The establishment of a fixed Christian view, of a lasting picture of the relationship between the Creator and creature, would necessarily mean that in taking today the insight given him today man hardens himself against receiving a new and better one tomorrow ... The knowledge received in enlightening and empowering by the Holy Ghost will never be closed but always open. (III/3, p. 56)

A third delimitation crowns the whole discussion, grounding what has been established in the first two. 'In its substance the Christian belief in providence is Christian faith, i.e., faith in Christ' (III/3, p. 26). Providence is not the outer court where Christian faith mixes with many other accounts of God and the world; it is not one species of a genus of belief in historical order. On the contrary; belief in providence bears the name 'Father', the name of the one manifest in Jesus Christ as God for us, and it is this one of whom we speak when we speak of providence. Belief in providence therefore 'looks to the history of the covenant which is fulfilled in the mission, in the person and work of the incarnate Son, of the "God for us". And through and beyond this it looks to the divine election of grace' (III/3, p. 29).

Throughout the entire discussion Barth is at pains to be Christianly specific. He accords priority to the particular content of Christian belief in providence, confident that these aspects are of far greater significance for theological talk about God's providential activity than any formal features which a Christian account undoubtedly shares with, for example, a philosophy of history. For Barth, attention to this particular content is sufficient to establish the uniqueness of Christian faith and its theology. He returns to this argument many times in the course of the discussion. Thus the thrust of the three lengthy depictions of *conservatio*, *concursus* and *gubernatio* in *Church Dogmatics* paragraph 49 is to try to display, by a series of theological meditations on Scripture, the particular character of providence as these acts undertaken by this God for these ends. However much a Christian account of providence may appear to be merely one more master-story, what establishes its difference is the identity of its divine subject.

> The rule of God as opposed to the control and outworking of a natural or spiritual cosmic principle is characterised by the fact that it is here in these particular events attested in the Old and New Testaments, in the 'I am' spoken and actualised by the King of Israel, in the covenant of free grace instituted and executed, promised and fulfilled by Him, that it has the centre which controls and is normative for everything else. (III/3, p. 183)

In sum: 'the Subject who speaks and actualises the "I am" in these events, the King of Israel, is the God who rules the world' (III/3, p. 177). Such a narrative is, we might say, non-degradeable; it will not permit any quiet removal of its central subject, so that the King of Israel could be smuggled off the stage and yet the story would somehow continue to perform its task of ordering history into a coherent scheme.

This leads to a second feature of Barth's account. He emphasizes the uniqueness, not only of the content of a Christian doctrine of providence, but also of the manner in which providence is apprehended. What he has to say here reinforces the anti-constructive nature of Barth's account of Christian belief in providence. To believe in providence is not to shape the scatter of the world's history but to confess the existence of a 'formative economy', a disposition of all things by the God of the gospel, on the basis of which 'occurrence acquires the character of a motivated history ... the individual thing receives its particular dignity and value on the basis of a formative economy which assigns to all things a place and time and function' (III/3, pp. 192f.). But form, we note, is acknowledged, not imposed. And so in a memorable statement Barth suggests a reversal of epistemological direction, in which we are answerable to the reality which it is given to us to perceive:

> we cannot treat of the perception and understanding of the superiority of the divine work in the same way as we can of a human opinion, or as indeed we must of even the most serious of human suggestions. In other words, we are not in any position to treat of this perception and understanding as though they were open to discussion. Naturally, our own comprehension and formulation of them are always open to discussion. By its very nature the matter is one which demands constantly a better formulation. But as it does so, it remains outside and above the sphere in which it itself can be called into question. It is a matter which questions us. Our relation to it can consist only in our rendering an account *to* it rather than *of* it. (III/3, p. 109)

And this, in the end, is why the condition for a correct perception of providence is spiritual; we are out of the region of technical reason. To see providence, we have to become certain sorts of persons, those from whom the Spirit has taken away both fear and vanity, those who are set free to pray. As Barth puts it later in *Church Dogmatics* IV:

> Jesus Christ is a living human person who comes and speaks and acts with the claim and authority of God, and in relation to whom there can be no question whatever of controlling and using Him to grasp or master this or that even in the sphere of thought ... What is there here to see and fix, to be the object of speculation

and disposition? The grace of God addressed to the world in Jesus Christ is that which exists supremely, but quite uniquely, only as on the basis of God's eternal love and election and faithfulness it was and is and will be event, inaccessible to all human or even Christian *hybris*, recognisable only in gratitude for the fact that it is real and true, and in prayer for ever new recognition of its reality and truth. (IV/3, pp. 706f.)

It is accordingly not incidental that Barth's doctrine of providence should close with discussion of faith, obedience and prayer as the marks of 'the Christian under the universal lordship of God'.

Conclusion

Barth was primarily concerned to recover for theology the full dimensions of the biblical witness in the light of his trinitarian starting point without the distraction of apologetics. Accordingly, the doctrine of creation was not a protological reflection on how the world came into existence, but a witness to God as creator who in his eternal purpose in love elected a people for a covenant in which the creation of the world provided the stage for this history of redemption. Creation encompassed both past, present, and future in an eschatological event of bringing forth and sustaining in mercy a created reality apart from himself.[4]

Barth's achievement in the doctrine of creation was, undoubtedly, to extract that doctrine from its entanglements in apologetic strategies and set it on its own feet as a piece of dogmatics, without allowing its shape to be skewed by forcing upon it tasks which it cannot perform without substantially revising its own inner conceptual structure. Although more theologically-oriented Old Testament scholars like von Rad and Kraus were generally sympathetic to Barth's intentions, his account did not commend itself widely, especially amongst English-speaking theologians, where its insistence on the priority of dogmatics was considered to offer little by way of help in fostering dialogue with the natural sciences.[5] Recently, however, some of Barth's major convictions have found their way back into treatments of the doctrine of creation – most of all, the linkage which he established between the doctrines of creation and the Trinity. It is, then, perhaps a little ironic that some contemporary proposals for a trinitarian theology of creation remain critical of Barth on precisely this score, namely that he does not have an adequately triune account of God as creator and God's relation to the creation. When such objections are raised, it is often in the area of the doctrine of the Spirit. Some fear that Barth's doctrine of creation, lacking a rich theology of the Spirit as the one in whom God relates to the creation, tends to fall back into an understanding of the created order which fails to give sufficient independent substance to the world. The creation, it seems to some, is not sufficiently 'other', and may, indeed, at times seem to be absorbed into Christ in such a way that its freedom and relative autonomy are threatened. From what we have seen of Barth's anthropology and his doctrine of providence, this criticism is very hard to sustain, for perhaps the most striking emphasis of what he has to say in those areas is that the order of creation is created for covenant – for free responsive life with God, for partnership with the divine Counterpart. Volume III of the *Church Dogmatics* is thoroughly personal in its construal of the relations of God and the created world, and there are few modern theologians who have been so stringent in excising from the dogmatics of creation the impersonal, abstract conceptuality of cause, with its almost inevitable tendency to produce monistic accounts of God as creator uncorrected by a trinitarian understanding of God's self-mediation.

Where Barth's dogmatics of creation could usefully be extended is in the area of the theology of nature. Barth was reluctant to commit himself to any cosmological reflections for a number of reasons: his frank distaste for the use made of concepts of 'natural order' by ideologists (political and theological) in the 1930s; what is sometimes thought of as his hostile attitude to natural science; and his sense that the core of the doctrine of creation is the relations of the creator and the human creature. Of these reasons, the last two deserve comment. It is certainly true that Barth evinced little interest in natural science throughout *Church Dogmatics* III and breathed a sigh of relief at the beginning when he asserted that 'there can be no scientific problems, objections or aids in relation to what Holy Scripture and the Christian Church understand by the divine work of creation' (III/1, p. ix). But Barth's statement a few lines further on, that 'future workers' in dogmatics will find 'many problems worth pondering' (III/1, p. x) in the relation of theology and natural science is usually passed over unremarked; and it may be that what Barth provides is the framework – if not the actual execution – of a dogmatic cosmology, one, that is, which approaches an account of the cosmos with a certain confidence in the mental furniture of Christian faith and a certain scepticism about the metaphysics of natural science. This leads to a second point. Part of what pulls Barth away from dealing with cosmological issues is the anthropocentric character of his doctrine of creation: like nearly all theology in modernity, he is an inheritor of that long process whereby '[h]istory rather than nature became the discourse of theologians'.[6] Yet Barth has one crucial advantage over most of his modern counterparts: he does not allow a focus on history to betray him into subjectivizing the doctrine of creation, so that it becomes merely a way of mythologizing the human experience of contingency. And Barth is able to resist the pressure of the modern tradition at this point precisely because his starting-point is the church's confession of the triune God.

Notes

1. For useful background material here, see C. Gunton (ed.), *The Doctrine of Creation. Essays in Dogmatics, History and Philosophy* (Edinburgh: T. & T. Clark, 1997); C. Gunton, *The Triune Creator. An Historical and Systematic Study* (Edinburgh: Edinburgh University Press, 1998); W. Pannenberg, *Systematic Theology* vol. 2 (Grand Rapids: Eerdmans; Edinburgh: T. & T. Clark, 1994), pp. 1–174; J. Pelikan, 'Creation and Causality in the History of Christian Thought', *Southwestern Journal of Theology* 32 (1990), pp. 10–24.

2. *CD* III/2, p. 3. Subsequent page references to *Church Dogmatics* III are in the main body of the text.

3. See also the discussion in *CD* IV/3, pp. 681–762.

4. B. Childs, *Biblical Theology of the Old and New Testaments. Theological Reflection on the Christian Bible* (Minneapolis: Fortress Press, 1993), p. 405.

5. The counter-example, of course, is the work of T. F. Torrance, who has consistently argued for the convergence between Barth's dogmatic method and the methods of natural scientific inquiry. See, from his many treatments of this theme, *Divine and Contingent Order* (Oxford: Oxford University Press, 1981; reissued Edinburgh: T. & T. Clark, 1998).

6. A. Funkenstein, *Theology and the Scientific Imagination from the Middle Ages to the Seventeenth Century* (Princeton: Princeton University Press, 1986), p. 360.

6

Reconciliation

In the 1950s Barth was in many ways the colossus of European Protestant thinkers, easily the most authoritative and celebrated theological figure. Even when his views were criticized or repudiated, his stature as the senior Protestant dogmatician was beyond question. He remained, of course, a controversial figure, not only theologically but also politically; his refusal to be trapped by the rhetoric of the Cold War was read by churlish opponents like Reinhold Niebuhr as softness to communist totalitarianism inconsistent with his stand against National Socialism in earlier decades. But what made Barth's political views controversial was the fact that he, the doyen Protestant systematician, held them. And within such eruptions of disapproval, Barth remained a magnetic centre of attraction for graduate students and other theologians. He was the subject of a bulky secondary literature which over the course of the 1950s was expanded by full-scale evaluations from Roman Catholics like von Balthasar, Bouillard, Hâmer and Küng and Reformed thinkers like Berkouwer; he was able to look back on a theological career of more than thirty years, in the course of which he had been the prime mover of a major change in the direction of Protestant theology and church life. But his prestige rested above all on the *Church Dogmatics*, eight part-volumes of which were complete at the beginning of the decade, and whose fourth section, the doctrine of reconciliation, was to become one of the incontestably great pieces of Christian literature of the century.

However, if the 1950s was the decade of Barth's greatest authority, it was also the decade which saw the beginning of the decline

113

which retirement and physical infirmity accelerated in the 1960s. He began the immense task of the doctrine of reconciliation in 1951 at the age of 65, deeply aware that this was to be his last full-scale project and that its execution demanded of him not only a determined focusing of theological perception but also a great measure of sheer energy to sustain the work which he had set himself.

> I have been very conscious of the very special responsibility laid on the theologian at this centre of all Christian knowledge. To fail here is to fail everywhere. To be on the right track here makes it impossible to be completely mistaken in the whole. Week by week and even day by day I have had, and will have (in the continuation), to exercise constant vigilance to find that right track and not to lose it.[1]

When Barth wrote those words in the preface to *Church Dogmatics* IV/1 (in June 1953) he retained his confidence that his powers were equal to the scope of the task. But as he moved from his mid-60s to his mid-70s, completion eluded him, even though he chose more and more to unburden himself of external commitments in order to give all his energy to the completion of this stretch of the argument. No account of the doctrine of reconciliation should present Barth's thinking as other than unfinished.

Because the doctrine of reconciliation bulks so large in the *Church Dogmatics* as a whole (five of the thirteen volumes are devoted to it), and because it is here that some of his theological principles find their most mature and expansive expression, there has been a temptation to read the work backwards and view the earlier volumes on revelation, God and creation as stages which Barth passed through on the way to his most spectacular achievement. The temptation is especially strong for those who look to Barth's later thought for a commanding example of a post-critical narrative Christology and doctrine of God, or for those who see in the doctrine of reconciliation the final turn from Barth's putative earlier transcendentalism towards the humanity of God and the gospel. But though Barth's tone is often more mellow in *Church Dogmatics* IV, the dogmatic content repeats and extends much earlier decisions about Trinity, incarnation and election which are in place early on in the work and, indeed, in some instances precede even the first volumes.

The intellectual structure of the doctrine of reconciliation is complex: no section of the argument is discrete, each part simultaneously building upon and expanding the others (this is one reason why *Church Dogmatics* IV needs to be read as a whole). Moreover, far from offering simply a treatment of the doctrine of salvation, the treatise interweaves Christology, soteriology, hamartiology (the doctrine of sin), pneumatology, ecclesiology and a theology of the Christian life. Furthermore, Barth's treatment of this great range of topics does not follow the more usual dogmatic convention of organizing the material serially, beginning with the person of Christ, moving to his work and then to the effectiveness of that work in the church, the world and the believer through the activity of the Holy Spirit. Instead, all these topics are assembled in three long passages of argument in IV/1, IV/2 and IV/3, each with a closely similar structure and together forming a carefully orchestrated set of repetitions, echoes and variations. Thus each part-volume begins with a substantial treatment of the person and work of Christ (Barth is quite clear that they are ingredient in each other and therefore cannot be expounded in isolation from each other). IV/1 considers this under the rubric of 'Jesus Christ, the Lord as Servant' and describes the 'obedience of the Son of God' in terms of his self-emptying and his taking judgement upon himself (in sections on 'The Way of the Son of God into the Far Country' and 'The Judge Judged in Our Place'), with the resurrection as the Father's 'verdict' upon the mission of the Son. What Barth is doing here is pulling into one complex arrangement blocks of dogmatic material from the Christian tradition: the Chalcedonian notion of Jesus Christ as 'true God', and two themes from the older Protestant dogmatics, that of the 'state of humiliation' of the incarnate one and that of the priestly office of Christ in which he effects reconciliation between God and sinners. Moreover, the flow is not so much argumentative as narrative, tracing the progress of the Son from eternity to eternity through self-abasement, the overarching plot-line being supplied both by the Christ-hymn of Philippians 2 and the story of the prodigal son (from which is taken the motif of 'going into the far country'). And, as a further variation on the classical traditions of Christology and soteriology, Barth ties together the deity of Christ and his obedience, thereby pushing the lowliness of the incarnate one back into the being of God himself.

In closely similar fashion, under the heading of 'Jesus Christ, the Servant as Lord', *Church Dogmatics* IV/2 considers 'the exaltation of the Son of Man'. Here the paradox of divinity in lowliness is reversed and the humanity of Christ is tied to triumph (rather than, as might be expected, abasement): where IV/1 explores deity in exile and humiliation, IV/2 considers 'the homecoming of the Son of Man' (taken from the prodigal's return), and binds the Chalce-donian 'true man' to the state of exaltation and the kingly office of Christ. In this way, the organizational structure of Barth's presenta-tion subverts the assumption that we should cluster together the divine nature, the state of exaltation and the kingly office, on the one hand, and the human nature, the state of humiliation and the priestly office on the other. *Church Dogmatics* IV/3 rounds off the presentation by considering more explicitly the unity of the two natures of Christ as the divine-human person and the unity of the two states of exaltation and humiliation, by looking at 'Jesus Christ the true witness', the light of life in his prophetic office.

More than anything else, Barth is struggling to escape christo-logical or soteriological abstraction; he will not allow dogmatic concepts to have any life apart from their function in helping the church gain some sort of purchase on the gospel's announcement of the wholly particular event of Jesus Christ. In one sense, the entire argument of *Church Dogmatics* IV is nothing more than an exten-ded paraphrase of the name of Jesus, in whom God's work as creator, reconciler and redeemer is fulfilled.

> The atonement is history. To know it, we must know it as such. To think of it, we must think of it as such. To speak of it, we must tell it as history. To try and grasp it as supra-historical or non-historical truth is not to grasp it at all ... To say atonement is to say Jesus Christ. (IV/1, pp. 157f.)

Having expounded this integrated account of the being and act of Jesus Christ as the divine-human agent of reconciliation, each part-volume then traces the effectiveness of the work of the reconciler, overcoming and healing human alienation from God. As the obedi-ent Son of God, Jesus Christ exposes sin as the pride which is the counter-movement to his humble self-offering, a pride which issues in our utter fall (IV/1, paragraph 60). As the victorious Son of Man, Jesus Christ exposes sin as the sloth which refuses to be caught up in his triumphant progress to the Father, and which takes the form of misery (IV/2, paragraph 65). As the true witness, the God-man Jesus Christ exposes sin as falsehood, which turns from truth and so condemns (IV/3, paragraph 70). In each case, sin is manifest for what it is as rebellion against the movement of divine grace which embraces and rectifies human life, a rebellion which, moreover, can only be understood for what it truly is in the light of the grace which it opposes. From here, Barth goes on to expound the ways in which the saving work of God in Christ effects the renewal of human life: first by considering it as justification (IV/1, paragraph 61), sanctification (IV/2, paragraph 66) and vocation (IV/3, paragraph 71), then through the work of the Holy Spirit in the community's gathering (IV/1, paragraph 62), upbuilding (IV/2, paragraph 67) and sending (IV/3, paragraph 72), and finally through the Spirit's work in the individual believer in generating faith (IV/1, paragraph 63), love (IV/2, paragraph 68) and hope (IV/3, paragraph 73).

Although it is a structure of remarkable fascination and not a little intellectual beauty, its form is strictly subservient to Barth's material aim, which is to present the heart of the Christian gospel as God's work of reconciling all things to himself in Christ. Matters of construction follow dogmatic conviction – about the inseparability of incarnation and atonement, about the being of God as the one who wills, establishes and realizes salvation, about the Holy Spirit as God's act of creating and commissioning the people of God, and about true human existence as glad acknowledgement of the free grace of God in restoring us to covenant fellowship with himself. How Barth sets out these convictions is the theme of the rest of this chapter. Given the exceptional range of what Barth undertakes in *Church Dogmatics* IV, and given its rhetorical and argumentative diffuseness, a full account of the volume as a whole is impossible. Instead, we start from an examination of the basic theological structure of the first part-volume, many of whose features recur in the later parts. From there, we proceed to look in rather more detail at one particular passage of argument from IV/3, where Barth develops his thoughts on the prophetic office of Christ; close reading of this material will help us see from the inside how Barth's arguments function, as well as identify what are often considered to be weaknesses in his christologically-grounded understanding of the church and its action.

Covenant and reconciliation

With the doctrine of reconciliation as the fulfilment of the covenant, Barth writes, 'We enter that sphere of Christian knowledge in which we have to do with the heart of the message received by and laid upon the Christian community and therefore with the heart of the Church's dogmatics' (IV/1, p. 3). His initial move in exploring this great theme is to offer a conspectus of the territory which will later be amplified in much more detail. This he does by three meditations on biblical phrases and texts: 'God With Us' (paragraph 57.1), 'I will be your God and you will be my people' (paragraph 57.2) and, in paragraph 57.3, the texts of John 3.16 and 2 Cor 5.19. Barth is deliberately very close to the biblical ground here, from the beginning displaying his belief that dogmatics may not adopt some higher, speculative or more sophisticated vantage-point above the texts of the prophetic and apostolic witness. The very genre of his writing – above all, the transparency of his conceptual materials to the discursive patterns of the church's confession – becomes the means of giving voice to his sense that, as a wholly irreducible act of divine sovereignty, the work of reconciliation cannot be deduced from anything other than itself, and therefore must be described or repeated rather than conceptually reconstructed. 'We are simply commanded to accept and acknowledge it in all its inconceivability as something that has happened, taking it strictly as it is without thinking round it or over it' (IV/1, pp. 80f.; cf. pp. 223ff., 248ff.).

The special theme which it is the task of the doctrine of reconciliation to describe is that of 'Emmanuel', the history of God with us, which is identical with the name (that is, the particular acting person) Jesus. Of this history, we are to say that it is event, not state ('the attestation and report of the life and act of God as the One who is' (IV/1, p. 7)), and a particular salvific event in which God acts to fulfil his will as creator and rescue those who through sin have forfeited fellowship with God. It is, moreover, the history of grace, grace which is both sovereign and covenantal, freely establishing reconciliation and therefore directed to re-establishing the grateful, active life of the fallen creatures of God. This is why 'reconciliation is the fulfilment of the covenant between God and man':

> 'Reconciliation' is the restitution, the resumption of a fellowship that once existed but was then threatened by dissolution. It is the maintaining, restoring and upholding of that fellowship in the face of an element which disturbs and disrupts and breaks it. It is the realisation of the original purpose which underlay and controlled it in defiance and by the removal of this obstruction. The fellowship which originally existed between God and man, which was then disturbed and jeopardised, the purpose of which is now fulfilled in Jesus Christ and in the work of reconciliation, we describe as the covenant. (IV/1, p. 22)

From this, three basic features of Barth's account of reconciliation can be identified. First, covenant offers a way of talking about the ordered mutuality of God and humanity in which God elects a people to have their being in obedient consent to their election. If sin is the wicked attempt to undo that determination of humanity for fellowship with God, reconciliation is sin's own undoing. To speak in such terms is, naturally, not a matter of some general ontology of relationality (which for Barth would be woefully idealistic); what grounds the account is nothing other than 'the concrete and unique story of Christ' (IV/1, p. 75). Second, therefore, there is the most deliberate christological concentration in what Barth has to say: 'Jesus Christ is the atonement. But that means that He is the maintaining and accomplishing and fulfilling of the divine covenant as executed by God Himself' (IV/1, p. 34). This last phrase indicates how part of what Barth is about in using the term 'covenant' is rooting the work of reconciliation in the being of God himself and, correspondingly, denying that what takes place in Christ's person and work is simply a contingent event. 'In Jesus Christ we really have to do with the first and eternal Word of God at the beginning of all things' (IV/1, p. 50). Covenant means that the God encountered in the gospel is (and does not merely represent) the one true God; there is no other – hidden, fleshless – God behind the divine act in Jesus Christ. Third, there is a soteriological or anthropological corollary: because covenant means 'God with us', it also means 'we with God'. Barth was as keen as any Christian existentialist to retain a vivid sense of the gospel as a human reality. But he did so, not by supplementing theological talk of God with philosophical or experiential talk of humanity, but by drawing attention once again to the gospel which already includes us:

If the fact that God is with us is a report about the being and life and act of God, then from the very outset it stands in a relationship to our own being and life and acts ... what unites God and us men is that He does not will to be God without us, that He creates us rather to share with us ... His own incomparable being and life and act, that He does not allow His history to be His and ours ours, but causes them to take place in a common history. (IV/1, p. 7)

What Bultmann found in a philosophy of existence, Barth found in the doctrines of Trinity, incarnation, election and creation, and their extension in the work of reconciliation.

The obedience of the Son of God

The christological groundwork of the entire doctrine of reconciliation is laid out in paragraph 59, which offers a unified depiction of incarnation and atonement as, first, a work of sheer divine majesty which is, second, directed towards human salvation and, third, effective in human history by virtue of Jesus' presence as the risen one.

The paragraph opens with an extended reflection on the divinity of the Son of God as the acting subject of reconciliation and the manner in which his elect path of humiliation and death is the manifestation of the true majesty of God. A central idea here for Barth is that reconciliation manifests the 'high humility' (IV/1, p. 159), the great condescension of divine grace.

> He does not hold aloof. In being gracious to man in Jesus Christ, He also goes into the far country, into the evil society of this being which is not God and against God. He does not shrink from him ... God shows Himself to be the great and true God in the fact that He can and will let His grace bear this cost, that He is capable and willing and ready for this condescension, this act of extravagance, this far journey ... God is not proud. In His high majesty He is humble. (IV/1, p. 159)

God's humility is high humility, from start to finish the miracle of free grace. There is no sense that in the humiliation of the Son of God, God ceases to be God, submitting to an alien fate or being forced to suppress or contradict his majesty and dignity as Lord of all. 'God is always God even in His humiliation' (IV/1, p. 179). But it is high *humility* which reconciliation embodies: the mode of God's sovereignty is self-emptying (this is the truth of the old doctrine of the 'state of humiliation'). What the Word became was flesh, and '[t]o be flesh is to be in a state of perishing before God' (IV/1, p. 175).

How can these things be said? How is it possible that 'the *forma dei* [form of God] consists in the grace in which God Himself assumes and makes His own the *forma servi* [form of a servant]' (IV/1, p. 188)? By way of answer, Barth points to the deep trinitarian roots of this theology of incarnation and reconciliation. The humility of the incarnate one is grounded in the being of God, who is 'able and free' (IV/1, p. 193) to act in this way. Barth's procedure, therefore, is to trace the work of God in the economy of salvation back into the immanent being of God and, correspondingly, to determine the nature of that immanent being from God's works in salvation. God is as God does; God's works manifest God's essence. This not only means that Barth refuses to negotiate away the conviction that Jesus' presence and activity are the direct and immediate presence and activity of God; it also means that what the work of reconciliation manifests is a movement or relation within God himself. In Jesus Christ 'God chooses condescension' (IV/1, p. 199), and on this basis 'we can speak of an obedience of the one true God Himself in His proper being' (IV/1, p. 200). Barth is emphatic that taking the history of salvation seriously involves rejecting 'abstract "monotheism"' (IV/1, p. 203). Indeed, well before 'social Trinitarianism' took the stage, and well before the theopaschite dramatics of some recent neo-Lutheran Christologies, Barth already found himself pressed to jettison the idea that unity in the case of God means 'singleness and solitariness' (IV/1, p. 202), and to question whether 'subordination in God necessarily involve[s] an inferiority, and therefore a deprivation, a lack' (ibid.).

The obedience of the Son of God, his treading of the way into the far country, is purposive; it is not only revelatory (as it threatens to become in some theologies of the cross) but effective. The answer to the question 'cur deus homo?' is 'propter nos homines et propter nostram salutem'. In other words, the Son's obedience acts out the fact that God is 'for us'. At this early stage in the argument, the aspect of this 'being for us' upon which Barth concentrates is his being 'the judge judged in our place', the one who makes his own the mortal peril in which we stand at enmity with God and thereby removes our condemnation. God became man

> In order to judge [the world] in the exercise of His kingly freedom, to show His grace in the execution of His judgment, to pronounce us free in passing sentence, to free us by imprisoning us, to ground our life in our death, to redeem and save us by our destruction. (IV/1, p. 222)

In particular, Barth draws attention to four aspects of this work of Christ as 'our Representative and Substitute' (IV/1, p. 230) in which he is for us. First, 'He took our place as our Judge' (IV/1, p. 231), displacing us from acting as our own judges, and therefore at one and the same time condemning and abasing us and liberating us by taking from us the 'evil responsibility' (IV/1, p. 234) of having to pronounce verdict on ourselves. Second, 'He took the place of us sinners' (IV/1, p. 235), conducting 'the case of God against us in

121

such a way that He takes from us our own evil case, taking our place and compromising and burdening Himself with it' (IV/1, p. 236). In our place, the Son becomes the one who is the object of divine judgment. Third, 'He suffered and was crucified and died' (IV/1, p. 244); his passion is 'for us' because its subject and agent is God. It is not just 'any suffering', but the suffering of God himself (IV/1, p. 247), and therefore that which reconciles and re-establishes covenant fellowship.

> As the passion of the Son of God who became man for us it is the radical divine action which attacks and destroys at its very root the primary evil in the world; the activity of the Second Adam who took the place of the first, who reversed and overthrew the activity of the first in this place, and in so doing brought in a new man, founded a new world and inaugurated a new aeon – and all this in His passion. (IV/1, p. 254)

And fourth, 'He has done this before God and has therefore done right' (IV/1, p. 256): the action of the Son is righteous, for it is an act of God which accords with the truth and good order which is God's being and will.

Having laid out the basis of reconciliation in the doctrines of Trinity and incarnation, and having indicated the directedness of God's being towards us as the one who is for us, Barth pauses and asks how we may move from these christological and soteriological affirmations to the anthropological sphere, the sphere of human life and activity. Though the question has always been a preoccupation of Barth's – even, as we have seen, in the so-called 'dialectical' writings – it is a question which faces him in the doctrine of reconciliation with especial force because of the pressure he felt from the Christian existentialism represented by Bultmann's theology. Close to the heart of Bultmann's project, as Barth understood it, was a conviction that it is in the anthropological realm that the Christian gospel is 'realized', that is, made real and actual for human existence. On Barth's account, this makes for a fatal exchange of subjects, one whose antecedents stretch back through the liberal theologies of the nineteenth- and early twentieth-century liberal theologies to Melanchthon and the early Luther. In this exchange, Christology becomes a function of human existence; the sovereign and representative nature of Jesus Christ as the God-man is replaced by the decision of faith. 'How', Barth asks in his (rather exasperated) attempt to understand Bultmann, can we expound the New Testament if we relegate God's saving act which is the foundation of Christian existence to a secondary position? How can we do it if we understand God's saving act only as a reflection in the mirror of Christian existence?[2]

Barth is no less interested than Bultmann in the human reality of the gospel. But he grounds it in what is, in effect, a quite different configuration of doctrines, in which the leading role is played by Christology rather than by teaching about human nature or faith. Jesus Christ's being real to us is a function of his free sovereign presence as the risen one, bestowing himself on us through the Spirit. Christology is thus not to be envisaged as so much abstract material which needs 'making real': on the contrary, Christology itself does the necessary work. The turn to the anthropological sphere, which theological existentialism works so hard to secure, has already been made. 'In our Christological basis, in Jesus Christ Himself, everything that can be said of His being and activity in our sphere is already included and anticipated' (IV/1, p. 285). Accordingly, paragraph 59.3 ('The Verdict of the Father') is given over to expounding the resurrection of Jesus as the fulfilment of the covenant and the ground of the contemporaneity of the event of reconciliation. What is most striking in Barth's account is his extensive deployment of the notion of Christ's presence. This notion had largely fallen into disrepair in modern theology, with its place taken over by a theory of human history or action. Spirituality, morals, experience, tradition, church are all under various guises substituted for a theology of the presence of Christ. Barth's response is as it were to pull the human present back into Christology: human history now is a function of Jesus' presence as the risen one.

> His history did not become dead history. It was history in His time to become as such eternal history – the history of God with the men of all times, and therefore taking place here and now as it did then. He is the living Saviour. (IV/1, pp. 313f.)

Thus: 'The event of Easter Day is the removing of the barrier between His life in His time and their life in their times, the initiation of His lordship as the Lord of all time' (IV/1, p. 316).

Having thus described its basis, the rest of *Church Dogmatics* IV/1 is given over to a depiction of the alteration of the human situation itself, in four interlocking presentations of sin, justification, church and faith.

The pride and fall of man

> The verdict of God pronounced in the resurrection of Jesus Christ crucified for us discloses who it was that was set aside in his death, the man who willed to be as God, himself lord, the judge of good and evil, his own helper, thus withstanding the lordship of the grace of God and making himself irreparably, radically and totally guilty before Him both individually and corporately. (IV/1, p. 358)

Barth's doctrine of sin is the consequence of, not the prologue to, his doctrine of reconciliation, for sin is perceptible for what it is only in the light of the act through which God intervenes once and for all to set it aside. The sinner, he says, is 'crooked even in the knowledge of his crookedness' (IV/1, p. 361), and so – despite a venerable Christian tradition – knowledge of sin is not innate. Rather than offering an account of sin oriented to that human self-awareness in which 'man is at bottom only engaged in a soliloquy which he has dramatised and mythologised with the help of biblical reminiscences' (IV/1, p. 372), Barth insists on a christological starting-point. If Jesus Christ is constitutive (rather than merely figurative) of the divine judgement upon sin, what that judgement discloses is that each person is what Barth calls 'the man of sin' (IV/1, p. 389); we are not simply those whose lives are deflected more or less frequently into sinful acts, but rather we *are* sinners, constituted as such and not merely occasionally affected by it. There is no 'neutral Ego which is different from its evil actions and hardly affected by them' (IV/1, p. 403):

> This disposes of the idea that actions are merely external and accidental and isolated. They are not, as it were, derailments. A man is what he does. Their wickedness and folly counts. They are his wicked works and by them he is judged. As the one who does them, who produces these wicked thoughts and words and works, he is the man of sin ... He is inwardly the one who expresses himself in this way outwardly. (IV/1, p. 405)

This is, indeed, a radical doctrine of human depravity, leaving no space whatsoever for innate human goodness. Yet, equally, it is not dualistic: the charge of a quasi-Manichean repudiation of the world as intrinsically evil, often enough levelled against the theology of the Reformed tradition, cannot be made to stick here. What prevents dualism, however, is not a restricting of the universality or gravity of sin, but a further extension of the divine sovereignty in reconciliation:

> From the act of atonement which has taken place in Jesus Christ it is clear that in evil we do not have to do with a reality and power which have escaped the will and work of God, let alone with something that is sovereign and superior in relation to it. Whatever evil is, God is its Lord. (IV/1, p. 408)

And so,

> We would be ignoring or denying what God has done for us in Jesus Christ if we did not hold steadfastly to the fact that the door has been closed on all dualistic views of evil by the eternal resolve of God which became a historical event on Golgotha. (ibid., p. 409)

From this, there follows the important corollary that the ontological status of sin can only be ambiguous. Barth cheerfully accepts that the price of rejecting dualism is disallowing that sinful acts are ontologically constitutive of their human agents. To sin is to do, and we are what we do. But what we do when we sin is that which is impossible or absurd, that whose reality cannot stand alongside the reality of God's good creation reconciled in Jesus Christ. Sin 'has, therefore, no possibility – we cannot escape this difficult formula – except that of the absolutely impossible. How else can we describe that which is intrinsically absurd but by a formula which is logically absurd?' (IV/1, p. 410).

From here, Barth moves to look at the first form of sin as pride. Two things are especially notable in his presentation. First, in line with the overall structure of the doctrine of reconciliation, sin is seen as a human movement in direct contradiction to the movement of divine grace. In the case of pride, this human movement consists in a self-exaltation which counters the lowly lordship of God, an assumption of dominion which counters God's service of us, an act of self-judgement which refuses to acknowledge God's truth, and therefore an attempt to come to our own aid rather than following the movement of Jesus Christ who cried to God in need. There is a vividness in this and similar sections of *Church Dogmatics* IV, deriving not only from the sheer human shrewdness of Barth's

125

depiction of the sinner, but also from the way in which he positions the reader within the biblical material and directly before its central figure, Jesus. This history is our history; here is irrevocably manifest who and what we are and what we do or fail to do.[3] Second, Barth's presentation shifts constantly between sin as real historical action and sin as absurdity, a contradiction of all that it means to act humanly. Barth rarely indulges in explicit ontological reflection, and even when he does (as here, or in the long treatment of 'God and Nothingness' in *CD* III/3) he displays his convictions descriptively rather than theoretically, as in this passage on the sin of judgement:

> man only wants to judge. He thinks he sits on a high throne, but in reality he sits only on a child's stool, blowing his little trumpet, cracking his little whip, pointing with frightful seriousness his little finger, while all the time nothing happens that really matters. He can only play the judge. (IV/1, p. 446)

And yet,

> When man sets out to exercise his own power to judge, is not the essential thing which he achieves something which for its insubstantiality is palpably and painfully real – the formation both microcosmically and macrocosmically of a world which is darkened and disrupted and bedevilled by its own self-righteousness? On the little stool which he thinks is a throne, man does create facts. He dreams, but even when he dreams, he himself is not a dream, but in all his corruption he is the real man who ... has in fact broken peace with God and himself and other men, who thinks he knows about good and evil, who in his factuality can only be described. (IV/1, p. 447)

Even in the doctrine of sin, then, we find Barth unwilling to think of humans as victims rather than perpetrators. If Christology presses Barth to deny any fundamentally constitutive role to sin in determining the being of humanity, the covenantal structure of his understanding of the gospel as concerned with agents in relation similarly presses him to deny that sin is anything other than what we do. One point at which this active character of sin is particularly visible is in Barth's treatment of original sin, where Barth argues quite fiercely against confusing original sin with hereditary sin. Sin is not fate or contagion but willed action – certainly action which turns back upon its agent and imprisons, but nevertheless that which the agent does. Original sin is 'the original and radical and therefore the comprehensive and total act of man', part of 'the voluntary and responsible life of every man' (IV/1, pp. 500f.). Adam's successors, therefore, are simply those who follow the 'rule and perverted order' (IV/1, p. 510) manifest in him.

Justification

Pursuing his task of reflectively tracing the dramatic movement of reconciliation from its ground in the inner being of God to its goal in the renewal of human life and activity, Barth turns to consider justification (a topic on which some, particularly Lutheran, critics believe Barth has little to say).[4] In each part-volume of *Church Dogmatics* IV, the presentation of sin is followed by a specific soteriological treatment of the act by which sin is overthrown; here, the divine act of justification counters the monstrous pride of sin.

Once again, Barth starts from considerations in the doctrine of God. Speaking of salvation as an event of justification presupposes God's 'harmony with Himself' (IV/1, p. 530), that 'God ... in Himself is ... law' (IV/1, p. 529). The concept of righteousness or justice, in other words, refers primarily to the being of God under the aspects of coherence, order and truth. Indeed, like all the divine attributes, God's righteousness is simply a way of indicating God himself. But God is God in act; and God's righteousness is thus inseparable from that act in which God sets aside human unrighteousness and establishes the right: 'The righteousness of God means God's negating and overcoming and taking away and destroying wrong and man as the doer of wrong' (IV/1, p. 535).

Barth is particularly interested in justification as an event of human renewal and devotes a good deal of space to spelling out the anthropological logic of imputed righteousness. To do this, he does not appeal to traditional notions of imparted or infused righteousness, which he fears compromise the prevenience and actuality of divine grace. Rather, he seeks to extend Christology and soteriology by tracing their anthropological effects. Again, this does not, of course, mean that he falls prey to subjectivism; it simply means that he is concerned with the ways in which God's omnipotent act determines the shape of human living. As always, anthropology is the conclusion, not the premise.

To what kind of human life and history does the notion of justification direct us? God's judgement in justification inaugurates a crisis, 'a separation which cuts' the sinner's 'existence at the very root' IV/1, p. 541). Not only does this mean that between the old condemned creature and the new, justified person there stands only the justifying act of God; it also means that the new existence of the justified is not evident, visible in any straightforward way, because justified human life and history is 'the being of God and man in a definite movement' (IV/1, p. 545). It is an event or process or history involving God's relation to and action upon us, which is not simply a predicate of our old being:

> the man who lives in this history of God with him is not in any sense perceptible to himself ... there can be no self-experience of this drama. The fact that it is our history which is in train, that we participate in this drama, is something which must be true and actual quite otherwise than in some depth of our own self, and recognisable as the truth quite otherwise than in the contemplation of one of the phenomena which meet us in these depths. (IV/1, p. 546)

What Barth is exploring here is an account of human selfhood in which the imputation of righteousness, its alien character when viewed from the vantage-point of our usual assumptions about self-identity, is taken very seriously indeed. It is not the history of consciousness or of self-deceived human activity which is primordial: the history of our justification by God alone is 'our true and actual today' (IV/1, p. 548). And 'our real today ... is always a strange today', namely, 'the today of Jesus Christ' (ibid.).

Read on its own, Barth's treatment of alien righteousness appears to promote human self-alienation and sheer passivity. It is therefore of the utmost importance to set what he has to say here about the anthropological entailments of justification alongside the anthropology found within the accounts of sanctification and vocation in *Church Dogmatics* IV/2 and IV/3 respectively. In both these later accounts, the work of Christ is understood as evocative as well as substitutionary: as divine action which calls human partners to acts of humble, dependent yet courageous following. Covenant means election and grace (and therefore passivity); but no less does it mean calling and partnership (and therefore activity). And it is Barth's consistent emphasis throughout the doctrine of reconciliation that grace and partnership, receiving and doing, are not – as an entire line of moral thought from Kant has insisted – contradictory, but complementary, when described with the right kind of Christian determinacy and attentiveness.

Spirit, church and faith

Barth's long progress along the first trajectory of his theology of reconciliation draws to a close with a more direct consideration of the subjective realization of the work of reconciliation in church and faith (paragraphs 62 and 63). In this last stretch of the account of the economy of salvation, Barth once again refuses to lay aside the strictly objective Christocentrism which has characterized the argument so far. Though there was much in his immediate theological context to dissuade Barth from holding to the point (the late liberal theologies of Christian existence which flowered in the 1950s, or the remarkable attention devoted to Bonhoeffer's prison writings on Christian secularity), Barth is characteristically uncompromising: indeed, he fears that a false step at this point will wreck the whole systematic structure of Christian teaching. If the objective orientation is not forgotten but in fact reinforced and deepened, it is because neither in its corporate nor its individual aspects is salvation detachable from that person and work of God in which grace is turned towards us and made real among and in us: namely, the person and work of the Holy Spirit. Here also we remain in the sphere of the Credo, of the confession of the work of God, on the basis of which alone we may speak of a human participation in reconciliation.

> If [reconciliation] is to take place in the Christian community and Christian faith, if man is to will what of himself he cannot will and do what of himself he cannot do, then it must be on the basis of a particular address and gift, in virtue of a particular awakening power of God, by which he is born again to this will and ability, to the freedom of this action, and under the lordship and impulse of which he is another man, in defiance of his being and status as sinner. God in this particular address and gift, God in this awakening power God as the Creator of this other man, is the Holy Spirit. (IV/1, p. 645)

The bulk of this first treatment of ecclesiology in *Church Dogmatics* IV is given over to a relatively uncontroversial but characteristically rich and full exposition of the four marks of the church: its unity, holiness, catholicity and apostolicity. Probably the most important feature of Barth's presentation, however, is the attempt to spell out an account of the relation between the being of the church and the being of Christ – a topic on which, as we shall see, he has been severely criticized. On the one hand, he wants to avoid any bifurcation of Christ and church, and for this reason puts forward the claim that 'The community is the earthly-historical form of the existence of Jesus Christ Himself' (IV/1, p. 661). On the other hand, he is unwilling to convert this claim into an undialectical assertion of identity between Christ and the church as a form of human association and activity and resists any idea that the historical–political reality of Christian society can be unconditionally described as the body of Christ. One means through which Barth tries to ensure the right kind of distinction is to emphasize that the church is event, that is, a teleological direction in human history rather than an achieved embodiment of Christ. Another is to speak of the church as possessed of a 'special visibility' (IV/1, p. 656), transcending the mere perception of phenomenal form. What is all-important to secure is that the church is what it is 'in virtue of the reconciling and self-revealing grace of God, in virtue of the mission and work of the Holy Spirit, and therefore in the power of Jesus Christ Himself' (ibid.).

What Barth is reaching towards here is, in effect, an ecclesiological version of what we have already seen in his account of justification: a theology of the economy of salvation in which the human dimension of reconciliation is grounded beyond itself, in the being and action of the non-possessable God of grace. Something very similar can be found in the last lap of the argument of *Church Dogmatics* IV/1, the account of 'The Holy Spirit and Christian Faith'. Its position at the close of the argument is not fortuitous, but a deliberate statement that the phenomenon of faith only makes Christian sense on the basis of the sweep of saving history so far depicted. Accordingly, Barth draws back from considering faith as 'decision' (which would suggest that the person of faith is self-constituting in the act of adopting an object of faith). The believer's choosing is 'choosing that for which he is already chosen by the divine decision' (IV/1, p. 748). And so, rather than decision, faith is more properly described as 'acknowledgement, recognition and confession' (IV/1, p. 751), deriving from and pointing towards the definitive alteration of the human situation which has already been secured in Jesus Christ and which is now present to the believer with awakening power through the active presence of the Holy Spirit. Of course, 'the question of the individual Christian subject has to be put' (IV/1, p. 755) – but only as consequence, never as some psychological or religious or moral reality which is 'the basis and measure of all things' (IV/1, p. 757).

No reader of this first part-volume of *Church Dogmatics* IV can miss the fact that (even at fifty years' distance) it is highly unconventional. This is above all because it deploys Christology to do the work more usually undertaken in modern theology by ethics, spirituality, or theories of community: the work of bridging the objective 'there and then' of Jesus Christ and the subjective 'here and now'. In its entirety, Barth's argument simply denies that any such gap exists. But the denial commits him to favouring a particular configuration of doctrines, one which is distinctly uneasy about thinking of created reality as having any mediating function and prefers to talk of church and faith as witnesses to, not bearers of, the prevenient reality of God. Just how consistently radical Barth became in his insistence on this point can be seen by reviewing one of the most original (and least studied) tracts of argument in the entire *Church Dogmatics*, the treatment of the prophetic office of Christ in *Church Dogmatics* IV/3.[5]

Jesus Christ as prophet

In older Protestant dogmatics, the prophetic office of Christ played a fairly restricted role, offering a way of talking of the earthly teaching ministry of Jesus and, sometimes, of the mediation of Jesus' word after his resurrection through the activity of church proclamation. In Barth's treatment, the concept of Jesus as prophet expands dramatically. To speak of Jesus as prophet is to speak of him as the immediate agent of the knowledge of himself: he is, literally, self-proclaiming. 'Reconciliation', Barth writes, 'is not a dark or dumb event, but perspicuous and vocal' (IV/3, p. 8). That is to say, the 'subjective' reality and effect of reconciliation is a function of itself. It is not the result of a co-ordination between God's reconciling act and some other reality, for the perfection of the work of reconciliation also includes its completion in the realm of human subjectivity, the 'Amen' or 'Yes' (IV/3, p. 11) to the purposes of God, which is not merely an act of human approval or consent, since '[f]irst and properly and basically ... it is pronounced by the very One in whom the Yes is also spoken' (IV/3, p. 12). The emphasis is not new, of course, but intrinsic to the overall design of *Church Dogmatics* IV, and its roots lie in the account of the three forms of the Word of God in *Church Dogmatics* I, in which the 'revealedness' or 'knowability' of the Word of God is a divine work. Barth consistently denies that describing the revelatory character of God's work involves us in a shift of subjects, by introducing (for example) a theory of cognition or human readiness. Any such move threatens to undermine the 'objectivity' of the revelatory character of God's work; and

> this objectivity of even its revelatory character must be emphasised so expressly because misunderstanding can so easily creep in, as if the problem of the knowledge, understanding and explanation of reconciliation, ... of the question how there can possibly be even the most rudimentary theology and proclamation of reconciliation, were really a problem of the theory of human knowledge and its spheres and limitations, its capacities and competencies, its possible or impossible approximations to this object. (IV/3, pp. 10f.)

Thus, when we talk of the effectiveness of reconciliation, theology remains in the sphere of Jesus Christ and his reality and, therefore, within the sphere of the eternity of God. In the last analysis, it is this which Barth's presentation of the prophetic office of Christ is intended to secure.

Barth proceeds by offering an extended analytical paraphrase of the biblical description of Jesus as the light of life, a paraphrase which consists of a series of moves through the material, in each of which the presentation is both deepened and enlarged. First, to say that Jesus the prophet is the light of life is to make a statement about *Jesus*, and therefore a statement whose meaning is wholly contained in its reference to him. He is neither its penultimate content, nor a symbol of a deeper layer of meaning, but is irreducibly and ultimately that to which the statement refers. Any account of him, therefore, has to be guided by the principle of 'starting from Him and His fulness' (IV/3, p. 7). Stylistically and structurally, this means that Barth unfolds the topic descriptively and not critically, on the basis of a conviction that, as prophet, Jesus attests his own reality and, therefore, is the active subject in our apprehension of him:

> The fact this One lives, and what it means that He lives, are not things invented or maintained of ourselves. If we say them responsibly, our own responsibility is only secondary. We really draw on the biblical attestation of His existence. For in this attestation He Himself lives. (IV/3, p. 44)

Second, to say that Jesus is the light of life is to say that 'He, Jesus Christ, lives' (IV/3, p. 39). This life, lived at once in the manner of

God and in the manner of a human person, is above all 'not an end in itself' (IV/3, p. 41), but rather life for the world, because Jesus 'is the Lord and Servant who lives, not for Himself, but for the sake of the creaturely world and humanity, for their deliverance' (IV/3, p. 42). As the living one, Jesus is universal in his particularity:

> The history as whose Subject He lives does not take place merely in a particularity, however distinguished, apart from the rest of world-occurrence or in isolation from even one of the countless life-stories of men. It takes place rather as the history of salvation; as the occurrence of the coming and eventuation of the salvation of the whole world and all men; as the happening which determines all history and embraces all other histories. (ibid.)

Nor is this saving life locked up in a sphere in which it is unavailable until made real or present by something beyond itself. For it is self-communicative life: 'As He lives, Jesus Christ speaks for Himself ... He is His own authentic witness ... of Himself He grounds and summons and creates knowledge of Himself and His life' (IV/3, p. 46). Reconciliation is revelation – not in the sense of some sort of gnosis, some insight into an arcane truth, but in the sense that the one who reconciles is equally the one whose glory shines in such a way as to demonstrate and proclaim him as who he is. Jesus' history, the history of salvation, 'is also as such the history of revelation' (IV/3, p. 46).

Such, then, is the initial description of Jesus' prophetic office: as revelation, reconciliation generates both the possibility and the actuality of the knowledge of itself, prescribing the manner of its own apprehension. But what is it that is so apprehended?

The content of the prophetic word of Jesus Christ is, very simply, 'Jesus is victor.' In him, 'there is enacted the history, action, drama, or conflict of the prophetic work of Jesus Christ, the shining of light in the darkness. As and because He, Jesus, is the acting Subject, the dominating Character, the warring Hero, it has this orientation' (IV/3, p. 172). The prophetic work of Jesus is best understood as a history of conflict between his self-declaration and its denial, a history in which Jesus' self-declaration is utterly effective, such that it is a history of the triumph of Jesus the light of life. In the prophetic action of Jesus Christ, it is once-for-all made manifest that the reconciliation which has taken place in and as him is now effective:

the fact that reconciliation is also revelation and Jesus Christ lives and works as Prophet means that objectively we can no longer be remote from Him in a private sphere, but that we are drawn into His sphere, into what takes place in Him. This occurrence becomes objectively our own experience. We experience here what takes place there in the supposed but only apparent 'there' which in reality encloses our here and in which our here is also there. That man's here (and he himself in his here) is truly there; that the there of that history is here in reality man's own history – this is what is disclosed as reconciliation is also revelation and Jesus Christ acts also as Prophet. (IV/3, p. 182)

From the beginning, then, the history of conflict brought about by Jesus' prophecy is not one between two equally balanced forces, nor a conflict in which it is yet to be determined whether reconciliation will prove itself effective. Nor is it that reconciliation is somehow incomplete until known and acknowledged to be such. In its character as revelation, the history of reconciliation is 'not merely *a* history of the usual historical or mythical type, but history in the supreme sense, history in which we have a share whether we realise and like it or not, history in which our own history takes place' (IV/3, p. 183). Nevertheless, as such a history, reconciliation is opposed by the 'open contradiction' (IV/3, p. 186) of the world and humanity: 'He meets the meaningless and unfounded opposition of this world, the absurd fact of ignorance of Himself, of His action, of the kingdom of God, of the accomplished alteration of the whole world situation' (IV/3, p. 191).

This opposition is in no sense final, however, because the history of conflict between the light of Jesus Christ and its antithesis in the world's darkness has a sure end in the triumph of light. It is a history in which darkness has already been and is being overcome. 'If we have a part in the problem of the Christ event, we also have a part in its solution in Him' (IV/3, p. 197). God's work of reconciliation is thus also God's effectual word which 'thrusts down its roots and wins for itself form and existence in this outside sphere' which is 'the Christian knowledge established, awakened and fashioned by the revelation, manifestation and prophecy of Jesus Christ' (IV/3, p. 211). To grasp the full extent of Barth's proposal here, two features need to be underscored. First, knowledge of the Word of God, considered as a qualification of human life and thought, is distinctly subordinate to the divine revealedness. God's being manifest is not contingent on being seen by human eyes. The primacy of 'revealedness' thrusts human acts of knowing away from centrality, in that knowing is not the point at which revelation first comes to have any force. 'Knowing' is a human reiteration of what is already well established and manifest. Second, this understanding of a prior objective knowledge of God is rooted in affirmations of the universal presence and activity of the man Jesus. 'God sets among men a fact which speaks for itself' – a fact which has the character of 'statement, word, *kerygma* and light' (IV/3, p. 221). This fact is the history of Jesus Christ, which in all its singularity is catholic and eloquent.

> As that which took place *illic et tunc* it also takes place *hic et nunc* in the present of other times, of our time. And present immediately in this way, it speaks and shines, not in distant echo of an old Word, but with all the clarity and urgency of a Word which, whether it is received or not, is spoken here today and is distinguished by its unique declaration. (IV/3, p. 224)

Barth's point is this: Jesus' perfect singularity includes the radiance of his history upon realities other than his own, for in his history, as 'outreaching, embracing and comprehensive', he is 'on His way from His own particular sphere to our surrounding, anthropological sphere' (IV/3, p. 224). As the risen one who makes himself present in the Spirit, therefore, Jesus is the prophet who is the reconciling act of God in its form of revelation. In sum: the doctrine of Christ's prophetic office articulates the fact that *kerygma* – the proclamation of revelation in its present effectiveness – is an activity of the risen Christ. It is the act of his effective self-glorification in which as mediator he manifests himself as truth and light, overcoming ignorance and darkness. Jesus is, and therefore is known.

Perhaps the most radical extension of what Barth is arguing concerns the understanding of the mission of the church. In essence, speaking of Jesus as prophet shifts the primary locus of activity away from the community of believers on to Jesus himself, who is the agent of his own realization. Thereby the church is redefined as a community whose task is not that of making effective Jesus' reality but of attesting its inherent effectiveness. The basic action of the church is what Barth identifies as 'service' or 'ministry', which he explains by distinguishing two forms in which Christ lives in the Christian. In the first form, Christ as new Adam is the 'Mediator, Head and Representative of all' (IV/3, p. 604); under this aspect, his work is incommunicable and can be participated in only passively, by faith. In the second form, Jesus imparts himself and calls others to be his heralds. 'He alone is the Speaker of the Word of God as well as the Doer of His work. But in the exercise of this prophetic office of His, even though it is He alone who controls it, He does not will to be alone' (IV/3, 606). For the Christian community and its members, this means that

> Being called by and to the Christ engaged in the exercise of His prophetic office, they have no option but to attach themselves to Him with their own action, to tread in His steps, to become with Him proclaimers of the reconciliation of the world accomplished in Him, heralds of His person and work. (Ibid.)

'He does not will to be alone.' The move Barth is making here at one and the same time relativizes and establishes the activity of Christian witness. 'Relativizes', because it asserts the entire adequacy of Jesus' own self-declaration; 'establishes', because the willed form of that self-declaration includes its echo in human declaration.

This initial account is filled out at the ecclesiological level in paragraph 72, 'The Holy Spirit and the Sending of the Christian Community'. The task of the community is confession of Christ. As Jesus 'constitutes and fashions' Christians 'as His community, He awakens them – this is the origin of their task – in order that they may and should confess *Him*' (IV/3, p. 796). 'Confession' here means a pointing to, a vivid attestation of, the 'single and unambiguous Yes' which God pronounces in Jesus: 'to proclaim Jesus Christ is to attest the goodness of God, no less, no other' (IV/3, p. 798). Why 'confession' as the basic act of the church's ministry? Partly in order to retain the primacy of that which is confessed in its sheer reality as self-positing glory. But partly also to ensure that the church's prophecy does not do anything other than indicate the prophetic work and word of Jesus himself:

> [The church] is not commanded to represent, introduce, bring into play or even in a sense accomplish again in its being, speech and action either reconciliation, the covenant, the kingdom or the new world reality. It is not commanded even in the earthly-historical sphere to take the place of Jesus Christ ... It lives as true prophecy by the fact that it remains distinct from His, that it is subject to it, that it does not try to replace it, but that with supreme power and yet with the deepest humility it points to the work of God accomplished in Him and the Word of God spoken

in Him, inviting to gratitude for this work and the hearing of this Word, but not pretending to be claimed for more than this indication and invitation, nor to be capable of anything more. (IV/3, p. 836)

The church is in no sense a bearer of Jesus' own prophetic self-utterance, but an indicator of a perfect and communicative divine activity. Accordingly, the way in which the church fulfils this task of ministry in its context is by 'explaining the gospel', an undertaking which Barth describes thus (and which in many ways *Church Dogmatics* IV as a whole seeks to fulfil):

> To explain the Gospel is to define and describe the nature, existence and activity of God as Creator, Reconciler and Redeemer, the grace, the covenant and the work of reconciliation with all that these include and in the living terms of the manifestation, life, death and resurrection of Jesus Christ ...
> The vital thing in so doing is that the whole content of the Gospel in all its elements and dimensions should be allowed to be its own principle of explanation, that under no pretext or title should alien principles of explanation in the form of metaphysical, anthropological, epistemological or religio-philosophical presuppositions be intruded upon it, that it should not be measured by any other standards of what is possible than its own, that answers should not be given to any other questions than those raised by itself, that it should not be forced into any alien scheme but left as it is and understood and expounded as such. (IV/3, p. 849)

Conclusion

Any work of such expanse simply resists assimilation or tidy characterization, and in Barth's case the seemingly endless detours, reinforcements or patternings of the argument make summary impossible. This astonishingly fertile and moving argument is, however, largely driven by a single, and relatively simple, conviction: that Jesus Christ is the summation of God's ways with the world and the world's dealings with God. It is this which gives *Church Dogmatics* IV its particular focused intensity, its deep unease about arbitrariness and its pretty ruthless criticism of the tendency for Christian theology to be dominated by themes whose provenance lies not in Jesus' self-testimony but in some human construct which he is considered to signify or embellish. Barth is fiercely anti-nominalist; he will not allow that the name of Jesus is a mere label attached to a conception of our own devising (this is part of his attraction for those committed to some sort of narrative theology). But, at least on his reading of the matter, the resistance to nominalism can only be sustained by tying the contingent history of Jesus to the eternal being of God, thereby indicating Jesus' foundational status, both ontologically and epistemologically, both for our understanding of God and for our understanding of human nature and history.

But if Barth's undeflected attention to the person and work of Christ as the root of all talk of God and humanity is the chief strength of his doctrine of reconciliation, it is also for many interpreters its chief weakness, even its chief offence. Barth's move is, in effect, to make the metaphysics of God, nature, history and morals consequent upon Christology, rather than vice versa. But in correcting the under-deployment of Christology in modern theology, it is argued, Barth in fact over-corrects, forcing Christology to undertake work which it is not intended to do, and expanding it in such a way that there are casualties both in the doctrine of the Trinity and in the understanding of the place and function of creaturely reality.

The trinitarian difficulties are usually considered to surface in the doctrine of the Holy Spirit which *Church Dogmatics* IV espouses. Barth evidently took at least the overall direction of his pneumatology from Calvin, who, in *Institutes* III describes the Holy Spirit as that divine agent who unites believers to Christ, making real and effective in them the benefits which Christ's work has secured. Barth often maintained that this christological definition of the Spirit in the Reformed tradition offered a way of rescuing theological talk of the Spirit from its fate at the hands of the theologians of immanence – whether that be in Schleiermacher's account of Christian subjectivity or in Hegel's metaphysics of absolute Spirit. The cost which Barth has to pay (it is suggested) is that the Spirit tends to be swallowed up by Christology. The personal agency of the Spirit in the life of the church and the Christian life is eclipsed and the trinitarian structure of the work of reconciliation deformed, or at least left in need of completion.

Whether such criticism of his pneumatology can be warranted from Barth's texts, and, even if it can, whether what is suggested as an alternative to Barth is self-evidently superior, are very much open questions. It may be that Barth is not so much deficient as simply different – less committed to a pluralist trinitarian theology, less anxious to identify the demarcations between the actions of Christ and Spirit in the world. But the cogency of the criticism is bound up with a further worry, for which our account of *Church Dogmatics* IV/3 has prepared us. His account of the prophetic office attributes to Jesus the prophet those acts which are more usually attributed to (or at least mediated by) the church. In taking this tack, Barth may be making an assumption of the incommunicability of God's action through creaturely agencies. This assumption has never been very far from the surface of the *Church Dogmatics*, even though there are places in the earlier volumes where Barth is much more relaxed about a theology of mediation. But by *Church Dogmatics* IV, creaturely mediation seems to have been collapsed back into the risen Christ's acts of self-mediation and self-manifestation. Once incarnation and atonement acquire the weight of sheer finality that they have in Barth, then there appears to be little place for any extension of Jesus' history in the world: any ongoing history is simply a matter of making accessible what simply is. 'All that remains ... is that we should see and hear and share in what has already been done ... Nothing is added to it except our histories.'[6] Once again, the price is that very great strain is placed on the notion of 'covenant': as Christ comes to look like a sole, and predominately divine, agent, the mutuality of God and humanity appears threatened.

The point at issue, therefore, is the role which Barth accords to the actions of human agents. What is not often grasped about Barth's argument is that his denial of mediatorial status to human action is not the assertion of some abstract principle of the unsuitability of creaturely media, nor is it driven by – for example – a deficient doctrine of creation or a weak theology of the humanity of Christ. In fact, the real force of the argument is often the opposite, rooted as it is in a desire on Barth's part to allow creaturely reality to be itself without having to bear the responsibility for mediating the divine. In effect, Barth's protest against creaturely mediation is in important respects a protest in favour of creation, ensuring that creaturely agents are not impelled by grace but enabled by grace to be themselves. That it is this which undergirds Barth's concerns not only in the doctrine of reconciliation but elsewhere in the *Church Dogmatics*, and not a deficient pneumatology, ecclesiology or doctrine of the Trinity, can, however, only be seen by examining the least studied sections of his dogmatic writing, namely his treatment of ethics. This is the task of the next chapter.

139

Notes

1. *CD* IV/1, p. ix. Subsequent page references to the *Church Dogmatics* are given in the main text.

2. K. Barth, 'Rudolf Bultmann – An Attempt to Understand Him', in H. W. Bartsch (ed.), *Kerygma and Myth. A Theological Debate* vol. II (London: SPCK, 1962), p. 94.

3. This is why Barth's phenomenology of sin is not drawn directly from the worlds of human history and experience but from biblical narrative: the Golden Calf story (Exodus 32), the story of Ahab and Naboth (1 Kings 21) and Jeremiah's material on the fall of Jerusalem.

4. A somewhat rough handling of the issues can be found in A. E. McGrath, *Iustitia Dei. A History of the Christian Doctrine of Justification* (Cambridge: Cambridge University Press, 1998[2]), pp. 357–71.

5. For what follows, see my essay ' "Eloquent and Radiant": The Prophetic Office of Christ and the Mission of the Church', in *Barth's Moral Theology. Human Action in Barth's Thought* (Edinburgh: T. & T. Clark, 1998), pp. 125–50.

6. D. Farrow, *Ascension and Ecclesia* (Edinburgh: T. & T. Clark, 1999), p. 245.

7

Ethics and politics

Barth's work has always suffered from partial readings which expound or criticize his thought on the basis of only a selection from his corpus. For example, his exegetical writings (both the early biblical lectures and the great wealth of expository material in the *Church Dogmatics*) have still not been studied with great thoroughness, and his interpretations of leading figures in the history of theology and Western philosophical thought are scarcely mentioned in accounts of his thinking. Much the same is true of his ethics: although over the course of the 1990s a number of studies of Barth's moral thought have sought to redress the balance,[1] much Barth interpretation goes about its business as if his writings on ethics do not exist.

Yet there are compelling reasons for giving much greater attention to what Barth has to say about ethics, not least the sheer bulk of his ethical writings: early essays and lectures on moral topics, a full lecture cycle on ethics from the late 1920s, as well as the very substantial ethical sections which close each volume of the *Church Dogmatics*. As we shall see, Barth always maintained that one of the distinctives of the Reformed tradition of theology and Christian practice was the high place it accorded to morals; as a consequence, his own dogmatic theology was designed with a two-fold theme – dogmatics *and* ethics – corresponding to the covenant between God and humanity which he regarded as intrinsic to a christologically-focused account of Christianity. The full scope and logic of Barth's work cannot properly be appreciated, therefore, without following it through to its reflections on the moral realm.

141

Moreover, Barth's ethical writings are a very important resource in handling a number of contested issues about the interpretation of his work. His relation to the Protestant tradition of the nineteenth century, for example, takes on a rather different aspect when he is seen not only as a dogmatician but also as a theological ethicist, no less concerned to address issues about human history and action than the Kantian and Ritschlian theologians whose projects he both subverted and re-established on a quite different basis. Or, to take another example, one of the central questions about Barth's early development, namely the influence exerted by his socio-political context, makes study of his ethical writings from that period imperative. Again, fresh light can be shed on the matter of the coherence and contiguity of Barth's theological project from its earliest to its last phases by examining the remarkably consistent interest in moral and political issues which Barth demonstrated from the time of his work as pastor through to the final sections of the *Church Dogmatics*. Inattention to these texts not only leaves us with a foreshortened picture of Barth's thought, but also deprives us of a resource for making a judgement about one of the primary objections to his entire project, namely the fear that his dogmatic decision in favour of a theology of the second article undermines a proper sense of the substance and spontaneity of creaturely acts.

Barth was a moral theologian, not in the sense that he was a professional Christian ethicist, but in the sense that questions of the ground, nature and goals of human moral action were never far from the surface of his work, and often form a major feature of its intellectual landscape. At first glance, however, this is not easy to see. This is chiefly because Barth's approach to moral theology involves him in both a radical recasting of the forms which it had taken in Protestant thought since Kant and some unfamiliar usage of its central concepts and terms. This refashioning is very far-reaching: inherited notions of command, freedom, agency, responsibility, the good – all the basic components of a moral metaphysics and moral anthropology – are subject to thorough theological critique and reconstruction. The result is that what Barth preposes by way of theological ethics is hard to recognize as such, especially for those who give greater authority to the conventions of modernity. The task in reading what Barth has to say on these matters thus involves a certain suspension of expectations, precisely so that what he is doing can be seen for what it is: a set of attempts, not to abandon moral and political activity, but to reorient it by directing attention to its ground in the activity of God which is attested in the Christian gospel and articulated in Christian theology.

Early ethical writings

One of Barth's major points of disagreement with the liberal theological tradition concerned what he saw as its moralism, its all-too-easy identification of the Kingdom of God with the moral, socio-political or historical processes of bourgeois society. He feared that the social ethics of liberal Protestantism contained a dangerously immanentist teleology and theory of moral value, and as a result became an ethics from which judgement and the transcendent otherness of divine action had been scoured out. One of the most explosive statements of these convictions is the famous address on 'The Christian's Place in Society' (known as the 'Tambach lecture' because it was delivered at a conference of those with Religious Socialist leanings at Tambach in 1919), which was Barth's first major treatment of an ethical theme following his departure from the liberal tradition. Like his last major piece of ethical writing forty years later (the lectures on 'The Struggle for Human Righteousness' in *The Christian Life*),[2] it treats of social ethics. Its theme is that God is 'origin', and therefore both the contradiction and the ground of social action. God's Kingdom is not to be equated with social action and yet the transcendent rule of God evokes Christian action in society. 'What,' Barth asks at the end, 'can the Christian in society do but follow attentively what is done by *God*?'[3]

The lecture is on any account a convoluted work, as Barth struggles towards a statement, trying at one and the same time to make sense of, and get out from underneath, a set of conventions common to bourgeois Protestantism and Socialism. Rather than constructing a position, Barth is attempting to bring home to the reader a spiritual and intellectual process in which he found himself caught up. Barth keeps turning the argument against itself, making it subvert its own affirmations. There is frequent use of pairs of contrasted concepts: 'Christian' and 'society', 'hope' and 'questioning', 'promise' and 'opposition'. And contrasting lines of argument are made to collide: over against the exaltation of social criticism, the Kingdom of God is the affirmation of social order; yet over against affirmations of natural and social order, the Kingdom of God remains the wholly other kingdom of glory. The danger in reading the lecture is that we give more attention to his denials

143

than to his affirmations, particularly if we interpret the text through the picture of the second edition of *Romans* which has become conventional.

To make sense of what Barth is doing, we need to attend with considerable care to what these 'dialectical' twists of argument are trying to accomplish; otherwise his purpose can be quite badly misinterpreted. The force of the dialectic is not an absolute contrast between superior divine action and (at best) inferior or (at worst) eliminated human action. Barth's aim is, rather, to ground both negation and affirmation in God as absolute origin. It is only at the end of the lecture that this aim finally becomes clear, however. Having at one and the same time affirmed and criticized both 'simple co-operation within the framework of existing society' and 'radical and absolute opposition to that society',[4] Barth writes thus in the final section of the address:

> as we had to guard ourselves against thinking that we could set up our overturned idols again by confining ourselves objectively to the world as it is, we must now fortify ourselves against expecting that our criticizing, protesting, reforming, organizing, democratizing, socializing, and revolutionizing – *however fundamental and thoroughgoing these may be* – will satisfy the ideal of the kingdom of God. That is really beyond us. There is no such thing as perfect naïveté in this age – and no such thing as perfect criticism. The unsolved situation in which God has placed us can no more be taken as an abstraction than the order of creation in which he has given us to live. The one must be understood by the other, and both understood as God-given. If we try to understand them otherwise we pass from one piece of worldly wisdom to another. Our Yes like our No carries its limitation in itself. While it is God who gives us that rest and this greater unrest, it is clear that neither our rest nor our unrest in the world, necessary though both of them be, can be final.[5]

Barth's point is that it is not just our 'Yes', our affirmation of the social order, which must acknowledge its limits, but also our 'No'. Both naïvely unambiguous affirmation of action in the social realm and 'perfect criticism' are finite; and their lack of finality is rooted in the fact that God is other, capturable neither in a determinate pattern of social action nor in revolutionary overthrow of any such pattern. 'The *other*, which we try to represent by parable in our thought, speech and action, the *other*, for whose actual appearing we yearn, being tired of mere parables, is not simply some other thing, but is the wholly other kingdom which is *God's*.'[6] More abstractly, this other is 'the original and spontaneously productive energy of the synthesis from which the energy of the thesis and the energy of the antithesis both derive'.[7] And so, Barth goes on: 'Beyond, *trans*: *that* is the crux of the situation; *that* is the source of our life.'[8] Put more concretely, this means that 'The synthesis we seek is in *God* alone, and in God alone can we find it'.[9]

> The naïve acceptance and the criticism with which in Christ we meet the lower order of things, both alike take their rise in the higher order which in God, but in God alone, is one with the lower. Naïve acceptance and criticism have their possibility, their authorization, and their necessity in the power of the resurrection.[10]

Where is Barth taking us? His emphasis on transcendence, otherness, the 'higher order', is clearly not designed to exclude social action but to relativize it: to sever the bond which liberal moralists like Rothe established between positive affirmation of the social order and the Kingdom of God, and at the same time to sever the similar bond which religious socialists established between social protest and the Kingdom. But Barth does not allow this two-fold relativization to lead him to abandon the historical, social world. And what prevents him from any such abandonment, even at this early stage, is doctrinal: the centrality of the resurrection of Jesus. Jesus' resurrection is understood as 'the appearance in our corporeality of a *totaliter aliter* constituted corporeality':[11] as life in the flesh remade. The doctrinal material here is somewhat rudimentary, devoid of the christological depth and richness of later work. But already there is a pattern of argument to which Barth will return many times in later treatments of ethics: the eschatological 'otherness' of God's action in Christ in fact liberates human action from the dehumanizing effect of having to be the bearer of the Kingdom of God, taking from it its false absolutism, whether of 'Yes' or 'No':

> We need not therefore be apprehensive of any pessimistic discrediting of our life here and of activity in our life here, *if* we conclude with Calvin to fix the place of the Christian in society within the *spes futurae vitae*. Thence the power of the consciousness of predestination! Thence the power of the decision to live to the glory of God! As a matter of fact we are restricted to this viewpoint as much in our naïve acceptance as in our criticism of

society. But restriction means confessedly not *loss* but *accumulation* of strength, the salutary damming of running water to prevent foolish waste and dangerous excess. And it is quite clear *why* we are so restricted. When we look from creation and redemption toward perfection, when we look toward the 'wholly other' *regnum gloriae*, both our naïve and our critical attitude to society, both our Yes and our No, fall into *right practical relation to each other in God*.[12]

It would be quite premature to find in Barth at this stage a rounded account of human social action. Nevertheless, it would be equally wide of the mark to interpret what he has to say as an eschatological annihilation of the human. At the very least, he is busy clearing the space for a positive theology of human action and beginning to suggest some of the basic shapes which such a theology is to assume.[13]

It is, of course, the rudiments of a *theology* of human action which Barth has here. Already at the end of the second decade of the century, he is clear that the ethical and political are predicates of the theological, and not vice versa. Certainly Barth's early theology cannot be separated from his social and political involvements and context, as some commentators rightly insist.[14] But theology is fundamental, because divine action is fundamental. However, theological talk of God's mighty acts necessarily, inescapably, includes talk of human action: this conviction, already present in Barth's earliest reflections on social ethics, was to remain one of his most consistently emphasized theological motifs. As Barth took up theological teaching and dug himself deeply into the classic texts of the Reformed tradition, the conviction gained profile and solidity. It is, for example, a major theme in his 1922 lectures on Calvin and finds expression in the lectures given the next year on the theology of the Reformed confessions.[15] An especially clear statement of it can be found slightly later in an address from 1925 on 'The Desirability and Possibility of a Universal Reformed Creed'. Here Barth insists that '[t]he doctrine, the proclamation of Christian truth among the Reformed, much more unambiguously than in the school of Luther, included the essentials for men's lives in society and in the state. In fact, it sets forth the problem of ethics radically in every line.'[16] Again: 'Acceptance of dogma among the old Reformed had nothing to do with abstract gnosis. It was wholly ethical. The *whole* man, the *whole* city was requisitioned by the *parole de Dieu* which was confessed.'[17]

Already, then, it ought to be clear that we do not need to wait for the *Church Dogmatics* to find the beginnings of serious attention to moral agency. Whilst the later doctrine of election and the 'theanthropology' to which it gives rise give deeper expression to the theme of human action, its roots lie in the early phase of Barth's thinking. We need to beware of presenting this early phase as one in which Barth is trapped within a competitive picture: *either* God's action *or* ours, *either* grace *or* history. For what Barth is denying is not that human action has any entitlement to exist, but that it can be considered as having self-evident status. The concern is not with the elimination of responsible human action, but with its placing or specification. At this stage, the placing is undertaken through a rhetoric designed to chasten the pretensions of the then-authoritative moral theory; but its final end (seen most clearly in *Church Dogmatics* IV, but already germinally present here) is the establishment of the right sort of status for the human agent.

Easily the most sophisticated earlier account of these matters can be found in the lectures on ethics from the late 1920s. First delivered only six years after the lectures on Calvin, they are considerably more complex and polished, and are in effect the first draft of the ethical sections of the *Church Dogmatics*. They lay characteristic emphasis on the inseparability of ethics and dogmatics and the importance of moral action as the locus of human response to the divine initiative – themes which will subsequently be explored at great length in Barth's *magnum opus*. The lectures remained unpublished during Barth's lifetime because he considered that he had been too generous towards the idea of 'orders of creation' (that is, relatively autonomous moral patterns in created reality), which he found abused by many pro-Nazi theologians in the 1930s. But even in their unrevised state, the lectures constitute a major treatise in Protestant theological ethics, at least as significant as Bonhoeffer's much more famous *Ethics*,[18] and, in fact, a good deal more comprehensive and doctrinally sophisticated.

Barth was always concerned for the correct ordering of divine grace and human moral action, and thus for clarifying the relation of dogmatics to ethics. Christian theology is concerned at all points with the Word of divine self-revelation. But because that Word has both indicative and imperative force, Barth felt a responsibility to explore the logic of two claims. The first is that Christian ethics is part of dogmatics and not a separate discipline (belonging perhaps to philosophy or the human sciences) which overlaps with theology at certain points. Christian ethics is *Christian* – that is, not a variant of some generic human morality, but concerned with that form of life which is established by God in Jesus Christ and commanded in the proclamation of the Christian gospel. It is, accordingly, a distinctively theological discipline, appealing to the same givens and governed by the same norms as Christian doctrine. The imperative is rooted in the indicative. Second, dogmatics is always ethical dogmatics, always, that is, concerned to elucidate how the indicative of Christian faith encounters us as moral imperative. Because this latter point is frequently missed, it is worth pausing over how Barth developed it in the *Ethics*. Dogmatics, he argued in the *Göttingen Church Dogmatics*, is the science of Christian preaching, critical regulation of the church's speech which claims to articulate the Word of God. But this Word is not a mere neutral factor; it has a certain direction, moving towards the will of the human hearer who hears the Word not in passive detachment but 'in and not apart from his act'.[19] The Word of God is not simply informational; its character as revelation is not fully understood even when it is thought of as a shattering intrusion of divine truth. 'The Word of God is moral truth.'[20] This is because it is the 'sanctifying Word', on the basis of which 'we have the right to state that the reality of the Word of God embraces the reality of the man who receives it and therefore gives the Christian answer to the question of the goodness of human conduct'.[21] Barth argued for the inseparability of dogmatics and ethics on the basis of two primary doctrinal affirmations. The first is anthropological (although derived from a consideration of what humanity is in the light of revelation): 'What we do, we *are*. Man does not exist and also act. He exists as he acts.'[22] The second concerns the nature of the divine self-revelation by which we are established as moral agents. 'The theme of dogmatics is simply the Word of God, but the theme of the Word of God is simply human existence, life, or conduct.'[23] Because – and only because – God speaks and acts in an imperatival way, the question of human conduct is ingredient within our talk of God. Thereby the task of Christian ethics becomes that of considering the Word of God in its character as claim.

Consequently, throughout the *Ethics* lectures Barth wove together two themes: the notion of the divine command and a certain 'moral anthropology', that is, a certain picture of the ethical agent. Both these emphases push the deliberative moral self out of the centre of the picture. The force of the notion of command is to stress that for Christian ethics 'the good' is to be identified with the purposive action and will of God and not simply with any projects or values which the agent may propose. To be faced with the divine command is to be faced with that which is utterly 'original' – that is, by a will absolutely other than my own, encountering me with critical energy. Barth consistently urged that the only way in which we can make headway in ethics is by grasping that moral reflection faces us with 'the transcendent factor'.[24] The alternative, as always, is a drawing of moral questioning within the sphere of the immanent, restricting ethics to inquiry into the psychology of the will, or to human moral culture and law. Only the most rigorously deployed notion of God as active commanding subject offers any effective resistance to the absorption of ethics into contingent moral history.

This notion of divine command is tied to a specific account of the human moral agent in which the self as judge is displaced. In a clear departure from the Kantian tradition, Barth does not consider that the claim of transcendent moral authority is discoverable by unaided moral reason. He was deeply troubled by the fear that moral reflection, ethical self-consciousness, might be thought of as somehow neutral, as a way of standing apart from and inspecting God's commands and reaching judgements about them. Such ideas, he believed, functioned as protection against radical demands for obedience, inserting a buffer of moral awareness between ourselves and the command of God, thereby evading its imperious summons to action. By contrast, Barth makes the divine act of salvation primary in our understanding of ourselves as reflective agents:

> Knowledge of the good is the self-knowledge in which we see that in our reflection on the good which precedes decision we are *not ourselves judges* and are in no position, through a choice of this or that act preceding our decision, to pronounce judgement on ourselves or to bring about our own determination for salvation or perdition.[25]

We are not judges, but the judged, measured by that before which we are made responsible in a final and irrevocable way. And so:

> The point of ethical reflection is that we become aware of our responsibility to this superior court so that the very next moment we act in awareness of this responsibility, not having chosen and grasped the good – how could we, that would be foolish effrontery – but in awareness that we are making a response with our act; in awareness of the absolute *givenness* of the command, over

and behind which there stands no higher general truth to which we can look apart from the command or appeal beyond the given command, but the command which is itself the truth, the truth of the good.[26]

Out of this Barth developed much else: his rejection of ideas of morality as straightforward application of laws; his use of the motif of justification–sanctification to talk of the crisis which is brought about and resolved by the will of God; his reworking of conscience as a moral faculty. In effect, Barth proposed an entirely different understanding of moral subjectivity and agency. To be moral subject and agent is to be made such by the imperative presence of God, before which I am no longer judge but both called into question and summoned not simply to reflection but to action in accordance with the declared will of God.

Because a good deal of the material content of the *Ethics* lectures is absorbed into the *Church Dogmatics*, little needs to be said of it here. In form, the exposition is trinitarian, with three lengthy chapters on the Command of God the Creator, the Command of God the Reconciler and the Command of God the Redeemer. This structure remains intact in the later version, and, indeed, the treatment of the ethics of redemption offers the only clue to what might have been the content of the fifth, unstarted, volume of the *Church Dogmatics*. This trinitarian depiction is a considerable advance on the rather formal attempt to reconstruct the moral world in the earlier ethical materials, and Barth looks in detail at such topics as marriage and sex, neighbourliness, the state, education and human rights. But as in the 'dialectical' writings, so here: what human beings do is determined by what they are, and what they are can be discovered only by attention to God's word and work.

Politics and the German church struggle

Barth's basic instinct in his earlier ethical writing was to insist that culture, politics and individual moral subjectivity are not autonomous or primordial realities but functions of the presence and purposive action of God. In this way, he sought to undo a metaphysics of morals which made ethical consciousness or the work of culture and politics into first principles, and to replace it by a trinitarian moral ontology of the command of God.

The considerable critical power possessed by this can be seen in the theology of the state which Barth worked out in the late 1920s and after, especially in the Nazi era. Some suggest that Barth's early account of the state (for example in his treatment of Romans 13 in *The Epistle to the Romans*) is quietist, the political realm being eschatologically disqualified from having positive claim on the Christian. Others emphasize the opposite: that the background of Barth's early eschatological theology is revolutionary politics. But by the time of the *Ethics* lectures, neither description works. Refusing to see the state either as 'the city of the devil deriving from the fall of the angels',[27] or as some kind of extension of the Kingdom of God, Barth commits himself to the state's provisional necessity. The state is

an order of the sustaining patience of God which is necessary and good because even those who have been blessed in Christ are wholly and utterly sinners. It ... presupposes that repentance before God and service to the neighbour are in an antithesis that has not yet been overcome ... It ... is a sign of the mediated fellowship between God and man. It ... once was not and one day will not be, so that it belongs with the church to the time between the times, to the kingdom of grace.[28]

The state is thus 'an order of reconciliation',[29] – a form of human fellowship which may claim Christian allegiance, though an allegiance limited by the state's historicity as the 'human work' of 'building up of society among men by establishing the sign of commonly discovered and accepted right and law, protected if necessary by force, and commonly sought education'.[30]

Something closely similar is found in the crucial fifth thesis of the 1934 Barmen Theological Declaration, largely written by Barth:

Scripture tells us that by divine appointment the State, in this still unredeemed world in which also the Church is situated, has the task of maintaining justice and peace, so far as human discernment and human ability make this possible, by means of the threat and use of force. The Church acknowledges with gratitude and reverence towards God the benefit of this, his appointment. It draws attention to God's dominion [*Reich*], God's commandment and justice, and with these the responsibility of those who rule and those who are ruled. It trusts and obeys the power of the Word, by which God upholds all things.

We reject the false doctrine that beyond its special commission the State should and could become the sole and total order of human life and so fulfil the vocation of the Church as well.

Given its context (the rampant ideologies of the state which had infected political and church life in Germany), the thesis is an astute refusal either to demonize or to give unqualified theological justification to the state. The crucial factor for Barth is 'divine appointment' (he uses the word *Anordnung*, a weaker term than *Ordnung*). Appointed by God to maintain justice and peace through coercion in the still unredeemed world, the state is a cause of gratitude to God; but it remains firmly subservient to God's dominion, command and righteousness, upheld by God's Word and therefore essentially restricted: it cannot be a total order for human life. Hence Barmen V repeats the content – and the order – of the biblical warrant which stands at its head: 'Fear God! Honour the emperor!' (1 Pet 2.17). More than anything else, Barmen secured the principle that systematic co-ordination of the gospel and political arrangements tends to absolutize the state, and that what is required is therefore a clearly christological definition of the nature of civil community. A later essay from the 1930s puts the matter thus in expounding Rom 13.1: 'the power, the State as such, belongs originally and ultimately to Jesus Christ ... in its comparatively independent substance, in its dignity, its function and its purpose, it should serve the Person and Work of Jesus Christ and therefore the justification of the sinner'.[31] In the 1930s, Barth laid special emphasis on the element of derivation and the dangers which attend the state's renunciation of its proper role: 'Caesar-worship, the myth of the State and the like'.[32] In later years, he continued to protest against the political nostrification of God, especially at the hands of Western opponents of Communism in the 1950s. Moreover, the element of the state's relativity nearly always found its way into Barth's political writing, as when he spoke of 'the external, relative and provisional sanctification of the unhallowed world which is brought about by the existence of political power and order'.[33] This relativity is reinforced eschatologically (the heavenly city, he once argued, is 'the only real state');[34] accordingly, Christian subjection is neither absolute nor direct. Indeed, the Christian may resist existing political arrangements, provided such resistance is not anarchic but an affirmation of the true order established by the Word of God.

The important essay from the immediate post-war period, 'The Christian Community and the Civil Community' (originally a lecture given in various German centres in 1946) draws many of the threads together: the role of the state as providential witness to Christ's rule; the state as protection against chaos by rule of law; the repudiation of direct identity between God's dominion and political society; the requirement that loyalty to the state be both unfeigned and yet critical. But the essay is chiefly known for proposing that 'the existence of the State [is] an allegory, ... a correspondence and an analogue, to the Kingdom of God'.[35] Sometimes the analogies which Barth spells out work well (the correspondence between the mission of the church and the search for social justice, for example); at other points (opposition to political secrecy on the basis that Jesus is the light of the world) the theological material seems to be conscripted. It is common to take these analogies as a sign that Barth only reached a positive theology of the state in the post-war period; but, as nearly always, such developmental accounts are too neat. There is material from the 1920s which suggests a 'positive' evaluation of political society; and the unfinished text on the ethics of reconciliation contains rather sharp protest against the state's ideological potential. It is more accurate to say that Barth has a relatively consistent but complex account of the state (provided one does not over-systematize his thinking), one or other element of which he emphasizes in particular circumstances: what needed to be said in 1934 against the total state was not what was needed in 1946 to encourage hopeful and responsible political reconstruction. The core features remain stable, however. One of the best expressions of them was in Barth's 1941 'Letter to Great Britain from Switzerland', where – as so often when he wrote on ethics – he began from a depiction of the kind of place the world is as the field of human action:

> the world in which we live is the place where Jesus Christ rose from the dead, and the present age is the time of God's long-suffering until the day when the same Jesus Christ shall come again in His glory ... Since this is true, the world in which we live is not some sinister wilderness where fate or chance holds sway, or where all sorts of 'principalities and powers' run riot unrestrained and rage about unchecked ... There is no doubt that such 'principalities and powers' ... *do* exist ... But at the same time it is written, and we can and must hold on to it even today: that although at the present the glory of the Kingdom of God is held out to us only as a hope, yet the Kingly Rule of Christ extends not merely over the Church as the congregation of the

faithful but ... over the whole universe in all its heights and depths; and it also confronts and overrules with sovereign dignity the principalities and powers and evil spirits of this world.[36]

But Christ's kingly rule is not a mere consoling warrant for indolence; because Christ rules the world, Christians are called to resist the passivity which totalitarian regimes breed, to be not simply political subjects but political agents: 'Jesus Christ does not dwell in some mystic, ritualistic, pietistic, individual-ethical or theological hinterland beyond the political sphere'; and

> Because His Rule is not confined within the walls of the Church, and because the political sphere is His, and does not belong to Man or to the Devil, we are irrevocably bound, precisely because we are members of His Church, to serve God in this sphere also.[37]

Ethics in the *Church Dogmatics*

'The task of theological ethics is to understand the Word of God as the command of God.'[38] The *Church Dogmatics* is a theology of the Word, that is, an attempt to indicate and depict the communicative history of God and humanity. As dogmatics, it accomplishes this by considering the Word as *truth* which summons; as ethics, it accomplishes this by considering the Word as truth which *summons*. Ethics is integral to dogmatics, no more separable from the task of doctrinal theology than the subjective aspect of revelation is separable from its objective aspect. This material decision, reached in the 1920s, finds its maturest expression in the ethical sections of the *Church Dogmatics*, where Barth returns to the theme on many occasions. In volume I, it emerges in Barth's stress on the inescapably ethical character of the Word: echoing the *Ethics* lectures, he proposes that 'the theme of dogmatics is always the Word of God and nothing else. But the theme of the Word is human existence, human life and volition and action'; and so '[d]ogmatics has no option: it has to be ethics as well'.[39] Or, as we have seen in his treatment of election, Barth insists that election is not simply the assigning of destiny but appointment to active fellowship with God, so that '[t]he Gospel itself has the format and fashion of the Law'.[40] But the most important concept for drawing attention to the inseparability of indicative and imperative is that of command – already, as the *Ethics* lectures show, a basic building block in Barth's moral thought.

Interpretation of Barth's ethics sometimes gets derailed by overlooking the fact that he uses this (apparently) purely imperatival

word in a way which embraces both the indicative and the imperative. Taken at face value, the term 'command' seems in danger of
grounding human action in a purely heteronomous divine will. In
fact, however, the term is deployed by Barth to do two tasks. The
first (imperatival) task is to state how Christian ethics is concerned
with the will of God in its absolute, obligatory force. But alongside
this there is a second (indicative) task: the term 'command' serves
as a shorthand summary of the moral field, the situation in which
human agents stand as those who encounter God's summons in the
economy of salvation. To talk of God's command, therefore, is both
to indicate the moral nature of reality (the space in which we stand,
the kinds of creatures we are, the gracious God whom we face), and
to highlight the fact that this reality may not be acknowledged in
mere passivity, since it comes to us as a call. Failure to see both
aspects of the notion of command often underlies misunderstand-
ings of Barth's ethical thought as irrationally voluntarist, organized
around the idea of aggressive and wholly discrete divine commands, uninterested in human flourishing, and much else. But
'command' is not equivalent to mere 'orders'; it is a summary term
for the vocation set before humanity in the merciful covenant
history of creation, reconciliation and redemption.

This is why Barth insists that command is event. God's command
is not a mere directive to be formalized, something statutory, but an
episode in and determination of the history of God's relation to us.
The content of God's claim is, very simply, 'the name of Jesus',
which is 'the substance of God's Law'.[41] In making this move, Barth
is not simply putting Jesus' moral teaching at the centre of Christian
ethics: action, not instruction, is what is referred to here. The
'name' of Jesus means his enacted history, that history which sums
up and completes God's covenant with humanity. According ethical primacy to the name of Jesus is therefore claiming that ethical
reality – the moral world we inhabit, our own moral natures, above
all, the God whose command we encounter – is defined at every
point by Jesus Christ. Acting in God's stead and in our stead, Jesus
establishes moral truth; good human action is action which corresponds to that truth. God's command is not merely that we should
submit to a power, but that we should act in conformity with the
reality of God's gracious history with us. 'What are we to do? We
are to do what corresponds to this grace.'[42]

Once this rather peculiar use of the term 'command' is accepted,
much else becomes clear. To give an example: command, Barth
says, is permission, 'the granting of a very definite freedom'.[43] If

command is mere orders, talk of freedom is nonsensical. But when command is seen as the imperative of reality, then it is no longer alien to our natures, in fact, quite the opposite: it is a command which requires us to be what the gospel declares that we are. Or again: command, Barth says, is decision, by which he means that God's command establishes us as creatures who have a specific nature in relation to God. 'The divine command is a statement about him [the human creature]. It not only subjects him to a requirement but in so doing, places him under a conclusion.'[44] Command, in effect, says not only: This is what you must do! But also: This is who you are!

Strange though it may appear, this means that what Barth is doing with the notion of 'command' is not wholly alien to what other theological traditions have talked about in terms of 'natural law'. Barth always opposed what he thought to be the epistemological defect of theories of natural law, namely, the assumption that knowledge of God's will can be drawn from a consideration of 'nature' independent of God's particular acts of self-communication. But he did not reject the ontological vision which the natural law tradition articulates, in which the good and the real are inseparable. Barth's idiom of command is characteristically historical, especially in its central idea of 'event'. But he insists (both in the ethics of creation in *Church Dogmatics* III/4 and in the ethics of reconciliation) that 'formed reference' to this event is possible and necessary.[45] The realities with which Christian ethics is concerned – God in his claim upon us, and the active human subject – are knowable and describable because they have a given nature, a specific 'shape'. That shape or nature is given only in Jesus Christ, and knowable and describable only in him. But this does not deny, only defines, its givenness:

Since the ethical event as an encounter of the concrete God with concrete man does not take place in an empty space but in that defined by the concreteness of both these partners and their encounter, ethics, too, does not stand before something which is general ... It has a text which it is its duty to understand and expound in relation to this event. It may also be said that it has a material principle, the perception and conception of something which is constant for all the singularity and uniqueness of this event. It knows not only the point of this event but also the field in which it takes place, to which it looks as it knows about the event as such ... But its text, material principle and field is the nexus, structure and differentiation of the history in which the ethical event has its place according to the Word of God, and of which it forms a moment.[46]

'Nature' is thus detached both from phenomenal history and from non-theological metaphysics and defined out of the eschatological reality which is established in the history of the covenant, supremely in Jesus Christ and the Holy Spirit. The most vivid depiction of this moral reality is found in the last sections of the *Church Dogmatics*. A fragment of this material, on Christian baptism, was published at the end of Barth's life as *Church Dogmatics* IV/4 and evoked a storm of protest, directed chiefly against its denial of the sacramental status of water baptism and the appropriateness of the baptism of infants. Read as an essay on sacramental theology, the fragment is rather obviously unsatisfactory. The exegesis is sometimes surprisingly shoddy, dominated by special pleading, as well as by what seems at times an almost Platonic distinction between water baptism (an exclusively human act) and baptism with the Spirit (an exclusively divine act). Moreover, the basic claim (that water baptism and Spirit baptism are clearly discrete operations) involves Barth in a sharp turn from the sophisticated accounts of sacramental mediation in earlier work (although his unease about baptism had already surfaced in the early 1940s). Clearly the Reformed tradition on sacraments had lost its appeal for him, though what replaced it lacked the nuance and weightiness of earlier discussion. In one sense, *Church Dogmatics* IV/4 does not cohere with the rest of the work – neither with Barth's earlier theology of sacraments, nor with his account of the mediation of revelation, nor, most of all, with the christologically-grounded refusal to divide divinity and humanity too sharply. In another sense, however, the baptism fragment shows strong consistency with the overarching theme of the *Church Dogmatics*, God and humanity in covenant relation. For part of what stimulates Barth to make such a clear separation of water and Spirit baptism is an ethical concern: a desire to indicate that at the beginning of the Christian life there is a distinctive form of human endeavour, subservient to the work of the Spirit but nevertheless genuine and real. However much Barth's decision to link this endeavour to baptism may be disputed, the point is clear:

the omnicausality of God must not be construed as his sole causality. The divine change in whose accomplishment a man becomes a Christian is an event of true intercourse between God and man. If it undoubtedly has its origin in God's initiative, no less indisputably man is not ignored or passed over in it. He is taken seriously as an independent creature of God. He is not run down and overpowered, but set on his own feet. He is not put under tutelage, but addressed and treated as an adult. The history of Jesus Christ, then, does not destroy a man's own history.[47]

One of the main reasons why this ethical impulse in Barth's later theology of baptism is not always appreciated is the separate publication of the baptism fragment, which was part of a set of lectures giving a more comprehensive account of the ethics of reconciliation: without the surrounding materials, the treatment of baptism is isolated from the larger argument and so looks like a rather inadequate foray into sacramental theology. With the post-humous publication of the immediately preceding and following materials, however, in the volume entitled *The Christian Life*, the ethical context becomes more transparent.

The Christian Life is Barth's last great piece of writing: even in its unrevised and incomplete state, it is an argument of remarkable theological and human resonance, nearly always superior to that in the baptism fragment, which by comparison is rougher and more angular in tone. The volume is structured as an exposition of the Lord's Prayer, for by now Barth is clear in his mind that the fundamental action of the Christian life is invocation of God: 'the humble and resolute, the frightened and joyful invocation of the gracious God in gratitude, praise, and above all petition' is 'the normal action corresponding to the fulfilment of the covenant in Jesus Christ'.[48] Why invocation?

'Invocation' catches exactly (and much more successfully than the separation of water and Spirit baptism) the relation between God's grace and the responsive human act of free obedience. Prayer can be considered the paradigmatic human moral action, firstly, because it is wholly referred to the action of God. Both in its origin (the prayer of Jesus himself and the activity of the Spirit) and in its goal (the action of God's grace), prayer is oriented to the work and word of God. Prayer is thus the counter-instance to moral autonomy, and in making it central to ethics Barth is once again rejecting an entire metaphysics and anthropology organized around undetermined human moral creativity. Yet, secondly, prayer is our act; indeed, it is in invocation of God that the active life is most properly entered upon:

What God the Father wills with us and for us ... is more than a solid but stationary relation or a firm but passive connection. He is the living Father of his living children. What he wills with and for these children is therefore ... living dealings between himself and them ... They too have to enter into these dealings on their side. They have to actualize the partnership in this history.[49]

Or – as Barth expressed it earlier in the ethics of creation – in prayer 'we stand before the innermost centre of the covenant between God and man'.[50]

Prayer, then, is at the heart of the ethics of covenantal obedience; but it is not the totality of the active life, for flowing from prayer, and corresponding to its basic structure as appeal to God, there is energetic human action. The prayer 'Thy Kingdom come!' is certainly no mere moral incentive; it is an appeal that God himself should act to manifest the majesty of the rule which has been established in Christ but whose full revelation is still awaited. Yet that same prayer is also the initiating act of Christian rebellion against what Barth calls 'the lordless powers' – the absurd forces which Christ has overthrown, but which persist in exercising an illusory authority over human life. Christian rebellion is not, of course, the attempt to *establish* God's righteousness, but rather the struggle to act in ways which correspond to God's own proper incommunicable activity. Yet this limitation does not undermine human action so much as indicate the space within which human agents are commanded to act. 'God's righteousness is the affair of God's own act ... God's righteousness took place in the history of Jesus Christ, and it will take place again, comprehensively and definitively, in his final manifestation.'[51] But now is

the time of responsibility for the occurrence of human righteousness ... On no pretext can they escape responsibility for it ... For if they are really grateful and really hope, if there is a brave prayer, then they are claimed for a corresponding inner and outer action which is also brave.[52]

There are some striking continuities between those late statements and early materials such as the Tambach lecture. Doubtless much has changed: the late lectures are more biblically and christologically dense, less abstract in their depiction of the transcendent freedom and uniqueness of divine action, possessed of a more rounded and humane moral ontology. But the primary impulse is remarkably similar – to propound an account of God's eschato-logical action which both relativizes and establishes human ethical reality. The moral world of the Reformed tradition, into which Barth stumbled in the early 1920s, and in which he immediately discovered a satisfying way of reconstructing the moral earnestness of liberal Protestantism, retained its attraction for him to the end.

Conclusion

However much Barth argues that dogmatics is incomplete without ethics, and however much he is therefore to be considered a moral theologian, it is dogmatics which has the upper hand in his ethical writings. His paramount concern is to give a rich and Christianly specific theological description of the moral field, invoking doctrine in order to answer questions such as: What is God's action? Who is the God who commands? Who is the human person who stands beneath the divine summons? The strengths of Barth's moral thinking are the consistency with which he deploys doctrine to depict moral reality and the critical power which such a depiction can exercise. That critical power was deployed at the theoretical level against modern traditions of moral thinking which detached ethics from ontology and made value into something we ascribe to the world, and at the practical level against the politics of state sovereignty in the 1930s. One effect of Barth's restructuring of Christian ethics was a quite different moral anthropology. Those who have read (or assumed) Barth to be saying that human action is of only marginal significance have badly misconstrued him, usually because of an expectation that such a radically theocentric account of Christianity must of necessity be opposed to giving much significance to what human beings do. But Barth refuses to be caught in the bind. The dichotomy of theocentrism and anthro-pocentrism simply does not exist for him: even in his 'dialectical' ethics, the contrast between God and humanity is an attempt to defeat liberal certainties and has to be balanced against his evident interest in reconstructing social ethics.

Because Barth is primarily interested in dogmatic depiction of the space in which God and humanity encounter each other and act in relation to each other, material ethical questions have a lower profile in his work. At times, he seems to proceed on the assump-tion that material questions can be resolved into questions of moral ontology: once a truthful account of the agent's situation before

God is offered, what the agent ought to do is evident. One effect of this is a certain lack of concretion in Barth's moral thought, particularly in his theology of politics. Partly this is the result of Barth's fear that when ethics becomes too prescriptive it runs the risk of anticipating the divine command. But a deeper problem may surface at this point: Barth's reluctance to discuss in detail the concrete instruments and ends of political community may be a symptom of the fact that he finds it hard to build in a sufficiently strong sense of human moral action as *making* history, rather than as testifying to history which has already been made. Of course, all sorts of qualifications to such a reading of Barth need to be registered: Barth *is* interested in history-making and is far indeed from the Hegelian metaphysics of world-processes. The lack is more a descriptive lack; Barth was content to remain at the level of the analogies between the Kingdom of God and civil society and did not consider it his task to specify all the implications.

Barth's unwillingness to immerse himself too deeply in the details of the human side of moral history can give the impression that his ethics lacks human depth. His heavy criticism of casuistry, for example, is certainly well taken as a refusal of the sovereignty of deliberation, but tends (at least on some accounts) to leave the processes of moral reasoning rather opaque. Or again, his moral anthropology sometimes appears to lack historical extension. At the level of the individual, he is wary of notions like character, virtue and habit, all of which suggest achievement rather than immediate dependence on grace. At the level of the Christian community, he has a rather slender account of the moral processes of common life. Whether these features indicate some deficiency in his moral anthropology is an open question: they may well simply show that Barth reached a different set of dogmatic judgements and worked with a different sense of what needed to be said in his particular situation. What is very clear is that Barth's hesitations over deliberation, character and so on should not be seen as undisciplined transcendentalism. If anything, it is the opposite which is the case. Lutherans have often urged that Barth's theology represents the moralization of Christianity, because of his (Reformed) stress on the significance of sanctification alongside justification. It is a criticism which is easily overdrawn, but it identifies something which this chapter has sought to draw out, namely that for Barth a Christian dogmatics organized around the fellowship of God and humanity in Christ must also be a theology of morals. This is one of the points at which Barth, for all his rejection of modernity, is a distinctly modern theologian.

Notes

1. See, for example, N. Biggar, *The Hastening that Waits. Karl Barth's Ethics* (Oxford: Clarendon, 1993); R. Hütter, *Evangelische Ethik als kirchliches Zeugnis* (Neukirchen-Vluyn: Neukirchener Verlag, 1993); P. D. Matheny, *Dogmatics and Ethics. The Theological Realism and Ethics of Karl Barth's 'Church Dogmatics'* (Frankfurt am Main: Lang, 1990); J. Webster, *Barth's Ethics of Reconciliation* (Cambridge: Cambridge University Press, 1995) and *Barth's Moral Theology* (Edinburgh: T. & T. Clark, 1998).

2. *ChrL*, pp. 205–71.

3. 'The Christian's Place in Society', *WGWM*, p. 327.

4. Ibid., p. 320.

5. Ibid.

6. Ibid., pp. 320f.

7. Ibid., p. 321.

8. Ibid.

9. Ibid., p. 322.

10. Ibid., pp. 322f.

11. Ibid., p. 323.

12. Ibid., pp. 324f.

13. This is why, in a 1926 paper entitled 'Church and Culture', Barth could claim that the positive assertion he makes there of the promise attached to the *regnum naturae* in God's reconciliation in Christ is not an abandonment of Tambach, however much he may speak in a different tone: see K. Barth, 'Church and Culture', in *ThCh*, p. 341, n. 1.

14. Most recently T. Gorringe, *Karl Barth. Against Hegemony* (Oxford: Oxford University Press, 1999).

15. K. Barth, *Die Theologie der reformierten Bekenntnisschriften* (Zürich: Theologischer Verlag, 1998).

16. K. Barth, 'The Desirability and Possibility of a Universal Reformed Creed', *ThCh*, p. 118.

17. Ibid., p. 132.

18. D. Bonhoeffer, *Ethics* (London: SCM, 1978).

19. K. Barth, *Ethics*, p. 15.

20. Ibid., p. 54.

21. Ibid., p. 16.

22. Ibid.
23. Ibid., p. 17.
24. Ibid., p. 5.
25. Ibid., p. 74.
26. Ibid., p. 76.
27. Ibid., p. 445.
28. Ibid.
29. Ibid.
30. Ibid., p. 447.
31. K. Barth, *Church and State*, p. 29.
32. Ibid., pp. 29f.
33. K. Barth, 'The Christian Community and the Civil Community', in *Against the Stream. Shorter Post-War Writings 1946–52*, p. 22.
34. *Church and State*, p. 38.
35. 'The Christian Community and the Civil Community', p. 32.
36. K. Barth, *A Letter to Great Britain from Switzerland*, pp. 9f.
37. Ibid., pp. 19f.
38. *CD* III/4, p. 4.
39. *CD* I/2, p. 793.
40. *CD* II/2, p. 511.
41. Ibid., p. 568.
42. Ibid., p. 576.
43. Ibid., p. 585.
44. Ibid., p. 631.
45. *CD* III/4, pp. 18, 23; cf. *ChrL*, p. 6 ('formed and contoured reference').
46. *CD* III/4, pp. 26–7. Hence in *CD* III/4, Barth offers lengthy depictions of moral reality in accounts of, for example, temporality, the relations of men and women, parents and children, neighbourliness, and much else.
47. *CD* IV/4, pp. 22f.
48. *ChrL*, p. 43.
49. Ibid., p. 85.
50. *CD* III/4, p. 93.
51. *ChrL*, p. 264.
52. Ibid.

8

Barth and the tasks of Christian theology

Barth was a theologian to the core. He considered theological work (not just dogmatics, but also biblical, historical and practical theology) to be indispensable and irreplaceable in the life of the Christian community. Without theology, the necessary clarification and critique of the church's speech and action could not be accomplished, for those tasks could not be devolved on to other intellectual disciplines. Barth thought of theology as a spiritual activity, an exercise of reason under the tutelage and judgement of revelation, undertaken in the sphere of the church and demanding of its practitioners a readiness for intellectual repentance and sanctification. He remained healthily ironic about whether any theology (especially his own) even approximated to this ideal, but the ideal animated his teaching and writing to the end. In one sense, Barth is a theologian's theologian. This is not because he laid great store by academic professionalism: he often felt rather on the margins of the scholarly guild and always considered the church, not the academy, to be his primary public. It is more that Barth was consumed by a sense of the importance of theology for the life of the church and expected his readers to share his passion. He was one of the few first-rate thinkers of the twentieth century whose mind was wholly mastered by the conceptual culture of Christian dogmatics, and he talked and wrote about its intricacies with single-mindedness, delight and seemingly limitless energy.

All this means that his writings have the characteristics of classics – a comprehensiveness of scope and reference, endurance beyond their immediate context, the potency to evoke a tradition of reflection and argument. But if Barth is a classic theologian, he remains only half-understood, because selectively read. This selectivity is especially apparent in attempts to place Barth in the history of modern theology. Placing any major thinker is difficult, especially in the case of a virtual contemporary who is too large and too near for us to be able to achieve the perspective of distance. Many attempts to locate Barth on the map of modern theology succeed only by trimming him to size, jettisoning one or more aspects of his work (the exegetical or ethical writings, for example), and then presenting him as an exemplary instance, or perhaps precursor, of some theological trend.

The point can be illustrated out of current debates about whether Barth is best described as premodern, modern or postmodern. Does Barth simply bypass modernity and continue the theological task in much the same way as did (for example) Calvin? Or is he a theologian who – despite everything – follows the trajectory of the Enlightenment; or is he perhaps the harbinger of the postmodern demise of ontotheology? It is not impossible to present Barth as if he were a premodern thinker beached on the shores of modernity, seeking (perhaps in some measure even succeeding) to make pristine again a pre-critical mode of theological activity by ignoring, subverting or changing the rules of reasoned discourse. This interpretation rightly sees the significance of Barth's polemic against 'modernist' dogmatics and morals and their foundations, but tends to be beguiled into thinking of Barth as a classical Christian thinker of the stature of Augustine, Anselm or Calvin who happened to find himself in the wrong historical epoch. Yet it was, we recall, Barth himself who near the end of his life remarked: 'I am a child of the nineteenth century.'[1] That is, the sensibilities which Barth brought to the theological task, the issues which continued to trouble and fascinate him, emerged from a collision between post-Enlightenment Protestant thought and his construal of the biblical message. Without the heritage of the nineteenth century, Barth would simply not have been the thinker that he was. It is not just that the rebel took on the lineaments of that against which he rebelled, but that the rebellion consisted in thinking through from the very foundations some of the most major preoccupations of the modern traditions of Christian theology. This is nowhere more evident than in Barth's inclusion of ethics within dogmatics, a move which takes up the moral concerns of nineteenth-century liberalism but gives them an entirely different grounding in the biblical theme of covenant.

Does this, therefore, mean that Barth is to be seen as a funda-mentally modern thinker – that, for all his repudiation of modernity, he nevertheless remained trapped within its religious or philosophical idioms and was not able finally to shake himself free? Certainly this case has been argued from a number of angles. Some critics of Barth, especially Lutherans, have persistently argued that his emphasis on revelation transposes Christian doctrine out of a salvific into an epistemological idiom, so that he takes knowledge of God rather than righteousness before God to be the organizing theme of dogmatics.[2] As we have seen, a similar critique has been pursued against Barth's doctrine of the Trinity, which some readers believe to be dominated by the logic of a self-manifesting, monadic divine ego, with the result that Barth not only consistently under-plays the theme of divine community, but also tends to make revelation a matter of epistemology rather than of participation in the divine life. This reading of Barth is connected with another account (associated above all with Trutz Rendtorff), according to which Barth's inability to wrest himself free of modernity can be seen in his understanding of divine selfhood. For Rendtorff, the idiom of Barth's understanding of divine sovereignty is determined by his transposition on to God of modern notions of absolute subjectivity: God is a kind of transcendental Fichtean ego, a magnified image of modern anthropology.[3] Others, again, have argued that Barth's theology, far from effecting any kind of breach in modernity, in fact trades on a capitulation to modernity, in conceding the force of Kant's restrictions, cordoning theology off as a special sphere of inquiry and so dodging the real task of mounting a theological critique of modern reason and its claims to omnicompetence:

> by refusing all 'mediations' through other spheres of knowledge and culture, Barthianism tended to assume a positive autonomy for theology, which rendered philosophical concerns a matter of indifference. Yet this itself was to remain captive to a modern – even liberal – duality of reason and revelation, and ran the risk of allowing worldly knowledge an unquestioned validity within its own sphere.[4]

Such readings of Barth are sustainable only to the extent that they exercise considerable care in handling his texts, taking the time to establish with some precision those strands of modernity with which Barth interacted and tracing the ways in which his thinking developed over the course of such interactions. Such care has been unfortunately rare; more often than not, readings of his work have been directed by polemical concerns (not infrequently a desire to deflate Barth or Barth's disciples by showing that – despite all claims to the contrary – he is as enmeshed in modern presuppositions as those whom he opposed). And, more often than not, the presentation consists of an alarmingly impressionistic picture of parallels between themes in Barth's writing (revelation, divine subjectivity and so forth) and putative trends in modern thought. None of this, of course, suggests that it is illegitimate to try to locate Barth in modernity and to criticize him accordingly; it simply draws attention to the difficulty of the project. The notion of 'modernity' is itself a complex evaluative construct, and Barth's writings are far too varied, intricate and ramified to allow schematic presentations to succeed.

Many of the same problems attend the discussion of Barth and postmodernity, this time exacerbated by the labyrinthine character of postmodern thought. In this case, there is the added difficulty that, whereas in placing Barth in modernity we are placing him by reference to his past, in processes of which he was in many respects fully aware, with questions of postmodernity we are about the much more speculative business of asking what Barth might have said, or perhaps, of trying to discern whether what Barth did say was, as it were, a kind of 'pre-postmodernism'.

The literature which has so far addressed Barth in relation to postmodern thought has generally presented one or more of three features. First, it has often proceeded by offering a thematic comparison of some aspect of Barth's work and the work of a representative postmodern thinker – 'the Other', givenness, totalities, negative theology, the determinacy of texts, the crisis of representation, are commonly the themes, and Derrida, Levinas, or Irigaray are the thinkers.[5] Such thematic comparisons are usually less than successful, since almost inevitably they have to abstract certain ideas or patterns of argument from their proper context in Barth's work and translate them into something more generic, less Christianly specific, in order to allow the conversation to proceed. One of Barth's basic rules of thought – 'Latet periculum in generalibus!' – is thereby lost, and what starts as a conversation quickly becomes a matter of adjusting Barth to a conceptual scheme quite foreign to his convictions.

A second feature is that of interpreting Barth's theology, especially in its so-called dialectical phase associated with the second commentary on Romans, as emerging from or representative of a proposed shift in Western culture in the early part of the twentieth century: the break-up of modernity and the rise of postmodernity. For example, it has been argued that Barth's early rhetoric of crisis is an indicator that his work is to be understood against the background of a wider 'crisis of representation' at the end of modernity.[6] From this, it is sometimes suggested that the second Romans commentary offers perhaps the greatest example that century of a postmodern turn from the metaphysics of theism – even though the pathos of Barth's later work is that he turns back from the brink and returns to a 'strident theological rhetoric of the "real" '.[7] Whether these generalizations about the epoch of the 1920s are anything other than impressionistic, and whether Barth's own denials[8] that his early theology is driven by the mood of European high culture after the Great War are enough to overturn this interpretation, are open questions. But it is very difficult to be persuaded by any interpretation of his work which routinely passes over the theological character of Barth's convictions, making his theology into simply a register for cultural trends. Barth was a theologian from the beginning; what he stumbled into when he stumbled into Romans in the summer of 1916 was a reality possessed of a unique, incomparable character which simply cannot be assimilated to anything else: the world of God.

Third, postmodern readings of Barth have shown strong interest in harnessing him to proposals about how Christian theology is to be undertaken in the present; for example, Barth can be read as an instance of genuinely theological transcendence of 'ontotheology', of a reserve towards representation of God which qualifies him as a negative theologian. In itself, of course, this is not an improper approach: unless one is reading great theological texts simply out of antiquarian interests, it is impossible not to have one's reading directed by constructive interests. The crucial question, however, is what constitutes the shape and the limits of the 'use' of a theologian's work. As with (for example) Aquinas and Calvin, so with Barth: the interpretation of a corpus of such range and depth is particularly exposed to being skewed by selection and partiality (Aquinas and Calvin are routinely read as if their biblical commentaries were not germane to the interpretation of their work), and by over-eagerness to make constructive use of ill-digested accounts of some or other of their preoccupations. The crucial factor in any account of Barth's theology is respect for the details of what he wrote. Such respect is not born of uncritical, slavish or deferential reverence; it is simply a safeguard against the tendency to annex

Barth to other projects by providing impressionistic readings of his work. Here it is particularly important that we keep alert to the theological character of Barth's work and do not allow ourselves to fall into the sort of interpretation which takes from him a certain ambience or tone, or relates some of his patterns of thought or characteristic turns of phrase to reconstructions of the culture of Weimar, or perhaps of today. If we once neglect Barth's strict insistence that the traffic always proceeds from the particular to the general and not vice versa, then he will soon share the fate of other major theological figures – becoming a mere emblematic figure whose authority is invoked but whose texts remain unread.

Because Barth's conception of the theological task is rather remote to many readers in different church and theological cultures, it is important to ask what may be learned from Barth about the nature of Christian theology and its responsibilities. Two lines of reflection suggest themselves.

First, Barth offers a theological construal of the situation of Christian theology. One of Barth's chief legacies is that he offers an example of one who told the history of thought and culture, and therefore the history (including the present history) of theology, from the perspective of gospel, church and faith. Because Barth mapped the situation of theology in the projection of the Christian gospel, and not by reference to any supposed givens of its surrounding intellectual culture, he was able to demonstrate a calmness and confidence in the face of the demands of the context in which he undertook his theological responsibilities. Barth was always about the business of 'doing theology as if nothing had happened',[9] refusing to be beguiled into believing that the history and context of theological work is somehow a fate, an iron necessity which requires us to recast the nature of our task. By contrast, he demonstrated a conviction that theological confidence requires, amongst other things, a properly cheerful sense of the relativity of context when viewed from the vantage-point of the gospel.

Barth's own way of reading the history of Christian theology is very instructive at this point. He was deeply interested in, and deeply knowledgeable about, the history of the various branches of Christian theology, especially dogmatics, and had a considerable facility with the history of modern philosophy, such that he could offer some brilliant (and partial) readings of classic modern texts, both theological and philosophical (the partiality of the readings is one of the things which makes for their brilliance). Moreover, from his early days as a theological professor, Barth was strongly gripped by a need to place himself *vis-à-vis* the history of modern theology, deeply conscious as he was that his work involved a rethinking and reconstructing of many of the established conventions of modern Protestantism and its place in the intellectual traditions of Western Europe since the eighteenth century. In trying to distinguish himself in this way, Barth had something in common with other seminal thinkers of the earlier part of the century: a sense of being at the pivot of intellectual change, and therefore of having to undertake a genealogical task in order to extract himself from the representations of modern life and thought which he was leaving behind by giving an account of them and displaying that they were no longer axiomatic. Nevertheless, Barth's account had a certain uniqueness which is germane to our theme. The kinds of judgements which Barth reached about the *context* of theology derive from a very particular understanding of theology's *content*. As he moved into the writing of Christian dogmatics from the mid-1920s, he discovered in a deeper way a manner of thinking and speaking about God which was not wholly consumed by notions of cultural, intellectual or moral crisis. As he came to invest more and more in his chosen medium, and as his thought world came to be peopled by strong texts of the exegetical and doctrinal traditions of Christianity, he was reassured about the possibility of a properly 'positive' theology, that is, a theology whose referents and procedures are given by the nature and free activity of the object of theology. The precise character of this givenness is quite crucial to understanding what Barth is about as he tries to read his own context. In essence, Barth developed over the course of the latter half of the 1920s and the early 1930s a specific theological and christological construal of the givenness of revelation to church and faith, and therefore to theology, which furnished the basis of a confidently theological evaluation of the contexts of theology, past and present. Right at the beginning of the *Church Dogmatics*, Barth puts matters thus:

> [Dogmatics] does not have to begin by finding or inventing the standard by which it measures. It sees and recognises that this is given with the Church. It is given in its own peculiar way, as Jesus Christ is given, as God in His revelation gives Himself to faith. But it is given.[10]

'It is given.' Construed through trinitarian and incarnational categories as the free, self-manifesting majesty of God's presence, that givenness made possible for Barth a kind of theological activity whose primary concern was not with anxious questions about its own feasibility in a culture in disarray, but with the sheer actuality of God's act of revelation, which has already as it were set theology on its path, thereby requiring the theologian to follow its given – spiritually given, but nevertheless given – presence and movement. The direction of that movement, Barth came to see, is towards the church, appointed by God as the sphere in which revelation meets the recognition of faith. Hence his 'positive' dogmatics is a church dogmatics, making confident use of the language of the church, above all as found in its textual deposit. Barth did not feel the need to maintain a suspicious bearing towards the church and its traditions of speech. He could castigate it for its idolatries and its capacity to convert God into an ecclesiastical ornament; but his account of the church was too deeply grounded in dogmatic principles to allow him to be fundamentally ironic or distant in his attitude. The ecclesial character of the positivity of Barth's theology was particularly manifest in his style of writing, which was never simply clever or sophisticated. And, moreover, he had a clear sense of responsibility to a determinate field of inquiry: where much postmodern theology, for example, is deliberately eclectic, dodging around in social and cultural studies, literary criticism, aesthetics, philosophy and religion, Barth is no *bricoleur*, but – in short – a positive theologian of the church of Jesus Christ.

This particular construal of the *positum* of Christian theology, his confidence in the spiritual presence of the object of theology in its gracious self-bestowal, enabled Barth to read the context of his theological activity through theological categories. Part of what makes Barth so foreign is his abiding sense that the difficulties which attend theological work are not solely or even primarily problems which have to do with cultural or historical or intellectual context; they are spiritual. For Barth, the real history of Christian theology is not only the history of its struggle to articulate the Christian gospel in a variety of cultures, borrowing more or less serviceable tools and enjoying greater or lesser degrees of success in retaining a sense of its own distinctive substance. Viewed at its deepest level, the history of Christian theology is a series of episodes in the wider history of God and humanity, and if we are to read the history of theology and our own responsibility for continuing that history in our situation properly, we must read it theologically.

It is this argument which Barth outlines in the opening chapter of his *Protestant Theology in the Nineteenth Century*. 'To describe and understand the history of Protestant theology from the time of Schleiermacher onwards,' he writes,

> is a *theological* task. Even as an object of historical considera-
> tion, theology demands theological perception, theological
> thought and theological involvement. Of course, there is no
> method, not even a theological one, by means of which we can be
> certain of catching sight of theology ... Nevertheless, it is a
> *condition sine qua non* of the success of our undertaking that it
> should be approached theologically, in accordance with its
> subject-matter.[11]

Barth's point is not simply that to do historical theology well we need a 'special participation' in its subject-matter,[12] and so cannot adopt the stance of the 'idle onlooker',[13] but something rather deeper. We are to read the history of theology as taking place in the sphere of the church – that is, not simply as a cultural activity, as an exercise or discipline participating in the general history of human inquiry. Rather,

> Every *period* of the Church does in fact want to be understood as
> a period of the *Church*, that is, as a time of revelation, knowledge
> and confession of the one Christian faith, indeed, as a special
> time, as *this* time of such revelation, knowledge and
> confession.[14]

Barth is deadly serious here: when we try to reflect on the history of Christian theology, we are firmly in the sphere of the one, holy, catholic and apostolic church. And, if that is so, then two important consequences which Barth discerns are to be noted. One is that we may not pretend to the kind of assurance in which we set ourselves up as critics of the past of theology, as if we in our situation had somehow transcended church and faith or been granted a clearer, more comprehensive grasp of theology than was granted to our forebears in the church.[15] 'History writing cannot be a proclamation of judgment.'[16] A second consequence is that it may not be inap-propriate for us to reflect seriously on our own situation and responsibilities in the same light; to ask ourselves whether – with all the differences between premodern, modern and postmodern – we should not also see ourselves as participants in the same history, facing the same demands, placed under the same requirements, offered the same opportunities. 'Over and above the differences,'

Barth wrote, 'a unity can continually be seen, a unity of perplexity and disquiet, but also a unity of richness and hope, which in the end binds us to the theologians of the past.'[17]

This is – emphatically – not to suggest that theological responsibility in our current situation means simply repeating what Barth or any other classical theologian said. Nor is it a matter of claiming that Barth's work encourages theology simply to carry on business as usual, if by 'usual business' we mean doing exactly what past generations attempted, pretending that our situation is theirs. We are where we are. But what Barth's construal of the situation of theology does press his readers to consider is the confession that 'where we are' is in the history of the church, in the history of revelation and repentance, confession and hope. It is that history which is to be allowed to shape the definition of the theologian and the tasks of Christian theology.

This leads to a second line of reflection. In trying to understand what Barth may offer theology in the present, the focus must be on dogmatic issues.

Neglect of the dogmatic character of Barth's work (that is, its character as the church's reflective inquiry into its coherence with its divinely-given basis) has led to some distorted pictures of Barth, especially in postmodern readings of him. Extracting certain themes from his writings and setting them alongside similar-sounding themes in one or other postmodern thinker, the result has often been precisely the sort of *mixophilosophicotheologia* which Barth so deplored,[18] and which is of very little use in establishing the real nature of his project, which was doctrinal to the core. The most important debates with Barth's work will always be exegetical and dogmatic, since it was as a biblical dogmatician that he thought and wrote. Some of the topics of debate have already been indicated: revelation, Trinity, creation, the mystery of salvation, sacraments. But this focus on dogmatics should not be thought to close Barth to conversation with what lies outside the theological sphere; in fact, it makes such conversation much more vigorous. This can be seen from Barth's frequent interaction with philosophy. Barth was unafraid to field dogmatic convictions when engaging and criticizing philosophical ideas; indeed, his most characteristic response to the philosophers whom he engaged (not only in *Protestant Theology* but also in the *Church Dogmatics*)[19] was to ask after their adequacy in the light of the God confessed in Christian faith. He did not set them alongside Christian faith as equal sources for theological reflection; still less did he think of philosophy as affording us a better vantage-point from which theology could be criticized. Rather, his accounts of philosophers show him concerned – with his usual mix of curiosity and determination – both to be addressed by philosophy and to respond with the only language available to him, namely that of the Christian confession. Barth did not think that engagement in conversation with philosophical texts and ideas could proceed only by temporarily abandoning or suspending the specific concerns and thought patterns of Christian dogmatics. Nor did he think that refusing (sometimes stubbornly) to abandon or suspend those concerns spelled the end of any conversation; indeed, it was precisely at this point that the real debate began. Barth's insistence on speaking on his own terms is not to be interpreted as obstinate reluctance to come out of his lair and talk to the rest of the world; quite the contrary: in writing, as in life, Barth showed remarkable openness to all manner of ideas, provided he is allowed to exercise Christian nonconformity. Nor is it a matter of Barth making a claim to have achieved a proper, fully sanctified, 'theological' way of thinking about and articulating the Christian faith unmixed with philosophy. On a number of occasions, Barth argued pretty firmly against 'the method of isolation'[20] in which theology confidently asserts its 'Christianness' over against philosophy. 'The Christianity of theology does not in any way rest upon itself but upon the revelation that is its theme.'[21] Nor, again, is it a matter of Barth irrationally claiming an exemption clause for Christianity by arguing that it is immune from such criticisms of religion and its imaginary as those offered by Feuerbach. Over against all these, what Barth is doing, and what we may learn from him, is that whatever interesting and helpful things Christian theology has to say in conversation with philosophy will derive from what it has learned as it has tried to attend to the gospel. And, furthermore, we may also learn here that philosophical criticism of Christian faith must engage genuinely Christian claims in all their specificity, rather than simply making do with whatever approximations to or substitutes for them are propounded, whether in philosophy or Christian theology itself.

Whether such a style of theological engagement can commend itself today is certainly open to question. Barth worked in a religious culture in which – possibly for the last time in Protestant history – sophisticated theological ideas were accorded great prestige, even when they were repudiated. The institutions and forms of Christian life which nurtured such a massive project as the *Church Dogmatics* scarcely exist, or exist only in somewhat embattled forms. Especially towards the end of his life, Barth himself already felt that the Christian theological culture in which he had been nurtured, and which he loved even as he quarrelled with it, was no longer in the mainstream. But not the least of his encouragements is his counsel to see the marginalization of theology in the contemporary church and in academia as an opportunity rather than a threat – as offering the occasion for theology to concentrate once again on its great, joyful subject-matter, God and the gospel of Jesus Christ, from which alone theology receives the law of its existence:

> Ever since the fading of its illusory splendour as a leading academic power during the Middle Ages, theology has taken too many pains to justify its own existence. It has tried too hard, especially in the nineteenth century, to secure for itself at least a small but honourable place in the throne room of general science. This attempt at self-justification has been no help to its own work. The fact is that it has made theology, to a great extent, hesitant and half-hearted; moreover, this uncertainty has earned theology no more respect for its achievements than a very modest tip of the hat. Strange to say, the surrounding world only recommended to take note of theology in earnest (though rather morosely) when it again undertook to consider and concentrate more strongly upon its own affairs. Theology had first to renounce all apologetics or external guarantees of its position within the environment of other sciences, for it will always stand on the firmest ground when it simply *acts* according to the law of its own being ... The 'place' of theology ... will be determined by the impetus which it receives from within its own domain and from its own *object*. Its object – the philanthropic God Himself – is the law which must be the continual starting-point of theology. It is ... the post that the theologian must take and keep, whether or not it suits him or any of his fellow creatures. The theologian has to hold this post at all costs, whether at the university or in the catacombs, if he does not wish to be imprisoned for dereliction of duty.[22]

Notes

1. H. Stoevesandt (ed.), *A Late Friendship. The Letters of Karl Barth and Carl Zuckmayer* (Grand Rapids: Eerdmans, 1982), p. 3.

2. Classically made by G. Wingren in *Theology in Conflict. Nygren – Barth – Bultmann* (Philadelphia: Muhlenberg Press, 1958).

3. See, for example, T. Rendtorff, 'Der Ethische Sinn der Dogmatik' in idem. (ed.), *Die Realisierung der Freiheit* (Gütersloh: Mohn, 1975), pp. 119–34, and J. Macken, *The Autonomy Theme in the* Church Dogmatics*: Karl Barth and His Critics* (Cambridge: Cambridge University Press, 1990).

4. 'Introduction. Suspending the material: the turn of radical orthodoxy', in J. Milbank et al., *Radical Orthodoxy. A New Theology* (London: Routledge, 1999), p. 2.

5. On Barth and Derrida, see I. Andrews, *Deconstructing Barth. A Study of the Complementary Methods in Karl Barth and Jacques Derrida* (Frankfurt am Main: Lang, 1996); G. Ward, *Barth, Derrida and the Language of Theology* (Cambridge: Cambridge University Press, 1995); W. Lowe, *Theology and Difference. The Wound of Reason* (Bloomington: Indiana University Press, 1993). On Barth and Levinas, see S. G. Smith, *The Argument to the Other. Reason beyond Reason in the Thought of Karl Barth and Emmanuel Levinas* (Chico, CA: Scholars' Press, 1983). On Barth and Irigaray, see S. Jones, 'This God Which Is Not One: Irigaray and Barth on the Divine', in C. W. Maggie Kim et al. (eds), *Transfigurations. Theology and the French Feminists* (Minneapolis: Fortress Press, 1993), pp. 109–41. More generally, see W. Stacy Johnson, *The Mystery of God. Karl Barth and the Postmodern Foundations of Theology* (Louisville: Westminster John Knox Press, 1997).

6. Besides G. Ward, *Barth, Derrida and the Language of Theology*, see D. E. Klemm, 'Toward a Rhetoric of Postmodern Theology: Through Barth and Heidegger', *Journal of the American Academy of Religion* 55 (1987), pp. 443–69; S. H. Webb, *Refiguring Theology. The Rhetoric of Karl Barth* (Albany: SUNY Press, 1991); R. H. Roberts, 'Barth and the Rhetoric of Weimar. A Theology on Its Way?', in *A Theology on its Way? Essays on Karl Barth* (Edinburgh: T. & T. Clark, 1991).

7. R. H. Roberts, 'Barth and the Rhetoric of Weimar', p. 196.

8. Such as in the 1922 lecture on 'The Problem of Ethics Today', *WGWM*, p. 150.

9. K. Barth, *Theological Existence Today! A Plea for Theological Freedom* (London: Hodder and Stoughton, 1933), p. 9.

10. *CD* I/1, p. 12.

11. K. Barth, *Protestant Theology in the Nineteenth Century*, p. 15.

12. Ibid.

13. Ibid., p. 16.

14. Ibid., p. 27.

15. Barth probably had in mind the over-eager students who first heard his lectures on historical theology and who looked to him to provide

reasons for not taking the nineteenth century seriously. See also K. Barth, *The Theology of Schleiermacher*, p. xvi.

16. *Protestant Theology*, p. 23.

17. Ibid., p. 27.

18. K. Barth, *Evangelical Theology: An Introduction* (London: Weidenfeld and Nicolson, 1963), p. iii.

19. For example, Descartes (*CD* III/1, pp. 350–63) or Leibniz, Heidegger and Sartre (ibid., pp. 316–49).

20. K. Barth, *Ethics*, p. 24.

21. Ibid., p. 34.

22. K. Barth, *Evangelical Theology*, pp. 15f.

Index

179